The Messenger House

Correspondence between now and then

Janet Sutherland

Shearsman Books

First published in the United Kingdom in 2023 by
Shearsman Books Ltd
PO Box 4239
Swindon
SN3 9FN

Shearsman Books Ltd Registered Office
30–31 St. James Place, Mangotsfield, Bristol BS16 9JB
(*this address not for correspondence*)

ISBN 978-1-84861-882-4

ACKNOWLEDGEMENTS

Acknowledgements are due to the editors of the following publications
in which some of these poems or earlier versions first appeared: *Envoi,
The Fortnightly Review* (online), *The Frogmore Papers, Litter* (online),
Long Poem Magazine, Mary Evans Picture Library (online), *Molly
Bloom* (online), *Riptide, The North, Poetry & All That Jazz, Shearsman.*

'The Parlatorium' appeared in *Locked Down, Poems, diary extracts and
art from the 2020 pandemic,* ed Susan Jane Sims. 'Nearly to the Axletrees
in Sand' appeared first in *Bone Monkey,* Shearsman Books (2014). 'On
Horseback in All Weathers' and 'The Ortolan Bunting' appeared in the
anthology *Echoes from the Old Hill,* ed. Jeremy Page (Frogmore 2022).

CONTENTS

Poems listed by title or first line

Thanks

Thanks are due to the Arts Council England and British Council for an Artists' International Development Fund awarded in 2018 for travel to Hungary and Serbia.

Thanks are also due to the Society of Authors for an Authors' Foundation grant towards travel in Europe awarded in 2019.
Thanks to the Association of Serbian Writers and the Petőfi Institute in Hungary and to the University of Debrecen for their hospitality and interest in this work. Personal thanks to Imre of Debrecen University in Hungary.

Thanks for translations to Ivanka Radmanović, Tony Frazer, Alexandra Loske, Kate Ashton and Gertraude Klemm.

I am particularly indebted to Ivanka Radmanović, Serbian poet and translator, for her help and support at all stages of this project. Her translations into Serbian of my poems and parts of George's journals, her introduction to the members of the Association of Writers of Serbia, her corrections to the Serbian parts of my manuscript, her enthusiasm for George's diaries, and most of all her friendship – made this work possible.

Thanks to my cousin Barbara Collins for her research over many years into our family history which provided rich details and avenues for further research in the writing of this book.

Grateful and warm thanks also to close readers of this work – Kate Ashton, Kelvin Corcoran, Charlotte Gann, Robert Hamberger, Maria Jastrzębska, John McCullough and Jackie Wills. Warm thanks also to the members of the Brighton and NZ Poets groups where early versions of some of the poems were shared. Warm thanks as always to Tony Frazer of Shearsman Books.

For Lesley, Joe and Moon, with love.

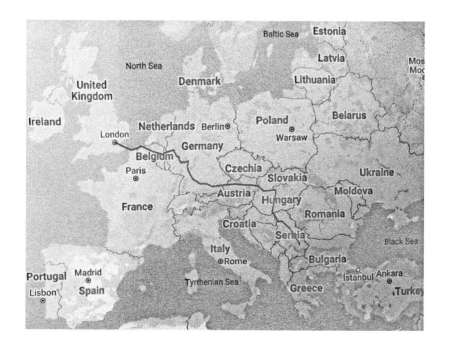

INTRODUCTION

Early Journeys

When I was a child my maternal grandparents lived in a cottage in a village called Cranmore, old English Crane Mere, the Lake of the Cranes, a derivation that rose from land and water before settlement, an unsettled place in which birds, disturbed, would take flight out of open water. I didn't know that then, only knew about the pond where we'd sometimes take scraps of bread for the ducks. The village is still small, population 650, just a few miles from the town of Shepton Mallet in Somerset.

My grandparents[1] had bought two adjacent stone-built thatched cottages in Cranmore when they retired. These were one up, one down cottages. The downstairs room in the cottage they lived in also had an adjoining dining room/kitchen, a scullery (a word I particularly liked) and bathroom which at some point in the past had been built on the side. The next-door cottage was used as a storeroom. In later life Grandpa had taken up farming, after having been a GP, and he kept tools there, including woodwork and turning tools and his artist's materials – he enjoyed sketching and painting. This second cottage was kept as an outhouse, dark and dusty, out of bounds. Outside there was a shared footpath to the rest of the row which ran straight past the front door. My grandparents' cottages were at the road end, and across this shared footpath was the garden where Grandpa grew flowers and vegetables. His sister, my great aunt [confusingly called Aunty Bill], lived in another house in the same village and we used to visit her occasionally although they'd always argue. The cottage was dark inside, cool in summer; it had thick Somerset stone walls and small windows. When we arrived, having driven from Salisbury, we'd park outside in the lane, run up the footpath, open the front door and walk straight in.

My Granny was disabled. She had a familial spinal cerebellar degeneration which set in when she was around thirty and progressed very gradually, until in her seventies and eighties it caused severe disabilities of both movement and speech. She subsequently passed this on to two of her five children, my mother, Paddy,[2, 3]

'əʊnli wiː kʊd ˌʌndəˈstænd
ðə əˈsɛmbld
'vaʊəlz ænd ˈkɒnsənənts
əˈraɪvɪŋ leɪt
ænd ɪn dɪsˈɔːdə

and my Uncle David.[4]

'əʊnli ðə θriː ɒv ðɛm
kʊd ˌʌndəˈstænd hɪz spiːʧ
fɔːr ʌs hɪz lɑːf
bɪˈkeɪm ðə ˌdaɪəgˈnɒstɪk tuːl

Her balance, because of this, was poor and her speech slurred. This meant that, as children, our communication with Granny was limited and we didn't hear her side of the family history. As a five-year-old I remember games of Ludo, and her standing propped over the kitchen sink peeling vegetables, but I don't remember her voice. I don't remember her walking much either, and if she did it would have been with a Zimmer frame, crutches or a curious stick with a three-pronged foot. Strangely, she was the one who slept upstairs in the small bedroom under the eaves although she would have had to haul herself up the narrow staircase hanging on by the handrail, with Grandpa following behind in case she fell. He always slept downstairs on an old fashioned dark brown divan in one corner of the sitting room. There was an open coal fire in the grate which he would light in the small hours and keep burning all day, encouraging it when it fell to embers by covering the firebox with a page of newspaper. A dining table was pushed against the outside wall by the door with a chenille tasselled tablecloth in a rich dark red, piled so high with books and papers it was never used for meals. There was a bookcase against the internal wall with diamond paned glass in its doors which held among others an illustrated medical reference book on skin diseases. A budgie in a cage by the window could say one or two words, unlike ours which had only learned to bark like our dog. Below the window was a metal chest which, I discovered when they died, contained various pieces of silverware including an old-fashioned chamberstick,[5] which had come, tarnished, out of the 18th century.

It wasn't that far, just a forty-five mile drive to their cottage. But in those days without dual carriageways on twisting narrow roads with blind spots and hidden dips it would take an hour and a half each way. We went with Mum. Dad would stay home on the farm – consequently, the Cranmore drive was more peaceful. There would be no unnerving accelerations away from tailgating drivers, no swerving round sharp bends, no anxiety over which exit should be taken from a well-known roundabout in Salisbury, no sitting right behind another car on the long stretches where passing places were few and far between and no irritable tensing of shoulders under a for-best tweed jacket, no huffing, no puffing. There would be no travel sickness either. Travel sickness was a perennial problem for me on the way to Dad's sister in Bath when he was the driver.

Milk Fevers

here we are again   my father and I
he's doing the fine work   inserting
the needle   anxious but handy

I'm the child fieldworker
lifting a brown bottle
(Calcium Borogluconate) high   higher

checking for twists in the tube
watching practical gravity shift
fluid from one place to another

his calloused hand still   after
all this time   massaging
the subcutaneous gathering of liquid

in her kinked neck   if we are
lucky   she will stand at last
on churned mud   on calving blood

in a cold wind   with rooks cawing
from the copse   as they do
as they always do

These trips to Cranmore continued every six weeks or so until my grandmother's death in the September of 1981 when she was eighty-six and I was twenty-four. By then she'd spent eleven years on a ward in a geriatric hospital just outside Shepton Mallet following a fall when my grandfather discovered he could no longer pick her up. He was eight-and-a-half years older than her, and her falls eventually defeated him. He continued living in the cottage with some assistance from home helps, after she was admitted to the geriatric hospital, and died in early February 1979 when he was ninety-two and I was nearly twenty-two. After he died the cottages were cleared and sold. The new owner demolished them and rebuilt a modern house there, even though they'd been listed.

> Wheat seed steeped
> in arsenic
> gives good clean crops[6]

The Materials

When we arrived, we'd hug our grandparents, then immediately ask if we could look in the Chinese Cabinet.[7] The cabinet was in a dark corner straight opposite the front door. Some of the damage to the contents had, no doubt, been acquired through age, but some was due to the exuberant handling of thirteen inquisitive grandchildren.

The five drawers included a South Seas folded piece of skin,[8] a piece of the Royal George,[9] a red bag containing 19th century German pfennigs, a *Brave Girls in War* booklet,[10] a handkerchief belonging to a Great Grandfather Corke in 1801,[11] a pair of Turkish slippers,[12] a measuring wheel, a bean containing six tiny ivory elephants,[13] a handmade doll with a head made from a walnut, and a whole multitude of other objects crammed into the drawers.

We knew there had been the journal of an ancestor's journey to Serbia in the cabinet. We had seen it, the closely handwritten pages, but had not been allowed to hold it – a sensible prohibition in the light of other damage. When my grandparents died this journal went to my Aunty Ann in Norfolk for safekeeping and later made its way back to my cousin, Barbara Collins who, as the eldest child of David, the eldest of the five siblings, was tasked to look after both it and the oriental cabinet.

I've always been fascinated with the items in the cabinet. They hold for me the mystery of lost things. They have been chosen over all other objects to be kept. To be held in a dark place like something sacred until no one alive remembers how they came to be, nor how they were acquired. I have a physical memory of many of the things in the cabinet, how they felt in my hand. There was a dried lime, wizened and hard, which came back from the First World War with my grandfather and what was described to me as a meteorite, but may not have been: a small but heavy lump of rock which he'd picked up in a desert. There were letters on such fine papers the light shone through them and others where the handwriting was doubled to save space and crawled diagonally over the horizontal until the words crossed and recrossed each other with fluid urgency but defied transcription. There were letters which had been scrutinised by the censor and heavily redacted. There were letters from soldiers and airmen who were billeted in Cardiff with Granny and Grandpa while on leave during the Second World War, or who were recuperating from wounds. There were letters from the parents of these men thanking my grandparents for taking in their sons, and photographs of their children born after the war. My mother's autograph album is full of signatures of men from Canada, the States, New Zealand, Poland and France with such notes as 'A swell time with a lovely family, A Chrysdale 19 Sep 43', a hand-drawn map of New Zealand, with superimposed sailing ship against a bright cloud, labelled 'Aeo-tea-Roa & Waitemata, God's own country, C Douglas Feb 15th 45' and 'In memory of Paddy and family who gave an American soldier the merriest of Christmases. May we be the best of friends always, sincerely Ed, Dec 25th 43.'

Each piece in these drawers had a story. Each piece lost parts of its story until all it had left was the fabric of itself. Consider the Measuring Wheel in the fifth drawer. We know nothing about it or the hands that used it, the mind that set out the numerals it measured and what was made of those measurements or why it was kept. We don't know who used the fans, feathered, carved, broken and plain, or who made or played with the dolls. The handwritten letters are orphans, both sender and recipient are dead, only the words remain on the paper, and we struggle with this because we

know how much flows through the mind before we pick the few words that end up on the page. What did the sender think as they wrote? How did the recipient respond? We try to reimagine the hand grasping the pen, the thought flowing with the ink, the decisions of what to reveal and what to hide, the swift eye of the reader, their anxiety, love, fear.

When my grandfather, a medical officer in the First World War, wrote (on September 7th 1915), a letter to his father in Dublin from Suvla Bay, (which later found its way into the cabinet and then to me), he drew a pen and ink picture of the dugout he made and wrote:

> 'I built a lovely dugout for myself, and there were plenty for the men, and made a fine dressing station of sandbags (& sweat). I would have developed into an excellent navvy if I'd stayed there a little longer – of course when I'd finished it, with the help of a company of engineers, I got orders to move – such is life.'

And later in the same letter:

> 'We are praying for one night's frost to kill the flies – you can have no idea of the appalling numbers there are here, nothing seems to drive them away, they sit on your food as you put it in your mouth, and walk all over your nib as you write. The most unpleasant ones are large and green and shiny, when you remember where they come from the idea is not pleasant.'

'I wish the muzzling order was not so stringent' he wrote 'or I might be able to tell you something interesting' and then:

> 'We also had a couple of furious shellings during the three days we were there, the net result, though plenty of shrapnel & H.E. [high explosive] fell round & into my camp, was one man wounded in the back (he was a sick man who had come in, to rest, having lost his way) & one of my men went potty with nervous strain – he sat in a corner & could not speak & kept rubbing his hands together.'

Towards the end of the letter, he wrote prosaically, 'Gothops sent me another tunic with a second Lt's Star on it. I don't know why they did this as I had already rec'd. the one I ordered, so I am returning this one sometime when I have leisure to do so.'

He ended the letter with the simple 'Addio John'. This is a son straightforwardly writing to his father about what he has experienced. The dips and feints in the letter are the normal undulations of tone, humour even, but the circumstances are extraordinary. He says 'you can have no idea of...' but tries anyway to convey what he is living through despite what he is not allowed to say. It's a workmanlike rendering of atrocity, of conveying on paper lived experience and palpable through the words in the quick flow of thought is the sense of trust this son has for his father.

George's Journals

The journals you are about to read are down to earth and un-self-conscious, like my grandfather's letter, and were written in 1846 and 1847 by a relative on Granny's side of the family, George Sydney Davies, my great-great-grandfather, who travelled with Mr Gutch, a Queen's Messenger for the Foreign Office. These journals prove the point that 'The most durable diarists have not always been those who mix in high society or are connected with the great and the good, the best diarists are those in which the voice of the individual comes through untainted by self-censorship or a desire to please.' (Taylor, 2000, p. ix).

Plant beans
three inches apart—
the common little horse-bean is the best[14]

In each journal George describes one trip from London to Serbia and back. The first is dated from 20th April 1846 to 24th July 1846 and the second from 27th September 1847 to 27th November 1847. On each journey they set out from 77 Great Portland Street in London which was Mr Gutch's residence. The stopping point in Serbia was the town of Alexnitza [Aleksinac] where there was a messenger house, near the then border with the Ottoman Empire. The messengers stayed there while despatches, brought from England by Mr Gutch, and the other Queen's Messengers, were taken onwards to Constantinople [Istanbul] by local couriers who would also bring despatches back from Constantinople to be conveyed back to London. Constantinople had been a source of the plague, typhus and cholera and travel in that area was also considered unsafe owing to brigands and robbers.

There are three main participants in the journals: George Sydney Davies (1822–1895) had just finished training to be a solicitor in his father's firm, Davies and Son, in Crickhowell, Wales when he set off on these journeys. His companion, John Wheeley Gough Gutch (1808–1869), was a Queen's Messenger, having previously been a surgeon, and was a keen early photographer. In 1847 they met Captain Edmund Spencer, in Alexnitza, a prolific British travel writer who writes about their meeting (Spencer, 1851). I have included more detail about the lives of George, John and Edmund at the back of this book, alongside details of Lewis Hertslet of the Foreign Office whose collections of papers at The National Archives at Kew contain the collection of accounts, vouchers, registers, regulations and other papers relating to Foreign Service Messengers and the background workings of the Foreign Office, including sick notes and letters Mr Gutch sent, some of which I have included here. I have also included some correspondences written by the Ambassadors in the Embassy at Constantinople, Sir Stratford Canning (1846) and Henry Wellesley, 1st Earl Cowley (1847) to give some idea of the political concerns they were dealing with around the time of these journals and, therefore, what urgent issues might have been included in the despatches Gutch carried.

I knew my letter-writing grandfather very well and had a strong connection with him. I still use his Shorter Oxford Dictionary which he left me because he knew that I would write. There is, of course, a much less direct connection with George; I know him only through his words on paper, but by reading his journals I've become strangely fond of him. He was in his energetic early-twenties when these journals were written; he's bouncy, bright, insouciant, inexperienced but having fun on these travels after years of study.[15] You can almost hear his companion, Mr Gutch, who was thirty-eight and had already lost his four-year-old son and had an ailing wife at home, sighing at times as George sets off for a twelve-mile gallop into the countryside, or insists on yet another hunt, through rough country, while he, himself, wants only to read, think, draw or quietly add to his beetle collection.

George is middle-class with Victorian values and can be thoughtless and xenophobic. He doesn't curb what he writes because he's writing not for publication but as a reminder of his travels, perhaps to show the children he's yet to have or his parents and brothers and sisters, so what you get in these journals is uncensored, aside from the self-censorship we all employ when we write. His descriptions range from succinct one-liners on a day's activities to pages full of detail, and if he finds a town 'dirty' and/or 'mean', that is exactly what he writes. He exhibits casual discrimination based on social class, religion, race, gender, for instance describing a judge's daughter who is to be married as 'ugly and old – a pretty little girl there' and he notes his 'disgust' at 'two great moustachioed fellows' kissing one another. A town with a large population of Jews is described as 'very dirty and poverty stricken'. He is also not above theft for which, all these generations later, I apologise wholeheartedly, as what was taken and never returned was a skull from the Tower of Skulls in Niš, Serbia.

The importance of 'class' in these journals should not be under-estimated. It is hugely important to both George and Mr Gutch to be seen as 'gentlemen'. The British class system is apparent in much of the journal, in George's aspirations to be thought well of, in his judgements of others, and in the Foreign Office notes which accompany the text[16]. The two weddings he attends in Serbia are completely categorised by class, George professing himself disgusted at the lower-class wedding shenanigans, whereas he is charmed by the middle-class wedding he attends. Classism and racism combine in some of George's more odious descriptions such as where he describes 'a Moorish visaged Gypsy'.

George is exuberantly and unashamedly British in his dress and manners so that Captain Spencer, the travel writer they meet, mocks him, saying 'Mr. Davies exhibited a most imposing exterior to the astonished Servians; his costume being the English hunting dress – scarlet jacket, top-boots and cap.' We do not know exactly what the Serbians he met made of him, except by his own record of meetings with them. He does note, unsurprisingly, that some of the locals thought the English 'arrogant'. He hunts avidly, a common pastime in those days, and shoots anything that moves; at one point, for instance, he writes 'shot a bee-eater, dove and two small birds' and offers the larks he has shot to Mr Gutch for breakfast one morning. But he is intensely interested in local customs and in the opinions of the people he meets; he is enthusiastic about the otherness of travel, for instance he is captivated by the clothes people wear, often describes them, and enjoys dressing up. He throws himself into new experiences. His descriptions of the landscapes and mountains are both charming and lyrical. He conveys a vivid sense of what it was like to travel across a fragmented and sometimes dangerous Europe in the 1840s while being, in other ways, the Englishman abroad.

His experiences were extraordinary, for example, on the 17th July 1846 and the 6th of October 1847, he tells of listening to Strauss and his orchestra in Vienna. He quotes Byron,[17] to him almost a contemporary, when describing thunderstorms in the mountains. He rides post horses across Serbia for hour after hour, misses a steamer and has to race to reconnect with it, meets a princess on a steamer and converses with her, cuts himself on a gun he has loaded for fear of robbers, and has cause to deal with a drunken postillion, but he also engagingly tells of making apple cakes for his companions, gets sick from the chemicals he uses to dye his moustaches, tells us how sad he feels when he receives no letters from home, and riffs on puns for the word 'leveret' when he fails to catch a hare on a hunting trip.

The first journal was written in a small brown leather notebook (4½ inches by 2 inches, approx.) with a pencil holder attached, in 1846. It was lodged with Cousin Barbara and, on a visit to her in July 2013, I photographed each page on my phone and used the photographs later to transcribe the handwriting[18]. I had been slowly transcribing it, a few pages at a time, when my sister, Alison, told me that Aunty Joan had shown her another journal written in 1847, describing a similar journey. I photographed that journal too, on a visit to see Joan in October 2014, and set to work transcribing it also. This journal is written in both pencil and ink in a black embossed pocketbook with pencil holder attached (5¾ inches by 3¾ inches, approx.) with a metal clasp. It has two watercolours of the messenger houses – the one they stayed in and the new one being built – and some simple line drawings of other buildings and landscapes. After my aunt's death in October 2017, I was given it to keep.

My Own Journals and Poems

In 2017, having finished the first rough transcription of the journals, I began to think about making the same journey as my great-great-grandfather with the intention of writing a journal as I travelled the same route as him, and writing poems when I returned. I applied for an Arts Council England/ British Council Artists' International Development Fund for help with travel to Hungary and Serbia and was lucky enough to receive it. The Artists' International Development Fund fosters relationships between writers and artists in the UK and those in other countries. I contacted The Petőfi Institute in Hungary, and the British Council arranged an introduction to Imre, a PhD student and lecturer at Debrecen University, Hungary where I subsequently did a reading at the university. Before travelling to Serbia I worked with Serbian poet, Ivanka Radmanović, on translations into Serbian of parts of the journals together with some of my poems and was invited to read at the 55th Belgrade International Writers' Assembly, September 19th to 23rd, 2018 which included readings in Belgrade, Malo Crniće and Veliko Gradište. Ivanka arranged additional readings for me in Vrbas, Pančevo and Niš. On 9th September 2018 I flew to Budapest with my wife, Lesley, and arrived home on 2nd October 2018. I took with me the 1847 journal which I was privileged to show to audiences at some of the readings. The journal I wrote during those three weeks is long and detailed and when planning this work, I decided to include sections of it where there seemed to me to be a point of interest between my journal and George's journals.

As I finished the fine details of the transcriptions of the journals and transcribed my own handwritten journals, all sorts of ideas began to take shape in my head: correspondences between then and now, progress and the lack of it. How our lives are measured, now as then, by the simple requirements of sleep and food and the turning wheel of day and night. How humanity takes itself forward in time but makes the same mistakes over and over and how imprisoned we are by our own moment in history. How what seems like progress for one generation – trains, steamers, etc – can become in time an ecological disaster for the generations to come. How we are all to some degree unreliable narrators, through forgetfulness but also through misunderstanding of other cultures or languages or deliberate misrepresentations of them. How the policies of earlier generations create the seedbeds for war and genocide. How complex political relationships can be. How personal responsibility, thoughtfulness and kindness may incrementally shape what is to come. How ideas of gender and power are used and misused. How sexuality is powerfully frightening to some people. How conformity relates to repression. How difference is dangerous. How religion, of all kinds, can be used as a tool of power and control. How colonialism and authoritarianism are used and misused. How uncertainty rides with us, because we are living creatures, and how facing that can be both uncomfortable and liberating. The idea of messages and messengers gradually became clearer. What do we take from the past? Can we improve?

I have given the Good Housewife, whose cockerel was murdered by Edmund Spencer, a list of concerns which she, and I of course, consider have not yet been adequately addressed in modern society. Considerations of feminist theory, gender inequality, discrimination, objectification, oppression, stereotyping, cultural imperialism and patriarchy lie at the heart of what I've been thinking about as I've navigated these journeys. There are many other concerns, of course. Some have shifted in the 175 years since George's journals were written, some remain constant. War and genocide remain with us. Dictators still rise to power and cling to it. Poverty and lack of social mobility still prevent people from fulfilling their dreams. The place of women in society is still fragile and unequal.

Our planet, our home, is now under threat; George spends much of his free time trying to shoot animals while we are faced with multiple extinctions. George benefits from the innovations of the beginning of the industrial revolution, powered by fossil fuels, while we, in continuing to use them, are facing global warming, extremes of temperature, floods, famines. George is familiar with quarantine and pandemics while we have been overtaken by the sudden appearance of Covid as a global emergency with lockdowns, quarantines and the development and rollout of new vaccines. For George communications are in their infancy – letters take weeks and get lost, despatches take months to arrive – while we are blessed (and cursed) with instant communications both personal and governmental. For George 'who we know' is important in getting on, and for us? I'll leave you to answer that question.

George and I share a little bit of our DNA – perhaps we also share something about the way we experience the world. His use of language, his sense of humour, his curiosity and fascination with otherness, his ability to be both open and closed at the same time, his joy in the physical world – all this feels familiar. He experiences that world through the prism and privilege of his gender. I do also, through mine, and through being lesbian in a mainly heterosexual world. How much is George aware of his privilege which comes from gender, class, wealth and education? How much am I aware of my own privileges? His youth, and my age, surely also affect our ways of looking. All of us, when we write, show our prejudices, whatever they are, and this comes through in a travel journal which is ostensibly about 'visits to places' as it does in more formal explorations of self.

For all of us it's hard to step outside our current lives. We try, perhaps in a piecemeal fashion, to get some perspective on the wider picture. George certainly can't 'see' Empire, with its ideas of borders and dominance, with white English men at the top of the tree, although he debates politics with his friends at Alexnitza who probably introduce him to some new ways of thinking.

It's a complex set of subjects and themes. The messages knock against each other in the messenger house. There are ambivalences and contradictions. My parallel journey and the writing of a journal about it, which like George's, does not comment overtly, or not very much, on the underlying thoughts of the writer was a deliberate act of equivalence. Where writing appears that is slant, it may offer views of other mountains, 'wild translations', hints at other messages.

Then and Now

Progress with the manuscript, after my return from Hungary and Serbia, was slowed by a period of ill health and by the Covid pandemic. We had booked a further trip, from London to Hungary, stopping in most of the places George visited en route. The start date for that trip was to have been the 15th May 2020, but on that day I was instead booked in to hospital for a biopsy preparatory to further treatment. Sick, and in full lockdown from Covid, we had to cancel that journey.

Poems, journals, letters, messenger regulations and other testimony, both imaginary and actual, sit side by side with each other here. All the writers are dealing with uncertainties of one kind or another as we all do in living our lives. I am interested in what they say, and don't say, to each other, how their, and my, testimonies rub up against each other. When I was a schoolchild, I didn't relate to the history books that were used to teach us: dry lists of wars and skirmishes, treaties, third party discussions of political decisions and their repercussions, which I couldn't connect with the pain and loss, the joy, the steady satisfaction, the multitude of emotions which must surely, I thought, lie underneath the words. Those history books seemed remote and disconnected from humanity – was that part of their purpose? The word 'progress' also was mysterious to me. As a post-war baby-boomer I was raised on the comforting notion that society moves forward in a trajectory of constant improvement, but I had a sneaking suspicion, even then, that things could and did reverse, politically, socially and catastrophically quickly and that gains in freedom and liberty could be as easily taken away as given.

The Balkans War of 1991 to 1999, with its horrors of ethnic cleansing, the suffering of refugees and the seventy-eight days of NATO bombing of Serbia are still, of course, raw and recent wounds in the memories of the people of the region. Some of the physical scars on the buildings of Belgrade have been left as witness to the bombing. I wondered if I could or should write anything about it, and finally decided that where people had talked to me about their experience of the war or what came after, I would, with humility, include some of what was said.

In Hungary the Prime Minister, Viktor Orbán, has shifted the political scene towards right-wing national conservatism and authoritarianism and has pursued anti-democratic reforms. His attempts to rewrite history include denying Hungarian responsibility for the murder of Jewish people in Hungary during the Second World War. I have included, in my journals, a description of a protest against a nationalistic monument which was erected covertly shortly before my trip to Hungary, and which we were witness to on our visit. In June 2021 Hungary's parliament passed legislation that bans, amid strong criticism from human rights groups and opposition parties, the dissemination of content in schools deemed to promote homosexuality and gender change. The new legislation wrongly conflates paedophilia with LGBTQ issues. Orbán has become increasingly extreme on social policy, railing against LGBTQ people and immigrants.

It has become clear to me, during the writing of this book, just how many of my – it should be acknowledged – comfortably-off 19th century relatives spent time living and working or simply fossicking about in Europe,[19] and what a natural thing it was for them to travel joyfully and extensively, to set down roots for a bit, to learn languages, to trade, to learn about other cultures, to look outwards. During the time it took to write this book the UK chose to leave Europe, chose Brexit and to listen to Little Englanders,[20] and I record here my anger at the politicians who enabled the whole debacle and who peddled lies to achieve it.

The welcome I was given from the people I met in Hungary and Serbia, and their many kindnesses during my travels, were extraordinary. I made many good, lifelong friends and I hope that this journey will be the first of many.

Whispers and Shadows

As Eavan Boland says of her poem 'Quarantine', 'the past is a place of whispers and shadows' ((UCTV), 2010). In transcribing these handwritten journals, I began to listen to some of those whispers.

While struggling with George's sometimes cryptic handwriting, place names which had changed, translations of the interjected German phrases (inaccurate German, impossible handwriting), the politics of the time, the social mores, I found I also wanted to know more about the people whose names are sometimes spelt phonetically, to learn about things we have mostly forgotten like quarantine[21] officers, types of sword, items of clothing, post horses and posting. I desperately wanted to know about people mentioned in passing – well known to George but who cannot now be found in the historical documents I've consulted. I wanted to better understand the society at home and abroad and look at the historical and political context of Serbia and other European countries of the time. I wanted to look at archives to see why things happened as they did. I wanted to know what diplomatic papers Mr Gutch might have been carrying. I wanted to look in from the outside to try to understand these men whose frames of reference were of their time, gender and class.

I haven't been able to find out everything – many things remain a mystery – life was as complicated then as now, but I hope you will enjoy these journals and my investigations of them, the poems and prose pieces, the whispers and shadows, the unsettled places where birds, disturbed, stretch out their wings before taking flight out of open water.

PART 1

Before Setting out, some letters
of a private nature on politics and health

To his brother William from Sir Stratford Canning[22]
British Embassy at Constantinople [Istanbul],
2nd December 1845

...I am told you would like to know a little more of my goings
on and so you shall. I must begin, however, by observing that my
goings on are often very much like standings still. At this moment
for instance, though I have long wished to be amongst you all once
more, and to rejoin my more especial belongings, it is to no purpose
that I spur with both heels, use horse language, and vip, and vip,
and vip ; the old hack will have its own way, sometimes with a
start, then with a kick, not always unaccompanied with a plunge
that bespatters one with mud, and not unfrequently with a dead
stop. Not so with the mails and steamers. On they go, whizzing
and whisking their paddles, or rattling their legs, and snorting out
loads of paper, instructions, reports, remarks, notes, letters, journals,
reviews, petitions, and Heaven knows what besides. In comes the
never-ceasing drift, under the doors, through the windows, down the
chimneys there is no possibility of keeping it out. I shovel it, attachés
shovel it, the dragomans shovel it, but the heap never disappears, and
all we can do by shovelling together is to save ourselves from being
choked by the accumulation. Where it all comes from and what it's
all about is sometimes a puzzle to me as well as to you; but you may
be sure that it is more pleasant to read about it than to deal with [...

...] Our new Embassy house, or palace as it is called here, is
rising rapidly above the ashes of the old one, and I have extorted a
few thousand pounds from the Porte[23] for the purchase of a row of
Turkish houses, the removal of which will open the garden on one
entire side to a fine terrace-view of Constantinople and its Golden
Horn.[24]

*

What can I say about the Ambassadors in Constantinople? I read their letters from the originals, or copies of the originals logged at the time by embassy staff. I wanted to know what they were dealing with when ggg [great-great-grandfather] was on his journey, what despatches they received and sent. I saw humanity in those ambassadorial letters, they moved me. That they had blind spots is undoubted but still their letters gave me a sense of who they were, and what they were dealing with seemed, too often, to be similar to what we deal with now.

'I have extorted a few thousand pounds from the Porte', writes Canning, 'for the purchase of a row of Turkish houses, the removal of which will open the garden on one entire side to a fine terrace-view of Constantinople and its Golden Horn'. This opens a can of worms. I wonder what compensation was paid for these houses, what happened to those who lived in them? The humanity evident in the letters and despatches is, of course, partial. The habits of the ruling upper classes are ingrained. The view of Constantinople and its Golden Horn is more important than its people.

To Hertslet from Thos. De Gr de Fonblanque
Belgrade March 28 [1845]

My dear Hertslet,
the inclosed from Count Pisani[25] scarcely leaves a doubt of the violation of the Dispatches[26] entrusted to Tatar[27] Tassa, and the delay, admitted by the man himself, makes it nearly certain that the criminal act was done here. To my mind, the consulates are quite absolved from even the faintest suspicion, and among the supports of various Political Parties here, I should say that Polish Emissaries are more likely than even those of Obrenovitches.[28] I have written to ask Sir Stratford Canning whether I shall adopt any measures in concert with H M Govt.

Ever faithfully yours, Thos. De Gr de Fonblanque

Belgrade March 28/45.

My dear Hertslet,

The inclosed from Count Pisani scarcely leaves a doubt of the violation of the dispatches entrusted to Tatar Jafea, and the delay admitted by the Man himself makes it nearly certain that the criminal act was done here. To my mind, the consulates are quite absolved from even the faintest suspicion, and among [...]

Be kind enough to return Ct. Pisani's letter when you have done with it. Tde F

Letter from Ct Pisani respecting certain Bags and Packets, forwarded by a tatar, which are suspected to have been opened [*explanatory note from Hertslet written above letter*]

*

To Hertslet from Mr Gutch
Calais Jan 27 1846

My dear sir
My wife lies here so dangerously ill[29] that I am reluctantly
compelled to beg that you will at your earliest convenience send me
my relief. Did I see any hopes of amendment I should not take this
step but with the chance of a surgical operation being necessary you
will I am sure imagine my anxiety to get her case seen to near our
home. Pray drop me a line saying when I may hope to be relieved.

Very truly yours, JWG Gutch

Mr Gutch Jan 28th. To be relieved from the Paris Station in
consequence of the serious illness of his wife [*explanatory note from
Hertslet inscribed top right of letter*]

*

From Hertslet to Mr Gutch
F. O. [*Foreign Office*]
28th January 1846
To JWG Gutch Esq.

My dear Sir
I have submitted your application (which ought to have been in
an official style, and accompanied by a medical certificate), to Mr
Addington; and I have the satisfaction to acquaint you that he has
complied with your request, and that you are at liberty to come
with Mrs Gutch immediately to England. Your place will be
supplied when your turn for Paris shall have arrived. Yours truly,

Signed Lewis Hertslet

*

From Mr Gutch to Hertslet
Foreign Office Feb 18 1846

Sir,

In consequence of the continued illness of Mrs Gutch, I do not think I should be justified in undertaking a foreign journey as although I had resumed duty I did so under the impression that ere my presence would be required, her health would be so far restored, as to render my further detention in England unnecessary; this I regret to say has not been the case, as the enclosed note, from her medical attendant will testify, and I trust that I shall be allowed under these peculiar circumstances to have my name placed at the bottom of the list[30]. I beg to remain Sir, Very truly yours, JWG Gutch, Queens For. [*Foreign*] Service Messenger

> To Lewis Hertslett Esq.
> Foreign Office
> Downing Street

From John Ashburner [Mrs Gutch's Physician] to Mr Gutch [forwarded to Hertslet as medical certificate and proof of Mrs Gutch's illness]
Private

55 Wimpole Street
18 February 1846
My dear Sir,

Your anxiety about Mrs Gutch is perfectly natural, and I cannot conceal from you the motives which have induced Mr Donatt and myself to postpone for a time the operation which was proposed. In some of these cases the uterus is in a condition to propagate malignant inflammations to the tissues in the neighbourhood, if the operation be had recourse to before it be ascertained whether the organ in truth be in a partially healthy condition. The last case we had at the Middlesex Hospital terminated fatally after the operation as a result of peritoneal inflammation which came on very suddenly[31]. We wish in Mrs Gutch's case, to avoid if possible the chance of such a result by taking a fair time to note other changes that may take place in the uterine tissues and to be enabled to assure ourselves that no untoward result may follow upon our endeavours to restore health. You must know well that to define a period under the circumstances when we can make up our minds, cannot be an easy matter. It may be ten days or it may be a few weeks, but you must be fully aware that we should not be warranted in our endeavours to hasten the time, or to precipitate our convictions on any account.

I remain, My dear sir, Yours sincerely, John Ashburner

Admonitions[32]

Never expose yourself to the night air
nor too much to the rays of the sun

Never sleep upon deck by moonlight
nor drink cold liquids in a state of perspiration

Travellers on foot should never sleep
under the shadow of a tree nor in a hemp field

If you pass over a bridge, or through a river in the night
never place confidence in your Postillions

who are sometimes intoxicated or sleepy –
never at that time traverse a large or lonely forest.

*

Travellers should never visit a sick person
in the morning before breakfast

nor in the presence of the sick
should they swallow their own saliva

Sweet or boiled wines inflame the blood
and are productive of the most dangerous consequences

The best posture for the 'siesta'
is half inclined and turned to the left side

Desist from exercise of a violent kind
and always keep the bowels moderately open.

*

The activity of the whole machine
is enlivened by cheerfulness

A degree of joy removes noxious particles
– gaiety, mirth, exultation and rapture

aid in the preservation of health
when not carried to an excess or too long continued

Before the tourist leaves England, he should lay down
a route from which he should never deviate –

a carriage for the Continent should carry linch-pins,
anti-attrition grease and a drag chain.

At home 2020/1: A&E for X-ray and CT 27th April 2020

I enter on footsteps, painted red,
this is the Covid part of A & E,
they think my cough might be a side-effect –
a blood clot to the lung.

The medical consultant has a chat.
Cancer, he says, and that's that –
it's written down with promises of tests.
I leave on footsteps, painted apple green.

9th September 2018: London to Budapest

Left the house and walked to the station with suitcases and a
rucksack. The train was just drawing into the station, so we ran to
catch it, both of us horrified at how we had nearly missed it!

Got through the departure lounge at Gatwick but had to take three kilos weight (books!) out of my large suitcase and into the hand luggage so as not to pay a surcharge. Good flight. L has a heavy cold. Arrived in Budapest at 4.30pm and caught a bus to the city centre only eight minutes' walk from the Hotel Palazzo Zichy. A short rest and unpacking then out for dinner and a walk in nearby streets. Took in the RC church where a service was in progress. Many young people singing. The church is large with two ornate wooden closed stalls for confession. Then back to the hotel and so to bed.

Journal, the first

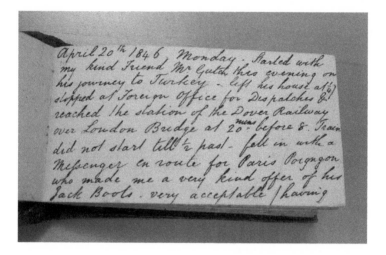

April 20th 1846.[33] Monday. Started with my kind friend Mr Gutch this evening on his journey to Turkey – left his house at ¼ 7 stopped at Foreign Office for Dispatches and reached the station of the Dover Railway over London Bridge at 20 mins before 8. Train did not start till half past – fell in with a Messenger en route for Paris (Poignon) who made me a very kind offer of his Jack Boots – very acceptable (having been disappointed of my own riding boots.)

After a journey of abt. 4½ hours we arrived at Dover – slept at The Ship a very comfortable Inn & started by one of the New English Packets (The Onyx[34]) at 7 am o'clock on Tuesday the 21st April. The Onyx is a very nice little packet and took us across to Calais in 1½ hour. It was a lovely morning which I looked upon as a favourable auspice for our journey. We pitched considerably & to my limited experience it seemed very rough tho. I understand it is seldom less so – every now & then got a perfect shower bath from the spray which broke over us –

At Home 2020/2: Base of brain to mid-thigh
FDG PET CT 4th May 2020

I wake with a migraine. No food allowed. A drive to Falmer to the imaging centre – run down at one edge of a car park. A nurse tells me they'll inject a radioactive tracer which contains a sugar to see if the cancer has spread to the lymph nodes. The operative talks about her cats, explains that I must lie without moving for one hour before the scan. No reading – that might take the dye to the brain where it's not needed. I take another migraine tablet. She brings the dye in a shielded box, wears an alarm at her waist which goes off as she opens it, injects it quickly, leaves the little room. I lie in the dark for an hour. The machine is big but the space above my head is very small. We move in increments, me and my tumour. I hold my breath when asked, repeatedly. Afterwards I walk out to the car park, ring L who comes to fetch me home.

– about half way we passed one of the French Steamers which had started about an hour & a half before us – a great unwieldy tub of a machine which takes about 4 hours to cross – mem. never to go by a French Steamer if I can go by an English one). At Calais having shown our passports at the Bureau des Passports and having the contents of our carpet bags turned out on the floor at the Douane (Customs) we proceeded to Dessins' Hotel where I left Mr Gutch to pack his carriage[35] & strolled out to see a little of Calais, an essentially French town, narrow streets, red brick houses chiefly with green shutters – stumbled upon Henry Stretton in one of the streets who was staying at Dessins' with his wife – We had breakfast at 10 for which I was quite ready having been up btn. 5 & 6 and a capital breakfast it was consisting of fried sole, mutton chops, omelette, cheese and a bottle and a half of Bordeaux (vin Ordinaire!!?!) I drank a bottle as good as the generality of claret one gets in England. Left Calais at about 11½ with post horses to Mr Gutch's carriage tow'ds Ostend – the Country flat sandy and uninteresting – the chief peculiarities being that the road was pitched the greater part of the way & ran thro' long avenues of trees as much as three miles in a straight line – passed thro' several small places Dunkirk & Nieport [Nieuwpoort] in Belgium strongly fortified – reached Ostende abt. 7½ this is also strongly fortified – most of the towns are – Ostende seems a clean and rather pretty town – stopped at the hotel d'Angleterre, the nearest to the railway – had a good dinner & went to bed to be ready for the Premiere Convoye du chemin de fer (1ˢᵗ Train)[*first train of the morning*] the following morning at 7.

Wednesday 22ⁿᵈ April had a cup of coffee and got to the station which as well as the carriages are very similar to ours – we travell'd in Mr G's carriage, uncommon snug, smoking allowed in all the carriages I indulged in to a great extent – not quite so fast as ours – 20 miles an hour. The country still very flat till we reached Lieges down to which there is an inclined plaine of abt 3 miles – from here to Aix la Chapelle [Aachen] the country is most picturesque, the road winding round thro. most beautiful little wooded vallies with a good deal of rock & passing thro' scarcely less than 16 or 18 tunnels. Reached Aachen [Aachen] abt. 7. dined & slept – had a capital bottle of Hockheimer – this is a large handsome & very clean town. Stayed at Nuellens a very nice hotel. & nicht so theur [*not so expensive*]

Thursday 23ʳᵈ April: started at 7 O'clock rail to Cologne.³⁶ Railroad not so good as the Belgian – country uninteresting. Cologne fortified city, beautiful, cathedral worthy of note begun in 1248,³⁷ not finished, crane on the top. Arrived here about 9½ and got horses as soon as we could (Germans not given to hurrying themselves) to take us to the Rhunishe Dampfschiffe [*River Rhine steamboat*] which sailed at 10. After sundry twinings & windings thro' narrow streets and many stoppages for other vehicles to pass behold us at last on the glorious Rhine. With the Rhine I confess I was disappointed, the greater part of the way the banks were low and muddy and the country flat and not till within two or three hours of Coblentz did it improve, it then became certainly very beautiful, undulating Bergs [*mountains*] beautifully covered with wood among which the most conspicuous objects are of course Drachenfels & Ehrenbreitstein – but I understand the most striking part of the Rhine is from Magenance to Coblentz which I hope to see coming back at a more favourable season and I shall then hope to have a more pleasing impression of the Beauties of the "Magestic Rhine" (Rafts on the Rhine, smoking dirt and feeding on board the Dampfschiffe – specimen of a German dinner – soup, fish, Boulli [*stew*], pigeon fried in batter, vegetables, roast fowl, pudding roast meat, cheese, dessert and wine in tumblers. We reached Coblentz abt. 7½ and started immediately with post-horses for Wiesbaden. Arrived at 4½ had a wash – breakfasted by myself at Duradly. Mr Gutch went to Mr Hughes, introduced to Mrs Hughes. Pump room and gardens worthy of notice here.

Friday 24th April went on by railroad to Frankfurt am Main, Hotel de Russie. Lunched. Splendid. Bronze statue of Goethe. Streets broad and clean and buildings handsome. Started at 2pm Darmstadt a large melancholy looking town. The Bergstrasse, road from thence to Heidelberg is a lovely drive along the base of a range of hills, thickly wooded and surmounted by old Castles – supped at Heidelberg at the Holländische Hof – Badische Hof [38] the best Inn, Mr Gutch made a blunder. From here we posted on to Stuttgardt where we breakfasted (Marcquardt's Hotel) a fine handsome town and prettily situated.

Saturday 25 April – posted on thro' Ulm to Augsburg took the rail road to Munich which we reached about 12½ on <u>Sunday 26th</u> had a Déjeuner a la fourchette[39] [*lunch with a fork*] at Schwarzer Adler [*The Black Eagle*] – another blunder the Goldener Hirsch[40] [*Golden Stag*] the best inn. The country round Munich flat and uninteresting but Munich itself nothing striking – the houses for the most part mean & dirty & with red tile roofs.

> Have an eye
> to your
> fallows[41]

Our drive from Munich continued for some hours thro' [*a*] flat bleak tract of country the wind blowing very cold from the Illyrian Alps of which we had a splendid view – a magnificent irregular range their tops covered with snow – after a time the country assumed a less desolate aspect – became more wooded & we passed thro' numerous villages – the roads thro' which are lined on both sides with Poplars – indeed thro'out the continent they appear a very favourite tree continuing in avenues for as much as 50 miles at a time – the pine forests too of great extent attracted my observation – giving to the country a very picturesque appearance. About 12 or 14 miles from Munich we began to ascend Mt Conjecture reached a great altitude. During the night we were awoke out of our sleep by a tremendous jolting which threatened the speedy dissolution of our vehicle at least we stopped and our Mr Gutch getting out he found only just in time – we had crossed a deep ditch at the side of the road and had got over on a rugged bank – two yds. more would have carried us over a fall of 10 or 12 feet – as it was, how we escaped being upset I know not – the roads thro'out are most dangerous, very rough & in some places an embankment of 4 or 5 feet with no defence whatever.

At Home 2020/3:
Percutaneous Lung Biopsy 15th May 2020

Before we head to CT where she'll push a needle in my lung
the doctor asks me if I've seen it on a screen.
I answer – that they let me know by phone –
because of Covid, I've been keeping safe.
She offers me a view. The PET scan of ten days ago
opens a window to my inner life. Drab is good,
in terms of diagnostics. We gaze together
at the swirls of force, the white explosive heat,
the supernova in my chest; its stubborn conflagrations.

<u>Monday 27th April</u>   Reached Braunau the Austrian frontier abt. 8 O'clock – when having submitted the carriage to a <u>slight</u> inspection / they were very civil here as I believe is generally the case towds. Cabinet Couriers we proceeded to The Traube [*The Grape*] to wash & breakfast – we were nearly putting our feet in it here, for whilst Mr. G. went out to put some letters in the post I was honoured by a visit from one of the Police Corps whose business was I learnt, when Mr. G. returned, to take me before the Commissaire de Police (I having omitted to have my Passport visé at Frankfurt by the Austrian Minister) – but this after some little chaff was remedied, Mr. G. representing that he had never known it necessary with a Cabinet Courier. We were shown in to his Bed room (a specimen of Continental manners) where he

& his wife received us, both in déshabille having just risen from their bed which was still occupied by two or three Kinchens in a state of somnolency.

From here the road continued hilly & pretty passing thro' unimportant places and on Tuesday 28th April about an 8 or 9 hours' drive from Vienna we came in sight of the waters of the "mighty Danube" – this is indeed a magnificent river & in some parts of it the scenery is very beautiful tho' the general character of its banks are low and muddy – We breakfasted at Molk [Melk] – town small and insignificant – but having a Benedictine Monastery beautifully situated on a rock rising abruptly from the right bank of the river to the height of 180 feet. From here nothing striking appeared in the road & we came in sight of Vienna about 5 or 6 o'clock pm. – I was disappointed with the capital of the Austrian dominions – the houses mean and dirty and the streets narrow – the most striking objects are the Emperors Palace and grounds. Schönbrunn of which you catch a slight glimpse on the right as you enter Vien [Vienna] it appears a magnificent Pile of building of great extent – but more consonant with our ideas of an antique Mansion House built of a lightish stone & having a red roof – it is surrounded with splendid forest trees – & on an eminence in the grounds is situated a sort of temple handsomely built to which the Public are allowed to make Parties etc and the cathedral a stupendous gothic Pile of architecture – the roof a sort of mosaic work of a diamond pattern, with tiles of various colours. We drove to the Kaiserin von Österreich [*Empress of Austria*], but their [sic] being no room we located ourselves in the Wild Mann ou de L'Homme Sauvage & found it very comfortable – we dined & slept – Mr Gutch received his dispatches & orders that night at 12!! to go by the steamer next morning at 6 – underneath

Wednesday 29th April we missed the steamer! Which gave us a few hours in Vienna which we spent in shopping and intended going by the next boat at 3 but that being a small one wo'd not take the carriage so we were obliged to have post horses to Presburgh[42] [Bratislava] – nearly the whole of the way is flat & monotonous – with scarcely an eminence to be seen – reached Presburgh abt. 8½ – like the other Austrian towns – more dirty if possible – dined, slept etc at the Grüner Baum [*Green Tree*] – Royal Palace – burnt by fire in 1811 finely situated on an eminence behind the Town – crossed by a Bridge of Boats similar to the one across the Rhine at Coblentz.

there is time to lie down/ those trees by the river/ platinum when
the wind blows/ flip-side wind driven/ deep green/ / look/ listen/
a raft/one side of a packing case/ drifting/ and creak of oars/ dog
in the gunwale/ / a cormorant / tied low to the curves of the river/
flapping like crazy /gains height where trees lean over/ where a
telephone wire crosses the water

Thursday 30th April 1846 Started at 8 by the steamer down the Danube
& enjoyed a similar day to that spent on the Rhine – the packet being
if anything more filthy & the company less select. The scenery very
pretty undulating well wooded hills surmounted by numerous old
Hungarian fortresses – chiefly dismantled by the Turks – curious
Mills on the Danube formed by two boats & a wheel between them
– a house in one where the Miller lived. Frequently as many as 8
or 10 together forming quite a village – arrived at Pesth[43][Pest] at 7
which appeared an improvement on Presburgh but it was too late to
form a very decided opinion of its merits (there is another bridge of
boats here – I saw it opened for a steamer to pass thro' – the boats are
severally anchored & at one end the boards across are not joined and,
on casting loose 6 or 8 of the anchors, that portion of the bridge sways
down with the stream and so forms a strait) this I saw at Presburgh
before we started. Now we found the inconvenience of having lost
the Steamer from Vien for on inquiry we found the Packet from
here to Semlin [Zemun] had sailed this very morning (30th) & that
the next wod. not sail till Sunday – so Mr. Gutch not deeming it
prudent to delay ordered horses to his carriage with all the pleasing
anticipation of 50 or 60 hours posting – we had time however to
visit a celebrated Pipe Shop here – where I invested a little "Geld" in
those depositaries for that universal panacea for the woes of human
nature "Bacco". We then returned to the Inn (Königin von England)
[Queen of England] & went to snatch a snooze at 10 o'clock with
strict injunctions to be called at 3 in the morning.

Friday 1st May – Got off about 4½ and now commenced the delights
of Hungarian Travelling – the Country is one vast plain bounded
only by the horizon & at least one [¼] of it an uncultivated sandy
common –

straggling
disjointed fields
are most perplexing[44]

there are no enclosures & no roads except such as are made by the waggons of the country – the traveller is entirely dependent on the farmers of the country for horses (Bauernpferde) [*farm horses*] to take him on his way and who we found thro'out very accommodating – though incontestably slow – keeping us waiting sometimes as much as 3 hours before we co'd make a start – we had fortunately provided ourselves with cold fowl, bread, & wine which was fortunate as we co'd get nothing this day but what extreme starvation wo'd have induced one to partake of – sour black bread, uninviting looking fragments of flesh & sauer kraut – cabbage leaves left together to rot & ferment and then cooked, boiled as a vegetable or made into soup – this night I awoke from a sound sleep by the calm which succeeded the pitching and tossing we had experienced all day & found ourselves in one of the vast plains – stuck fast nearly to the axletrees in sand – the moon just sinking – 2 o'clock morning & with every prospect of finishing the night there – the country is thickly overspread with large pools of water – at last we moved slowly and gained the next station about 6 o'clock having accomplished abt 14 miles since 9 the night before.

Nearly to the axletrees in sand

I awoke from a sound sleep
the pitching and tossing

had ceased
and now   stuck fast

in opal light
we opened our mouths

amphibious children
of the night

to let the cold come in
our voices strange

even to us
who have been used

to travelling dangerously
Ge thouu, geshvinkt thouu[45]

as we were taught
we entreat them

at last the farm horses
buck and leap with teeth bared

and shivering
gain a firm purchase

While waiting for the horses I made love to a Farmers Daughter for some capital coffee & bread and butter of which we were very glad. Cost 1 zwanziger. We continued journeying on in the same slow way that is to say with long delays for the actual speed is great the Hungarians being splendid whips & driving 4 in hand with an ease that wo'd eclipse many of our coachmen – the harness made [*of*] mostly rope – most of their waggons & carts are made without any iron.

Very glad were we to find ourselves on <u>Sunday 3rd May</u> about 8 o'clock at Peterwardein [Petrovaradin] where 5 or 6 hours wo'd complete our journey. This is a large & strongly fortified place on the Danube – in leaving it we crossed at least 3 or 4 moats & drawbridges. We breakfasted at Peterwardein or rather Neusatz [Novi Sad] (the other is the name of the fortress)…

Friday 14th September 2018: Budapest to Novi Sad via Vrbas

…made smoked salmon sandwiches at the breakfast table of the Budapest hotel and took pastries, free bottled water and filled the flask with hot peppermint tea for the train which has no buffet. The taxi driver swerved about so much we were both nearly sick.

Arrived at Keleti Station at 5 to 11 am for the train at 11.57. Waited in the grand and ornate station entrance hall with its beautiful murals. On the train a young man lifted both heavy cases up on the rack for us. There was a little metal pull-out rubbish bin below our table. I opened it to put in some rubbish – found a previous passenger had kindly left us several inches of urine.

The country all the way is very flat. Where corn has been harvested the edge of standing corn still left seems to mimic the horizon which here and there is broken up by trees. Small hamlets lie not far off or are split by the train lines. At minor stations people heft luggage over other tracks to get to and from the train. Station masters (men and women) wear a red cap with two gold bands. Crops we passed included grape vines, asparagus, maize. We passed a field with four pale long horned cattle. Hardly a bird in the sky.

do you remember that journey?
our train stopped   and we saw them
walking away   already stranger

I could be that old woman
in a blue coat   she the laggard
apex of a triangle   on whom

light falls   uneven but arresting
you could draw lines
from her   to any of the others

walking away from us   across tracks
mysterious souls   she is always
the stalled marker   impatiently

waiting to take the next step
the shadow glued to her heels
shaped like a mountain

At 20 to 4 we stopped at the Hungarian border for 10 to 15 minutes. Female border guards came on and checked our passports by running them through a slot in a hand-held machine. No obvious border – just a small border post by the side of the track. Then we set off slowly again into Serbia which seems less cultivated just here and with more derelict buildings close to the track.

Ten minutes down the line the train grinds to a halt and after fifteen minutes or so burly Serbian guards get on, collect everyone's passports, and take them away. Eventually underway again at 4.30 and, once our passports have been returned, new passengers get on. A family sit opposite us, two men, a woman and a child. They put their bags on the overhead rack and after a minute Coca-Cola cascades down all over them as their cola filled water bottle bursts. L gives the little boy some tissues.

The train trundles along at a very slow speed past acres and acres of flat farmland. I say to L 'It's not really a bullet train, is it?' As the train draws into Vrbas, L stays on the train and I prepare to get off; a man lifts my case out of the train for me and puts it down where it promptly rolls into the midriff of a woman waiting to get on. So my first words on Serbian soil are 'Thank you, thank you, sorry!'

Bane was there to meet me and took me straight to the Vrbas library where the reading would be, led me to where Ivanka and Vidak waited. A short interview with Serbian local TV before the reading at which Vidak extemporised on an essay he'd written about my work then I read poems interspersed with Ivanka reading her translations. In an uncomfortable moment when I read a poem about Suvla Bay a 90-year-old gets up and speaks about how it affected him, comes forward to shake my hand. I am moved to the point of tears, but later Bane says, this old man is over-emotional, his behaviour very unpredictable. Apparently, he also said that poets, including me, should have more influence over British politicians so that they like Serbia better.

I showed George's journal to the audience and they were very interested. Vidak said later of the picture of the messenger house that the place is still there, and we should be able to go and see it. It's a government building now and has a plaque on it, he says.

Run through

There's something about a railroad which passes through a village,

no station to sanction its passing, just an opening people slide through.

A farmer might pause before driving on. His load at right
angles to the rails,

no barriers to this crossing, just the train which passes
slowly, the road

little more than a track, some tarmac, some stones, the
fields behind him,

and houses to the side, dishevelled, with dogs on long
chains and scruffy

chickens scratching earth and open plots that run to the
rails in disorder – he pauses,

that farmer, sweats, rubs his head and looks like my
father stripped to the waist

on his way home for supper, chaff stuck to his skin. Dust
will adhere.

The day darkens towards nightfall, nothing is permanent,
so we go onwards,

the village broken open like a husk of corn and all these
sentences unfinished

After the reading Bane invites us for a meal. We drive in Ivanka's
car to the restaurant. As we arrive a van goes past with an array
of nozzles from which a fine mist sprays the air around the road
and the verge. I recognise the smell from the farm – insecticide;
for mosquitoes says Ivanka. We must walk through the fog of
droplets to get to the restaurant. Later Bane and his father drive
me to the apartment, Fortress View, in Novi Sad, where we'll stay
for two nights. L has gone ahead (on the train I got off at Vrbas)
and got settled, got Serbian money, gone shopping for eggs, milk
and bread for breakfast.

En route Bane explains the toll road system. Top speed here is
130 km/hr. Ivanka should stop for coffee in between the booths to
make the time longer, he says. He worries that she may be fined

and tries to phone her. I ask if he's been to the UK, as he's told me his wife studied at Essex – coincidentally in the same department as I did. He says he is not allowed to enter the UK, he came to Serbia as a refugee during the conflict, then plays me a song on his mobile phone:

Selma [46]

There's a toll road from Vrbas to Novi Sad
the ticket timed from one end to the other
and if you go too fast you'll get a fine.
On his phone he plays the hard rock ballad
and says that Selma never did arrive.

Selma is leaving for college
She's leaving while I carry her suitcase
Look it's heavy, but it's hers
and so I love that suitcase too

Between two toll booths in the headlight's flicker
he tells me he's a Bosnian refugee,
says War is better than what comes after.
This desolation dropped in silence
over the song of loss and non-arrival.

I wanted to tell you something sweet
something with lots of concern
but I said only goodbye Selma
and please, do not lean out of the window

We soon arrive at the flats in Novi Sad. Bane and his father check we are at the right place and leave while I phone for L to come down to meet me at the café below. The key sticks fast in the lock as we enter the flat and L rings the owner, Damir, who comes over to investigate. A locksmith will be needed the next day. The door cannot now be locked.

We look over towards the Fortress that night from our apartment on the fifth floor – below us on the promenade by the river are hundreds of young teenagers talking, playing, eating, drinking – beer, juice, vodka (L shopped with them in the local shop). They promenade until late – the bridge across to Petrovaradin lit by thousands of rainbow lights.

Saturday 15th September 2018: Novi Sad

Damir has come to the flat to wait for a locksmith while we go out to explore Novi Sad.

At the waterside, where the teenagers roamed last night, we look at the monument to the Jews and Serbs murdered in the Second World War by the armed forces of Hungary.[47]

Later we notice seven army boats drawn up nearby – with camouflage etc. Further on a merchant vessel, the 'Kapitan Shirkov', has washing strung out on a line along the deck which catches my eye, the domesticity a contrast to the military, then we walked across the bridge to the Fortress side, where the museum is, and round the old buildings marvelling at their clay-tiled roofs. These are of the age to have been here when George was here. Some of the streets are cobbled as they would have been. There were no hotels on the Novi Sad side of the Danube when George stayed here.

George continues:

...and were on our road again at 9 o'clock – the road is very pretty & near the Danube the whole way – reached Semlin [Zemun][48] about 4pm – a large but extremely mean and dirty town, in which you see the Servian, Hungarian, German and a few Turkish Costumes – found Holmes, one of the messengers & Mr Fonblanque, Con. Gen. [*Consul General*] at Belgrade – took up our quarters at the same Inn [Beiusel's] 3 fl. a day – tolerably comfortable – dined at 6. Belgrade very picturesquely situated – Pacha's Palace a mean looking building – Turkish Mosques Minarets etc partly Turkish & Servian – went in Turkish part to a Tobacco & Pipe shop – bought a pipe stick & some "Bacco".

Wednesday 19th September 2018: Belgrade

Woke at 7.30am to another scorching day, 30 degrees C, which it has been since we arrived on the 9th September. No rain, occasional clouds. Ivanka came at 11am to show us Belgrade, this being a mostly free day, with only the opening Serbian Writers event this evening. She took us on a tour of Belgrade – the Fortress[49] and then the Konak Building[50] – an early 19th century Turkish-style mansion, built by Prince Miloš Obrenović as a Residence for his wife Ljubica Obrenović, showing the architecture, furniture and interior design of the period which brings George's descriptions of clothes and interiors of the time to life. We had lunch with Ivanka and later she took us for ice cream and coffee before we came back to the flat for a short rest before the evening at the Association of Serbian Writers.

Ivanka told us that she was in the States during the war in Serbia and said it was reported in the USA as if it was a war game. She would phone her friend in Belgrade while watching the USA news and the friend could hear and feel the bombs dropping close by from the planes Ivanka was watching on TV. Ivanka, at that time, had a flat in New York and sheltered 12 Serbian friends and family at various times during the war. She told us about the sicknesses that have followed the war. Many more cancers in young people – the 15-year-old twins who have both been diagnosed with breast cancer. The role of depleted uranium.[51]

Thursday 20th September 2018: Belgrade

Slept badly, coughing much of the night. Breakfast, then out to the Association of Serbian Writers. We gathered for coffee and then walked out together to lay flowers on the statue of Ivo Andrić at 10am. Unfortunately, our group, all foreign poets, did not know the way and walked in the wrong direction to the wrong park! Eventually we arrived at the monument too late for the flower laying. Ivanka was there waiting – worried in case I was lost.

...into the Assembly of the City of Belgrade[52] for the official opening ceremony. Sat next to Ivanka and her historian friend, Mrs. Zorka Mirković, who told me the building was the Obrenović Dynasty court, that George's diary is precious because in general she had come across very little information, and almost no written documentation of that period. We had three speeches including one from the Culture Minister, translations of all the speeches into English, music from a famous guitarist and readings from Serbian poets. The halls are very splendid with chandeliers, pillars, large mirrors.

Afterwards the poets attending the gathering were given an open-air bus tour of Belgrade with commentary. We passed buildings partially destroyed in the '99 war which have been left with their war damage. The commentator also told us about the building of New Belgrade and how young people did National Service in the late 1940s by manually filling in the swamps and constructing roads.[53]

Friday 21st September 2018:
Belgrade to Rakovica to Malo Crniće to monastery of Zaow

Said goodbye to L, who is exploring Belgrade on her own for the next couple of days, and set out for the Serbian Writers Association at 9.40am with backpack, clothes for two days.[54] Arrived there and found Petar our guide, Amos the Italian poet and Aleksandr Kozhedub, the Russian. Got into Petar's car and set off in heavy traffic. I had no idea where we were going as Petar's English is small and my Serbian non-existent. The windscreen of his car had a very long diagonal crack right across it. We stopped once on a roundabout and veered gently into the kerb a couple of times to answer his phone or look up directions.

Our first stop was at Rakovica[55] monastery not far outside Belgrade. We arrived at 11am and went into an enormous auditorium with raked seating and a stage. A choir of adolescent girls and boys, dressed in black, sang, then there was a speech by an orthodox priest and some readings. There had been a spiritual poetry competition, which I later found out Petar had judged, and all the winners read and were awarded certificates and prizes and had pictures taken. Then it was our turn on stage where Petar read our poems in translation. There were other songs from the teenage choir, ecclesiastical in nature, and another ensemble, a woman singer with three male backing singers. Many poets came up and read their poem and finally it was over. A hasty trip to the loo, no time for lunch, we had 100km to drive before 3pm. We arrived with ½ an hour to spare. Petar had rung ahead to a motel for food...

...Drove on to the first engagement, a meeting with the mayor of Malo Crniće. We were ushered upstairs to his office in the municipal building for coffee and an introductory chat. They have much planned for us – we have no idea – it all unfolds. We go first to another monastery, monastery of Zaova, and are shown round by the orthodox monk. The inside of the church is covered in frescos. He tells the story of how it was founded. A legend about a married couple and her jealous sister. The sister tries to break up the marriage by killing first a falcon, then a dog and then the couple's child. She hides the knife under her sister's pillow. The wife is sentenced to death by her husband – tied to the tails of four horses, torn into four. This explains the founding of four monasteries where the pieces of her body came to rest. Nine years later the sister confesses and is also torn apart – thus explaining four local lakes. The tomb of the mother lies in the chapel engraved with an illustration of this horror.

We go to an awning in the monastery garden for drinks, slivovitz, mead etc, then the cavalcade of cars moves off – I am transferred into another car here along with Aleks, the Russian poet, and we soon arrive at one of the lakes near Veliko Selo, photos then back to the cars and along more small country roads. We park on a verge, get out, and see a carriage and two horses, a coachman, and then, in the porch of a ruined house, a couple sitting in 19th century costume. It is the poet Đura Jakšić, who wrote poems here, and his wife! He reads to us from his poem, 'Road to Gornjak' (*Put u Gornjak*). We go on a carriage ride up and down the lanes which feels doubly appropriate for me following in George's carriage tracks and finally arrive outside a village hall in Veliko Selo. There are children dressed up in 19th century costumes, a long table covered with drinks and sweet snacks, cakes etc. Slivovitz again. There is mead and honey and there are lots of wasps. I see a woman picking two out of the honey by their wings.

The coachman parks up under some trees we get out and the horses are patted. We chat to the local people, as best we can, and to the mayor and his people. Lots of smiling etc. Round the base of a monument, not far off, some young men posture, acting tough. I cannot work out their place in this.

After half an hour or so we go into the hall and are there from 4pm until 6pm. There is fantastic Serbian dancing in national dress, speeches from the mayor, singing, several solos from a young woman, and the children perform a piece in fancy dress which I do not understand at the time[56] but which later we are told is a mime of 19th century poets (some of the kids have drawn on what look like Hitler-style moustaches in felt tip pen which adds greatly to my utter confusion).

Many certificates are given on stage, and we get a certificate each too, there are more speeches – it's hard to know exactly what's going on. We are in the front row as guests of honour with the mayor. Afterwards we come out for cakes. Then to the library for a reading. 7pm till about 10pm. I lose my backpack briefly – it turns up in Petar's car although I am pretty sure I left it in someone else's – I think I changed cars twice!

We go into the reading – everyone in the audience reads one poem. We do too. People are very kind and chat afterwards and we have wine and more sausages. My leftover chicken from lunch which has been in Petar's hot car all afternoon is brought in for me to finish. Still coughing lots. Then we drive back to the motel outside Malo Crniće where we had our quick 3pm lunch and I take up residence in room 4. I catch up with messages to L, Facebook and so on and cough, cough, cough! Finish writing this at 11.50pm by which time I am more than ready to lay my head down. We are due to leave tomorrow at 10am.

Saturday 22nd September 2018:
Malo Crniće to Veliko Gradište

Went down to breakfast at ¼ to 9 after a night spent in uncontrollable coughing. The air conditioner took the temperature down to 16 degrees centigrade, but really, I slept very little.

After breakfast onwards to Veliko Gradište to the library where we are due to meet the library director, Milena Dimitrijević, the president of the Serbian Writers Association, Radomir Andrić, and some other officials. Petar kindly went off to get me cough syrup before the car full of poets arrived from Belgrade and we went into the library to be introduced to Milena. After greetings we went off to our new hotel. I have a self-contained studio flat with a small kitchen area, bathroom, sofa, double bed and desk. Perfect, and much more comfortable than last night's motel which had holes in the nylon sheets and was dusty. After dropping off bags and finding a photo of my driving licence on my phone – thank goodness as I really needed my passport which is still in Belgrade, and which was needed to register me with the police – we all went out to lunch. Petar drove us to a restaurant where all the poets were – two Russians, me, Amos, and all the Serbian poets from the Writers Association. Lunch took time – fish soup, main courses, coffees, puddings etc. Finally got to the little flat for an hour and a half before the reading at 6pm at the library.

The Association were launching an anthology about the Danube, which here makes the border between Serbia and Romania. I had wondered at lunch why one of the older male poets was wearing white nautical captain's hat, white shirt and trousers (now spattered with soup). There were the usual introductions and then long poems in Serbian from several poets. Then it was our turn to read. My voice is ropey from the cold and Milena read Ivanka's translations. Amos read his translated poem in Italian and in English translation. Then more poems from both Russians and we moved on to the Danube Anthology, more speeches and readings. At this point I got an unbearable tickle and had to leave to cough uncontrollably outside...

At Home 2020/5: Dunlin

this small flock/ takes flight/ skims the low waves/ flashes white till they/ tilt / brown against blue/ so close / to water/ breakwater/ tumbled stone/or ache/ blue sea-flick to reverse/tilt shift /to invisible/ drift/sift/ here/ not here/ a thought / material / but not /a trick of the light/ or joyful vanishing

The older poets left to go back to Belgrade and Petar, Amos, Aleks, Milena and I went for a drink and a bit of supper to the same restaurant we lunched at. Lots of back and forth conversation in various languages. Milena speaks excellent English. We discussed education in secondary school in Serbia, UK and Italy. She had been a teacher for a couple of years before joining the library service. I'd noticed earlier that the library had a good selection of English and American literature in Serbian translation including Virginia Woolf, Graham Greene and Walt Whitman. She told us it had been refurbished recently with district money and had a reference room, a children's room and the general adult borrowing room. Beautifully run and with an entrance hall with busts, statuettes and paintings.

After supper – back to the apartment (Amos went off for a walk in the dark around the lake). We are due to meet for breakfast at the same restaurant at 9am tomorrow. (Cooler tonight).

Sunday 23rd September 2018: Veliko Gradište to Belgrade

8.30am packed everything up in the apartment, shoved it into the backpack then out to the car. Petar, Amos and Aleks were sitting waiting under an arbour in the front garden. Drove to the restaurant for breakfast. Plain omelette, coffee, warm bread roll. The library director, Milena, joined us again. I asked about library opening hours – 7.30am until 8pm at night and shorter hours on Saturday – much better than in the UK, where libraries have been decimated by Tory spending cuts and are sometimes run by volunteers.[57]

After breakfast we walked to Srebrno Jezero (Silver Lake), a section of the Danube by an island which has been dammed at each end to form a lake. It is a holiday resort with many restaurants and cafés, a campsite, a river lido with ladders down into the lake, pedalos and a walkway by the lakeside. Amos said there was a fountain in the lake which was lit in many colours at night. It is end of season now, so quiet, but Milena says it shines silver when the sun is out. You can see Romania in the distance behind the island.

We begin the drive back to Belgrade. The country is very beautiful, much maize, slightly hilly wooded slopes and then suddenly a great plain before us and lower down – autumn farmland, full of golds and browns and greens. I shut my eyes for some of the trip having not slept much the night before and drift off to the music Petar is listening to on the car radio. Some classical, some traditional and finally pop which he turns off saying 'Enough!'. We reach Belgrade on a modern toll road and then enter Belgrade and head for the Centar and the Serbian Writers Association. There is nowhere to park so Petar stops in a side road, and we unload and say a quick goodbye and thank you to him and I walk back to our Belgrade apartment.

L is there talking to J on Messenger – so we have a long chat and catch up with him. L says she'll go out for a walk to the fortress to make the most of the good weather. It is due to get much colder tomorrow and rain is forecast. I rest on the sofa, reading. L comes back about 5.30pm and watches a film on her phone, sometimes laughing out loud, I have no idea why as she's using headphones.

Later out to supper in Skadarlija, a cobbled pedestrian street, full of restaurants. First, to a restaurant L had been to with J's friend, Matija Franklin, a few days ago. L said, even with Matija who was brought up in Belgrade, the staff were cantankerous! We were offered a small, cramped corridor table by a very grumpy waiter so slipped away and went to another place Ivanka had recommended, in a pleasant open-air forecourt with friendly waiters. After supper a ten-minute walk back to the apartment and bed. Coughing very bad with waking dreams which were nightmarish. Finally slept a bit.

Monday 24th September 2018:
Belgrade to Pančevo and return

Spent most of the day in bed coughing and resting and taking various medicines. Also dealt with Facebook and Instagram and put up more pictures and descriptions of the trip. Read, dozed etc. The weather has turned. From 30 degrees plus it is now 10 degrees C and it rained for much of the day. Messages from Ivanka re meeting up before the reading tonight. Vidak met us outside the Association and we walked to a main road above it to pick up the taxi he had ordered. Lovely ride to Pančevo. The skies had cleared and were full of frilled apricot clouds. Came out through the Belgrade suburbs into the countryside, went across the Danube and then into countryside with crops and what looked like ex-army huts near industrial areas. So, into Pančevo with its large central square. Drove straight to the library for the reading and met Ivanka and the library director, Dejan Bosnic, an ex-lawyer. We went into the hall, laid out with desks like a classroom. There were about fifteen or twenty people there.

Afterwards walked through the town, past the square which has grand houses built around the time George was in Serbia. Then down a long pedestrian street which has a prison on it about halfway along. An old prison with a wall next to it with razor wire on top. Dejan Bosnic joked that it is called 'the longest street'! Ivanka tells me that when she was a teenager in the 1970s, these pedestrian streets were used as promenades in the evening for all the local youth. You had to know which was 'your' area – the gymnasium and university students used one area, the blue collar, another. Ivanka points out some of the buildings, a particular favourite having ornate swags of plaster fruits below its windows. She tells us about a contemporary of hers at school who lived in one of these majestic buildings which had only broken windows (in the very cold winters) and was derelict – a whole family living there who all died very young.[58]

We arrived, then, at the restaurant for the evening – the cellar of an old brewery. At the back of the cellar a man with a microphone was singing accompanied by an accordionist. They both stood in the middle of a group of women in their 70s who were dancing a disco/traditional Serbian combo. It was loud. Ivanka explained a few things and we laughed about what I'd misunderstood during the writers' events. I told her how our group of poets had bonded over photos on our phones of our children, and vegetables we'd grown, as we didn't have a language in common (all having either allotments and gardens or children, or both). After dinner back into a taxi with Vidak to Belgrade. The taxi dropped us right outside the apartment. After which, conversation, coughing, bed.

Monday 4th May 1846. Went over to Belgrade with Fonblanque and Holmes to see the latter off on his ride to Alexnitza – a most picturesque Cavalcade. Baggage slung across one horse and two or three Servians (Tatars or guides) costume very like the Greek except that some of them wear the Turkish trousers & no petticoat. (Yowan) the Tatar was so habited, dress of crimson cloth embroidered and a Fez cap – Fonblanque's (Paundwr[59]) or groom wears quite the Abbacinian [sic] dress – with the exception of a Turban with a fringe falling behind. We here met the French Consul Monsieur St André a very agreeable man. Mr Fonblanque also a very gentlemanly man returned with us to Semlin to dinner at 5. The country is overflowed by the Danube in Winter & abt. this time begins to subside when comes fever with all its train of horrors.

the antiseptic used
to clean the skin
is cold as a plunge pool

I should think the distance across to Belgrade could not be less than abt. 2 miles abt. ¾ of an hour's row – the boats are heavy and flat bottomed – the amazing noise made by the frogs here astonished me – thousands of them tuning together which we could hear well in our rooms about ½ a mile off – well described in the German by "Quar!" tho' the notes of some are not unmusical – not unlike a humming to[p] – the stork too as indeed all through Hungary & in Belgium in great numbers building on the house & chimney tops – swallows very large.

'When comes fever with all its train of horrors' – that statement jerks at the stomach. Death was a close companion, life snuffed out as easily as blowing out a candle. Here that phrase comes with a child's spinning top, for comfort, and charming frogs, of which he says 'the notes of some are not unmusical', bringing a phrase of poetry into that uncertainty, and settling it. Parts of his text unhinge from story, fragments link and unlink, items on a nature table. Natural poems, little wild phrases. The prose around them lets them shine like fallen leaves on a riverbank.

Meanwhile in Constantinople

Sir Stratford Canning to his wife. 4th May [1846]

"Though I am not yet quite free I am dropping my shackles one after the other – The Persian negotiation[60] is still the main, if not the only, difficulty. I have, however, taken leave of the Sultan, who was graciousness itself. He thanked me for my services to his empire, was satisfied of my devotion to his interests, regretted my absence, and longed for my return. What more could the fondness of a lover have suggested? The audience was a private one, and Reshid,[61] by accident, was my interpreter".[62]

Tuesday 5ᵗʰ May 1846 Went for a ride up the course of the Soave at <u>2 o'clock – the country flat. [Returned] to dinner at 5 – pipes ever [present]</u>

<u>Wednesday 6ᵗʰ May</u> We went over with Mr Fonblanque abt. 1. dined with at 2 – a steady dinner for a Con. Gen. [Consul General] – met Mousr. Le Docteur [a quarantine doctor]. Mousr. St André came and smoked with us after – chibouques & Coffee as a matter of course quite in Turkish style – returned at 5 – no communication allowed after 6[63] – pass quarantine at Custom House.

Tuesday 18ᵗʰ September 2018: Belgrade to Zemun

Woke at 8.30 after a disturbed night. Had woken at 3.30am coughing and had read for an hour or so. Brought coffee in bed by L and then breakfast made for me – egg, toast, tea, grapes. We decided to go to Zemun on the bus. She had researched routes the night before – not easy as Google Maps/transport doesn't work here. Left the apartment and walked towards the Ethnographic Museum and purchased tickets, 200 dinar each, and spent a couple of very interesting hours there looking at room settings of rural 19ᵗʰ century Balkan life, tools, trades, clothes (though a part of the clothing exhibit was, unfortunately, closed), habits, housing etc.

After the museum we walked to get the bus. Got the 706 which should go to Zemun but we missed the right stop and were bowling along in the middle of the countryside by the time we realised. Five or six fellow travellers tried to help. Eventually we got off, asked at a lorry drivers' hostel opposite, and were told to go back the other way by ten to twelve stops (all done in sign language holding up the number of fingers!)...

Saw the old Custom House in Zemun, where people would have been quarantined in George's day, now a restaurant, and sat drinking beer at a waterfront bar for a while, taking pictures, writing this journal, messaging J.

Wandered up to the tower on Zemun hill. Fantastic view from there of the Danube, Belgrade in the distance with its grey concrete towers and the old roofs of Zemun immediately below. We took some pictures and walked back down the cobbled street to the riverfront. I asked a woman where the restaurant L had picked out for us was and she kindly walked us most of the way there saying it was a nice place and she ate there herself. TripAdvisor recommends it, but L professed her chicken casserole to be the worst meal she'd ever had – chicken skin and jelly, no vegetables in an uncooked pancake batter, burnt on top! My dish – edible but poor (I shared mine with L). Disappointed.

Thursday 7ᵗʰ May Went over to Belgrade at 11 to <u>do some shopping</u> – called on Mousr St André – smoked a chibouque not etiquette to decline this proffered mark of friendship. A festival (St Mark) all the shops closed, dined at 4 & went for a ride after a very pleasant cooling shower of rain – the weather had been scorching all the time we were here.

<u>Friday 8ᵗʰ May</u> Intended to go to Belgrade – no boat – heavy rain.

<u>Saturday 9ᵗʰ May</u> Went early to Belgrade – went shopping – lionizing with Mr. Fonblanque – Prince's Palace, barracks, Senate house. Dined with Mr. Fonblanque at 2 – Pipes taken at the Custom House – won a bet of Monsr. St André – 2 Guld. No rain before we got in.

<u>Sunday 10ᵗʰ May</u> Wrote no end of letters. Fonblanque dined with us at 2.

<u>Monday 11ᵗʰ May</u> Dined at 3½ & went to bed early – to be ready for boat for Mehadia[64] at 4 tomorrow morning.

Tuesday 12ᵗʰ May Got up at 2. A cup of coffee & went to the boat. Excessively amusing to see all the passengers asleep – some on Deck & some below in the saloon. The scenery from Semlin of Orshova [Orşova] abt. 150 miles down the river is the most magnificent I ever saw – running nearly the whole way between Rocky & beautifully wooded mountains rising perpendicularly to the height of 2000 feet. Curious old castle at Semendriou with abt. 24 towers. Made an agreeable acquaintance on board with a Walachian[65] Princess

(Kqüche)[66] spoke Germ. French. Greek, Walach, Eng, Ital, Span. Had read Sopl. [*Sophocles*] Xenoph. [*Xenophon*] Herod. [*Herodotus*]

The Wallachian Princess adds notes to her journal, evening Tuesday 12th

7.30pm: Quiet again, thank God! Supper and reading.

8pm: "See how he struts, the uncivilised brat –
amazed at my studies, my erudite chat –
he met a Princess, but I met a prat."

8.05pm: "I drown in the sweetness of the Greek –
Xenophon[67] brought me to Babylon,
and I returned with him, over wasteland
and snow-packed mountain passes. From him
I learned flanking manoeuvres, rear-guard
combat. Long was the way, and hard,
till we met with Thibron, the Spartan."

– arrived at Orshova at 6½ – no room in the inn – an Embassy to greet the Sultan came with us – going on tomorrow to Ranschituck – ordered a "<u>Wagen</u>" to Mehardia – three horses abreast – a lovely night & the scenery exactly similar to what we had had by water – the road winding thro' narrow vallies with the most stupendous rocks interspersed with the most luxuriant foliage rising abruptly to a great height above our heads. Mr. Gutch compared it to the commencement of the ascent of the Simplon – arrived abt. 10. – 12 miles – 5 Guld.

Wednesday – Mehardia[68] most beautifully situated in a narrow valley among the Carpathian mountains – on a foaming mountain torrent surrounded by such scenery as I have attempted to describe but to convey an idea of which description must be quite inadequate. The only scenery I have seen at all like it is near Ly[n]mouth and the neighbourhood of Llanwrtyd – but quite in miniature compared to this. There is a very strong hot sulphur well here – baths supplied. & also saline not strong – went up one of the hills after breakfast for a walk – zig zag walks – magnificent view – caves – found one from a Chasm in which the steam came out so hot that one could not hold ones hand at the mouth of it – heard the water boiling beneath. Government Lodging houses – beds 1 fl. a night – breakfasted and dined at a ghasthause [sic] 300 people here last year. 50 families could not be accommodated.

Thursday 14th May Went with a party (the Doctor, Apothike [*Pharmacist*] etc) an expedition up one of the mountains the highest peak in this valley (3000ft) we commenced our ascent at 6 a.m. up a zig zag path through a most delicious wood – we then came to a line of frowning Rock 500 or 600 feet perpendicular which we had to surmount by passing along some distance by a narrow ledge abt 3 ft wide called the "chats pfad" [*cat's path*] & then climbing thro' a narrow cleft in the Rock – then ascending though almost perpendicular woods again interspersed with gigantic Rocks (lime stone) – the woods are chiefly ash and oak & from the summits & clefts of the Rocks Italian Pines shoot out in every direction – the lilac also grows here in profusion. Bears frequent these mountains, the tracks of which we saw – the scene from the summit was magnificent in the extreme & perfectly baffles all description – standing upon the topmost crag, eagles soaring above my head, which rose quite to a point I looked down on the village of Mehadia 3,000ft below on the glistening torrent we could only see, while on every side the Carpathian range reared their craggy and forest clothed summits to the skies – the highest of them is 8000 – the highest we could see was abt 5000 or 6000, its top piercing the clouds and covered low down with snow. This towards the north. To the south over the wood covered hills the blue mountains in the distance thro' which the majestic Danube wound its mighty way now losing itself and then again becoming visible thro a chasm in the mountain. We reached the top about 10 & began to descend at 11 passing through a magnificent wood of forest trees – I should think about a 100 or 200 years growth & then through a narrow & precipitous gorge for perhaps 2 miles, gigantic pine crowned rocks 500 or 600 feet nearly meeting above our head –got down about 1½ – 3 hours descending – had a delightful warm bath on my return.

Friday 15th May Bathed first time this year in the river Cherne [Cerna] at 7½ deliciously cold. Went butterfly hunting etc and dined at the Pavilion at 4. Mousr. L'Italian dined with us.

<u>Saturday 16th May</u> Bathed. Went after breakfast a delightful walk along a beautiful path up the bank of the river. Stupendous crags appearing at every break in the dense foliage – 500 or 600 feet from the brink of the river whose waters laved its base – saw several snakes, some 1 yd ½ long – all venomous here. Black spotted with blue – fawn and black – black and white.

Tuesday 25th September 2018: Belgrade

Woke @ 9a.m.-ish, slightly better night with more sleep. Had breakfast and decided what to do with this, our last full day, in Belgrade. We walked back to the Ethnographic Museum to see if we could view the ground floor costume room which had been closed for work on our previous visit. Spent a couple of hours looking at the traditional costumes on display, many features of which I could recognise from George's journal – wedding dresses, coins used as necklaces and decoration on belts and tabards, shaggy shepherds' costumes. All the exhibits are labelled in English as well as Serbian. I particularly liked a collection of carved walking sticks – one of which was covered in snakeskin. Had a coughing fit in the museum at which 3 or 4 people gathered round me in consternation.

Grave[69]

The first's a squared off shepherd's crook with a rounded hook, uncarved, utilitarian. The shepherds used their sticks as hooks. A muscled wolf snarling, snarling, dives over the top of the second, a symbol of status for a kmet, a knez and an obor-knez,[70] with a goose between its splayed front paws. His tail flies down the shaft to groves under groves, where other wolves, a bridled horse and helmeted rider, an eagle grasping a dove in its talons, trees, leaves and flowers all live extraordinary lives in the untamed forest. The third is a feminine clenched fist in a very dark wood. The old, the infirm, the heart of its rage hardened in darkness. The fourth is tightly covered from head to foot in a snakeskin, because a stick that touches a snake that has caught a bird carries magical powers and the knowledge of wild language is never given by the bird but always by the serpent. Scales on the curved handle are softened and worn. Regular faint markings pattern this staff which seems to be always on the brink of a wild translation.

Grove

At the Ethnographic Museum in Belgrade
is a small display of walking sticks
above which is written a note in English
which explains they'd be staked
to a man's grove, a misunderstanding it turns out,
as it should say grave[71] not grove.
But in the meantime, we've already
decorated the place with vines,
an orchard, goats and an outdoor table
where the man's family are having supper;
fish, bread, wine and a good plum brandy.
In the background the walking stick
casts a thin shadow staked to its grove,
rooted in evening light, implacable, ready.

Grieve

for the beautiful path
for the breath of wind in the branches
for the dense foliage
for the coiled and uncoiled
for the curled word
for the laving of water
for the laying out of time
for the knowing of a fierce language

There's a file in my 2019 OneDrive folder called 'snake stick notes'. Here are findings on Serbian and Eastern European folklore in which wild language is obtained from snakes and birds. Isn't that what we want in poetry, the unsayable spoken? Like poetry that gift isn't easy to find – elaborate conditions need to be met to find wild language, and once found, it might need to be secret. The research, as always, is a thing of itself, esoteric and delicious. George notes he,

'saw several snakes some 1 yd ½ long, all venomous here. Black spotted with blue. Fawn and black, black and white'. There is poetry both in his phrasing and in the snakeskin covered stick I saw in the museum.

'It was not only man, in ancient times, who could speak', say my notes, but also animals, stones and trees. They could reveal why they were good for man and why they were meant for him. In Serbian folklore, a stick with which a man touches a snake that has caught a bird carries magical powers. In folk tales from Slovenia anyone eating a snake's heart could transform into another creature (Möderndorfer 1946/1801–1802: 238) and it was said 'if you want to hear what flowers say, you have to eat a soup in which a white snake is cooked' (Kotnik 1942: 1) (Radenković 1996: 23) and whoever 'licks a white snake, becomes all-knowing' (Möderndorfer 1946/1803: 238). In Serbian folk tales those who hunt snakes with bare hands, have the power of prophecy (Djordjević 1958: 180). Some versions of these stories say the voice of the white serpent is like the whistling noise of a flying dragon, the dragon which is

therefore like a bird. That the knowledge of wild language is never transmitted by the bird, but always by the serpent is taken from these stories.

I wrote an 87-line poem in blank verse, which sits in this folder, but never used it, a retelling of a Serbian folk tale in which a shepherd rescues a snake, child of the king of Serbian snakes, and is given the gift of the language of animals but may not tell of it on pain of death. The folk tale ends with the shepherd taking a stick to his wife because she won't stop asking about his secret knowledge. There are too many folk tales where women are blamed for everything and too many where violence against women is condoned. I won't be part of it.

Tuesday 25th September 2018 (cont): Belgrade

...Later we decided to have another walk around the Fortress – here were groups playing chess and cards. We took a photograph for a couple – him German and her Maltese. Came out via the Zoo entrance and then through the local streets and via a supermarket for eggs, watermelon and chocolate and back to the apartment. After a rest we packed our bags. Our bus leaves at 1.45pm tomorrow from the bus station. Posted today's pics on Facebook. Had supper – fried eggs and toast, watermelon. Then to bed.

Belgrade Fortress, 2018

I took no notes, but the photos say we were there,
high up, looking over the Danube,
the Danube and the Sava at the place where they join,
on the 25th of September at 4.32.
It was sunny and bright, each cloud haloed,
everything bleached, the rivers wore bands of silver,
even the small path that slanted down
to the overlook above a busy road
had moon-white paving. By the side of the path
a drystone wall retainer

and at every step, I remember, there were lizards
splayed and motionless then gone
one after the other, basking in the heat then gone.
It was then you told me, and I don't know why
it seems important to remember this,
how on another day, you'd seen a car lose all control
spinning across both carriageways,
the noise of it, and then

Sunday 17<u>th</u> May Like anything but Sunday – shops open. Billiard playing etc. Rom. Cath. Ch. [*Roman Catholic Church*] Disgusting mummery (bathed heute auch [*today also*]) met an agreeable man Bohemian – officer in the Austrian Service – he talked English to me & I German to him. Mutual obligation.

Monday 18th May Bathed – butterfly hunting etc. beg. to write Germ. The mineral springs vary in temperature – 2 degrees hotter today. Usually about 34 Germ[72] or 112 Fahrenheit. A magnificent thunderstorm this evening abt. 7 – lasted till 9½ – the vivid lightening shone "from rock to rock the rattling crags among, leaped the live thunder"[73] & rain in such torrents as I never saw before. Played billiards with a German – beat me 4 out of 6.

Tuesday 19<u>th</u> May bathed, walked, dined at 4 and started at 5½ in a "Wagen" for Orsova to be in time for the packet in the morning – in a Wagen wicker work – two seats like a Britska – covered like an English Market Cart. Arrived at Orsova at 7½ – went to the Bureau to have our passports vised, ordered beds and went to the packet office – found there was no packet, the Sultan having put them all out of their regular order. One having started for Semlin that very morning. But a Wagen was to take passengers to Drenkova to meet the Dampfschiffe. Turned in.

The Parlatorium, Orsova [74]
[Trading Standards]

A central no man's land contains a table,
the Austrian Quarantine Officer, and a guard
of soldiers; fixed bayonets, loaded firearms.

This market's in a wooden shed. Austrians,
Wallachians and Servians assemble,
by realm, behind three breast high boards.

No mixing is allowed. Money falls from fingers
into a long-handled ladle an attendant offers,
then drops into a basin charged with vinegar

which is passed to the other side. Goods
must be washed or fumigated. Two yards
separate us all, but we gesticulate and roar.

<u>Wednesday 20<u>th</u> May</u> Got up at 5 as they told us last night the Wagen
would go at 6. When we got down to the office found it would not
go for an hour. Waited 1½ hour & got under weigh [sic] eventually at
7½ – slap up turn out – leather harness etc – Nusr warm [*just warm*].
Stopped two hours to eat at a little village abt. half way – got bread,
eggs & good wine – a beautiful drive – did not regret the change – the
road running the whole way along the left bank of the Danube at
the base of the rocks – scooped in some places – the rocks hanging
right over our heads & on the opposite side rising perpendicularly
nearly 1000 ft. reached the packet abt. 4 – dined & slept on board –
very mean bed on the horse hair seats with only a quilt over us in the
Dampfschiffe – slept well notwithstanding fleas and everything.

A letter from Mr Gutch to the Foreign Office concerning £100

Semlin May 20 1846

My dear Sir, Many thanks for your friendly note reminding me of
my culpability respecting the draft for the £100 drawn at Vienna. I
herewith enclose a note which you can leave for Mr Cunningham
and which will I trust plead my excuse. I had already written a letter
from Vienna, but which would appear to have miscarried. I was
perfectly well aware of the irregularity of the proceeding, but I had
no alternative. I trust that the Chief Clark[75] will see it in that light.

Obediently my very dear sir, Most truly yours, JWG Gutch

I have not written the letter on the official paper in consequence of the postage.[76]

Thursday 21st May Waited this morning (after a most acceptable jump into the Donau [*Danube*] from the steps of the Packet) till Mittag [*midday*] for the Dampfschiff from Orsova but none arriving we resumed our journey as far as Drenkova (two or three houses close to the water) found our travelling companion in the Wagen the previous day very agreeable – walked and talked in Latin and German (he an Italian) slept on board again.

Friday 22nd May En route again about 6 a.m. mountains vanished. Country flat and plain – arrived at Semlin abt 3pm dined and went for a walk with our Italian friend (Giuseppe Abramisk) No end of letters from home etc. One from Fonblanque – Consul on Sunday.

Mrs Gutch, at her writing desk
77 Great Portland Street, London

My pen hovers above the page;
I am not well, and you
my love, are oh so far away.

My thighs are stained
with blood. I yearn for him,
and he, my darling boy, is clay.

Shall I reveal *My heart*
is breaking? Or confess
I ache for him each day?

What can I tell you? Not *I bleed.*
No, I shall reassure, and say,
The treatment's working.

Saturday 23rd May Went to Belgrade "shopping" – called on the Consul. M. St André who introduced us to a naval officer, a Frenchman in the Turkish Service (Lerman) who had brought the Pascha down & was just going to return to Constantinople / stopping at [Rauschta][77] to accompany the Sultan – came to Semlin together – he stopped at our Hotel – had supper and smoked – very agreeable (Monsr. Lerman I mean). Costume blue frock coat – white trousers, fez cap, sword etc. he was at the battle of Navarino[78] – every language spoken in Constantinople.

Sunday Bathed in the Donau. – went to Belgrade at 10. Found Fonblanque in uniform – blue & silver etc waiting for his visitors – disappointed in the court – they came one by one – 1st French Consul – blue coat and trousers embroidered with gold. 2nd Two Servians – Semitsch, President of Counsel & Vächitsch[79] Instigator and leader in the last Revolution, fez caps, ample cloth cloaks & Turkish slippers – 3rd Col. Danilevsky Russian Consul. 4th Austrian Mousr. D' Lescar, 5th Russian Secretary and 6th. abt. 1 O'clock the Pascha (Vehigil) – disappointed with the Pascha – the present Sultan has changed the costume from Turkish to European. He wore a fez cap, blue surtout exuberantly embroidered with gold over the chest, back and at the corners. Blue trousers with gold lace & patent leather boots which looked as if they had come from Regt. [regiment]. Sword with a diamond hilt and gold scabbard and a diamond star of his rank on his breast, diamonds on his person worth about 5000l[80] has a ring a single diamond worth 3000l weighs 24 carats[81].

> The poor will
> come
> a-gleaning [82]

Harem consists of 50 women. We dined with Fonblanque and returned abt. 4 – had supper at 9 with Mousr. Lerman – had received 5 wounds! Knew Lord Byron in Greece – Sultan always goes in his ship – a steamer with two rows of guns – 25 in the Turkish Service. 100 ships of War – we exchanged cards and he told me if ever I came to Constantinople there was a room for me in his house (opposite Sir Stratford Canning's) and If I went to an Hotel he would never speak to me again.

Monday 25th May Breakfasted, dined etc with Mousr. Lerman – played a game of billiards with Mr Gutch. Mousr. Lerman started at night promising to return to go with us to Alexanitza –bathed this morning in the Danube.

Tuesday 26th May Bathed, had a nice ride and wrote letters.

Wednesday 27th May Ditto. Went to Spälers Gardens and played billiards

Thursday 28th May Ditto. Went over to Belgrade – shopped – dined with the consul and brought over our pipes which had been taken at the Douan [*customs house*] and sent to the consul before we went to Mehadia – and a tobacco bag.

Friday 29th May Bathed etc

Saturday 30th May Do. [*ditto*] Went for a ride – Mr Fonblanque came over to dine with us at 3. Mousr. St Andre could not come

Sunday 31st May Bathed. Col. Townley[83] arrived at 7 O'Clock.

Falls from Horses [84]
Townley's journey from Belgrade to Therapia

By the second night in the saddle
I was reeling backwards and forwards
in an odd and ridiculous manner.
So black was the whole horizon,
so dense the forest through which we passed,
that although the Tatar had a white horse
we rode in loneliness all night.

Descending a hill my horse fell hard
in ground so soft I lay unharmed,
the roads quite saddle-girth high in mud,
my ears dinned by the howling of wolves.
In grey dawn my horse fell again

twisting the spur on my right boot
to a scrap of bent wire. Those hours
of watchfulness and mud!

I rode near the brink of precipices
through defiles that closed overhead
deep in trance till a nearby muezzin
called out the earliest prayer.
He called me to wakefulness too,
dawn light tender on the mountains.
How thankful I am to Him who has thus
been merciful through this long journey!

Packed up traps and went over to Belgrade at 12. Dined with Mr.
Fonblanque at 3 and having arrayed ourselves in white caps, German
blouses, Turkish trousers (with abt. 12 yards of stuff in them), Jack
boots (mine red morocco) & spurs – our cavalcade moved off out of
the Court at 5, consisting besides ourselves of 2 baggage horses, the
Tatar in fez cap, red embroidered jacket and vest and Turkish trousers,
tatar boots etc and the Surojee or post boy with fez cap, yellow jacket,
flannel Turkish trousers & red slippers – after abt. 5 miles the country
becomes beautiful, very hilly and splendidly wooded – the road
running the whole way thro' magnificent oak forests – at night the
scene was very striking, the silver moon every now and then piercing
the dense foliage and revealing to us our picturesque appearance while
every here and there we came suddenly upon encampments of caravans
from Stambul. The Buffaloos Waggons and wild forms of the men
spread out in a circle round a blazing fire – abt. 7 stations between
Belgrade and Alexnitza – changing horses took about an hour when
we usually refreshed ourselves with some bread we brought with us
– some coffee when we could get it and our pipes, the revivifying
and soothing effect on the nerves of a pipe of Turkish tobacco after a
hard ride of 5 or 6 hours passes all description. Reached Pack Polanka
[Smederevska Palanka] abt. the 3 or 4 stage at abt 12½ or 1 O'clock

Messenger Regulations:[85] concerning distances to be travelled
On the Second Principal Road

Miles by the clock or dial/ For the ordinary post/For Tatars & Couriers (scale hours)
[The first column and the figures below the list of places are written in pencil]

Belgrade to Grotzka [Grocka]	5	5	3½	3
Grotzka to Kolar [Kolari]	4	4	2¾	2½
Kolar to Palanka [Smederevska Palanka]	6	6	4½	4
Palanka to Batochina [Batočina]	8	7	5	4½
Batochina to Jagodina	7	6	4½	4
Jagodina to Tchupria [Ćuprija]	4	4	2¾	2¼
Tchupria to Alexanizza [Aleksinac]	8	6	4½	4
	42Hrs	38	27½	24¼

To the Cordon at Alexnitza   4½   -----   ½ hr   3½
                                                                                 at each

2½ hours more   168   27¾
                              21
                              189 miles

Journey usually done in 32 hours

Monday 1st June in the morning – when after having had some bread and slivovitch and water we were very glad to lay ourselves down on a hard board and slept very soundly for 2 hours. At 3 after having had some capital boiled milk and a pipe we were again en route – at a small town about 3 hours ride this side of Jagodina at 11 we were very glad of some cold lamb, bread and some red wine which we fell in with and then reached Jagodina abt. 1 from whence I was delighted to hear we only had two stages to Alexnitza – long ones however they proved for we did not reach Alexnitza till abt. 20.12 where as soon as a bed could be got ready (a straw palliasse on boards across trestles) I rolled in and never turned till 9 the next morning – as fresh as a lark except a little stiff.

At Home 2020/7:
Taxi to Guy's Hospital for surgery 11ᵗʰ June 2020

the taxi arrives at 5.30 am and we swing by
a suburb of Brighton to pick up one more.
She's had a transplant *then* cancer. Fortunate,
she says, they came in *that* order. The driver

dabs at his accelerator without reason and I
swallow vomit. He's erected a temporary screen
between him and us. The cling film stretches,
creases, sags and causes early morning light
to ripple uneasily, fog the road ahead.

Alexnitza

Reading and shooting
– an extract about Queen's Messengers in Serbia

'Alexinitza was, in fact, the point to which her Majesty's messengers formerly went during a long period that Constantinople may be said to have been in its quarantine with the world; consequently, the messengers halted there, sending on Tatars to the capital and remaining there till they returned. It was therefore absolutely necessary to have some recreation, and as the wild country around abounded in game, dogs and guns were in great request; and I believe I am not wrong in naming, that every succeeding messenger who came from England was expected to bring out and leave a few books, till a very tolerable library was formed in the miserable Bulgarian abode where for a time they lingered.' (Hall, 1865, p. 83)

George continues:

<u>Tuesday 2nd June 1846</u> our landlord and attendant Risto[86] gave a grand spread to which he asked us. Mr Holmes the messenger at Alexnitza and I went. Mr Gutch was too tired. The scene was picturesque in the extreme in a pretty spot well shaded and close to a sparkling stream which turned a Mill close by. The party was fast collecting. The host and hostess were superintending the cooking of the dinner on the spot. There was a large hole in which there were the smouldering embers of a fire and over this were roasting two whole sheep and about half a dozen fowls with a stick run thro' them resting on two forked sticks and two boys in the picturesque costume of the country performing the office of turnspits. Mine host brought me a pipe with which, and a little conversation in German, I whiled away the time till dinner was ready.

When the ladies had arrived we sat down to a table about 1½ ft high, the ladies, Holmes and myself on cushions at the upper end and the rest on the ground – I sat next to the wife of the Capitain of the place and considering we neither of us understood a word of what the other said we got on pretty well, drank out of the same glass etc, her dress was very pretty – a good specimen of a Servian Woman – (a red fez cap and blue tassel / sometimes gold) the hair dyed black and twisted round on one side, ½ round the head a string of ducats and a treble row round the neck. Like the Greeks a tight under vest and purple velvet jacket beautifully embroidered in gold and silver, a silk petticoat and red morocco shoes. The men were habited variously, military costume, maroon red embroidery and red band round the cap – blue frogs and silver lace down the trousers, red fez and ample cloak lined and bordered with sable – after dinner we all moved from the table – the women sat round in a circle & talked. The men smoked, drank, sang and proposed health's – Prince of Servia, Queen V [*Queen Victoria*], The Sultan. Holmes proposed the Commandant, Capitain, Magistrates etc and I the ladies. We then danced a Servian dance in a circle round the musician who played an instrument like a Scotch Bagpipe and then I had a capital Waltz with the Capitainitza (deux temps) [*waltz in two beats*] and we then escorted the ladies in procession home – I having the honour of having the Capitainitza and the next best looking woman on either arm. The Commandant Capitain and one or two others then came up into our house and "finished the evening like children of mars".[87] The people appear very sociable and well disposed. Alexnitza is a struggling dirty, small town with one principal street where all the houses look like a collection of Welsh blacksmith shops as indeed they do in all the Servian towns – it is notwithstandingly beautifully situated in a fertile valley thro' which the Morava serpentines surrounded by beautifully wooded hills – as you face Constantinople you see before you part of the range of the Balkan and on the right the blue mountains towards Albania.[88] There is another beautiful little mountain stream running thro' the valley where I enjoyed matutinal [*morning*] immersions. This night I got into the bedroom I was to occupy till Mr. Holmes went.[89] The entrance to which was effected thro' a hole abt a yard square like the entrance to an ash hole. It adjoined the kitchen with which it communicated so as to enable me to luxuriate in an atmosphere of wood smoke & fragrant viands – they were both detached from the house – the house an extraordinary old shop built of logs of wood, wattling and mud and covered with red tiles – there are two bed rooms, a sitting room which is a passage, formed with bricks & on each side an open balcony – one of which is of wood and deliciously cool in the evening.

Thursday 27th September 2018:
Sokobanja to Aleksinac and back

We went to breakfast – lots of dishes – cheeses, meats, a corn mash, potato salad, sour milk, milk, juices, cereals, fruits, fish fingers! – a huge array of possibilities plus salads of course. Tea/ coffee etc. Walked round the outside of the ancient thermal bath and then along the main pedestrian street, which is tiled underfoot, with restaurants and shops on either side. An area off to one side is full of tourist-tat huts. We decided to have a quick lunch at the Irish Pub having ascertained at the bus station that the next bus to Aleksinac would leave in an hour. Had a Greek salad each and some flatbread. The salads were very good as was the bread and both very cheap. The women's toilet was less good – no lock on the door and the seat so unattached to its china it was likely to throw you off mid flow!

To the bus station in time for the bus to Aleksinac from which we saw two herons standing in a field, hunting, another flying. The weather clear and less cold as the day went on. We arrived at the bus station in Aleksinac and walked from there into town. The intention was to find the messenger house which Vidak had told me was still standing and had been refurbished and was now used as a municipal office and had a plaque to commemorate its previous use. We walked here and there for some hours but could not find it. Disappointed but my fault as I had not pressed him for its exact location. The museum and library were closed today so we could not enquire there.

There are second-hand shops in Aleksinac – the only place we have seen them. The housing is mixed with older style orange roof-tiled houses towards the very pretty wooded hills and old flats in the centre, mixed in with much older square 19th Century buildings. We passed one such building which is now a fire station. A couple of long streets are pedestrianised with bars and tables and chairs in the centre of the road, quite busy. The people look generally poorer than in other places we have been. The infrastructure needs upgrading – metal pavement insets for drain covers and the like are worn to holes, there are missing paving stones, uneven surfaces. We had a beer at one of the bars and then decided to head for the bus station. Confusion here – we cannot buy a ticket to Sokobanja. The woman shakes her head. Eventually a man comes to our aid. We are directed to cross the road away from the bus station and wait. Eventually a very small minibus draws up, perhaps 15 seats, and we buy tickets from the driver.

Wednesday 3rd June went for a short ride over the mountains covered with oak underwood – beautiful view of the Balkan – got a good wetting and came back to dinner at 6. Began bathing in Moravitza.

Thursday 4th June Rode to St Stephano, a small convent, about 12 miles off, prettily situated in a narrow valley – something of Mehadia in miniature – a small Greek chapel with painted scene etc which the two old monks who live there were very civil in showing us – the ride there is exceedingly pretty – now over and then winding round the bases of these densely wooded hills.

Friday 5th June Went for a ride thro' similar scenery and got intensely wet.

Saturday 6th June Rode part of the way to Bagnia [Sokobanja] to a beautiful pass between the mountains, rocky and prettily wooded but I must confess it seemed to me tame after Mehadia. Bears and Deer frequent these woods. Tracks near the brook.

Sunday 7th June Went to church. Way very civilly made for me to the front of the screen beautifully painted and gilded. Candles etc burning, something like the Rom. Cath. Priest very handsome Greek splendidly dressed in green embroidered robe & gilded mantle, no seats, floor strewed with grass.

Monday 8th June Captain lent me his gun. Took it out with Mr. G. who went butterfly hunting – did not get a shot – went out riding at 3 towards the blue mountains on the right – across the ferry thro beautiful oak underwood, a very pretty ride.

From 'An Off-the-shoulder Number' [90]

blow
with a soft breath
then breathe in
Continue
as if you mean it

through the thunder
a blackbird's
liquid
voice–
You are riding

into the blue mountains
through beautiful
Oak under-woods
listening
listening–

<u>Tuesday 9th June</u> Bathed, rode & Mr Gutch & I mutually performed the office of Barber on one another. .n. [*note*] employ him again

<u>Wednesday 10th June</u> Dispatches arrived from Constantinople; Mr Holmes departed for Belgrade. Went the first stage (Shipiliae[91]) in Risto's Vagen, a wicker-work van without springs. We went out riding – a magnificent thunder stürm in the evening came up from the S.W. splendid forked lightning & three or 4 crashing claps of thunder just over our heads – the echoes of which continued rolling through the mountains round for several mins. afterwards "from peak to peak the rattling crags among leaped the live thunder etc"[92]

<u>Thursday 11th June</u> did not bathe. Took a pretty ride thro' the woods over the hills – caught a tortoise.

<u>Friday 12th June</u> Bathed. Took a gun and accompanied Mr G towards the Turkish frontier. Shot a bee-eater, dove and two small birds.

<u>Saturday 13th June</u> Wrote to the Governor with letter for Ld. Brougham.[93] Went butterfly hunting & rode the pony after dinner. Did not bathe this morning. Heavy rain.

<u>Sunday 14th June</u> Butterfly hunting. Called on Capitainitza. Bedroom reception room – 3 or 4 ladies sitting there and a Pole Quarantine Officer who spoke German and French – rode the pony along the banks of Morava.

<u>Monday 15th June</u> Rode after dinner with Mr Gutch up the valley over the hill into the Belgrade Road and home – beautiful sunset.

<u>Tuesday 16th June</u> Dyed moustaches – went for a ride to the frontier. Felt very ill in the evening – concluded it proceeded from the dye some of which I had accidentally swallowed – served me write [sic]. Vanity well punished.

> Dislodge maggots with a knife
> set a scrape of soft white lead
> amongst the wool[94]

<u>Wednesday 17th June</u> Still seedy – went for a ride towards Albanian Hills. Determined to defer our trip to Bagnia till Friday instead of tomorrow as we intended.

<u>Thursday 18th June</u> Intensely hot as indeed it has been for the last week – stayed in during the day – out in the evening.

Meanwhile in Constantinople

Sir Stratford Canning to his wife
18th June 1846

[...] Why stay so long, you say? Because I am goose enough to aim at settling every possible question before I go, not only for my own credit, but because the position is a favourable one for acting with success. The Sultan came back two days before his time, and by sea in a steamer, as I had most strenuously advised. His journey has done him good, in health, self-confidence, and reputation. He seems to mean generosity as well as humanity [...] Reshid[95] is in high content and desires his particular remembrances and those of his ladies to you. Mrs. Redhouse[96] will tell you a good deal about the Sultan. I really seem to have a hold on his kindness, and he is doing or preparing to do as much as the wretched state of his people and empire will allow. Think of fatty Rif'at[97] fairly throwing his arms round my neck the other day, and half crying with affection. He explained by saying that he had always liked me, but now perceived I was a better friend to the empire than all his colleagues [...][98]

<u>Friday 19th June</u> Expedition to Bagnia – started at 10½ Rhisto Brindish – our Tatar – blue embroidered Turkish trousers, red boots, white jacket and fez – road pretty & winding thro' the vallies. Bagnia prettily situated in a plain surrounded by mountains – one abt 8 or 10 miles off – 3000 or 4000ft – one beyond not in sight 6000 – went on a voyage of discovery after dinner to the top of one of the hills. Glorious sunset "one unclouded blaze of living light"[99] Sat on rocks – "mused over flood and fell" "slowly traced the forests shady scene, climbed the trackless mountain, leant o'er steeps and foaming falls" brawling torrent rocky bed and channels very narrow – reminded me of Wolf's Leap above Llanwrtyd. Slept on hay with a horse cloth spread over it in bath house. Magnificent cold spring water for drinking.

<u>Saturday 20th June</u> arose from our point-du-tout [*not at all*] "Downey" at 6½ to enjoy the luxury of a tepid bath. An old Roman bath – circular, 4 ft deep, from 12 to 16 [*feet*] in diameter at the bottom of a place like a dungeon with little round holes at the top. Water slightly sulphurous, hot 112 deg. – had breakfast walked to the source of the cold spring – intensely cold and brilliantly clear from a cleft in the limestone rock – in the saddle again at 9 to return to Alexinatz. Wasn't it baking? Oh So!

Friday 28th September 2018: Sokobanja

We resolve to walk into the hills to see Soko Grad, an old fortress. L has directions from the Bradt guide. We walk through town towards the Moravica, a shallow stream, past the ordinary end of town –

small clothes shops, the honey shop with beehives and specialist beekeeping clothes, fruit and veg shops. Just before the river is a park with trees, a children's playground and shady paths. Women have laid out cloths on some of the benches or on the ground and are selling bunches of herbs, hand-embroidered clothes, hand-knit socks etc. I am reminded of the hand-knit socks George was given as a present when he left Alexnitza in 1847. The paths lead to a taverna at a bend in the river, there are steps down to the water which flows gently over gravel with steep wooded slopes behind. The river has stones ridged across it making some small dams through which the water finds its way almost unhindered. I watch a tiny boy pick up little pebbles and attempt to throw them in – his grandfather says 'Bravo!' each time a stone plops into the water. We have a drink in the taverna. A small beer each at a table above the water. Mostly I sit eyes closed just listening. We are visited by wasps.

We retrace our steps to a low concrete bridge that crosses the river. A sign at its other end advertises Hotel Moravica. We cross and climb steps to a gravelled path up through the woods. The woods are mostly mixed broadleaved trees and bushes, some conifers, and some bushes with a pungent smell, when bruised, which have already turned all shades of pink and apricot.

The path ahead seems to shine in the gleams of light. The stones are polished from other feet. Through a tunnel of leaves, the grey-green misty light of distant forests arrives. There are craggy rocks, hills clothed in forest, some trees now harvest-yellow with all the greens and rose tints joining in. Slope upon slope with long rocky parchment-coloured cliffs, red glints where a bush has already turned more vivid than the rest. The sun is bright and there are some scree stretches which are hot and dun-coloured. The paths are well maintained, easy to follow.

We meet others walking, some elderly using walking sticks, and some with bags full of twigs they have collected which look like herbs. One was using a knife in the soil – we could not guess why. We kept going forward, not sure where the path would lead. There were several signs in Cyrillic text with walking times beside each and arrows pointing the direction but we did not understand, so simply walked on. After 45 minutes or so we came to a wooden open-sided circular hut with a built-in table and benches inside – a high point for a picnic and beside it a metal cross on a plinth. People had left offerings there, religious pictures of Christ or Mary, bank notes, hand-written messages – all held down with stones to stop the wind blowing them away. We drank some water and marvelled at the views – we could see over to Soko Grad, the fortress built into the rock across a steep gulf or chasm in the hills, and the tiny shapes of people climbing among the fortress stones there. To the left of this was a faraway plain with fields and scattered trees. Farmland at harvest time, maize fields, and beyond that the grey pyramid-shaped line of hills we'd seen before. L's landlord[100] had told us people go there on pilgrimage and, he said, talk of aliens.

A young woman and her grandfather came up then and stopped too. We exchanged 'Dobar dan's' and after a while we packed up and walked back the way we'd come. Saw a lizard climbing a little bush – it stopped long enough for me to look at it, a delicate green, so camouflaged I could not later find it in the photograph I took.

Saturday 29th September 2018: Sokobanja

The plan for the rest of the day was to take another walk to Soko Grad by a different route. We walked out of town the same way as before but crossed the river Moravica and bore right on the paved road beyond it. As we crossed there was a terrific roaring, a biker doing wheelies along this straight stretch of road.

We went on up the hill towards Moravica Hotel. A signpost, which might have helped, was on the ground, face up, and seemed to have been for a while. The road rose gently, and we passed a football pitch and then a children's playground. Three paths splayed out in front of us in scrubland. The middle one took us through thorn bushes and rough grass – soon we were in thin woodland on similar paths to yesterday. The land on the right side of the path going steeply down so that sometimes the path took us across scree. Then more woodland, lit here and there by the marvellous pink hues of the shrub we had seen yesterday

We carried on, hoping the path would take us to the Fortress Soko Grad we'd seen from across the valley yesterday. At a big picnic spot I spied a sign in Cyrillic pointing the way to **Соко Град**, under some trees and by the river. The surface of the path, a mess of intertwined tree roots.

Codes and archives:

On earth we turn in time/then lit by love/ atone

middle one which took us through scrubby land with thorn bushes & rough grass. Soon we were in the woodland — similar paths to yesterday, gravel and earth and shiny rocks smoothed by many feet. The trees seemed to have turned more colours since yesterday & leaves were falling. We came to the same spot we reached yesterday where we had previously turned left uphill. Today we took the path ahead of us which sloped gently downhill into a sloped valley. The land on the right side of the path going steeply down so that sometimes the path seemed to be going across scree. Then into more woodland, lit here and there by the marvellous pink hues of the shrub we had seen yesterday. At one point we climbed down steps cut into the rock, there was an old iron railing to cling on to & soon came to a river, very clear, pebbled. A labrador came past us then & waded into the river, started chewing sticks the woman who came after it threw for it. We carried on, having the

The path got steeper and steeper zigzagging up the side of the hill. Great boulders hunched among the trees, white and mossy. At points the path was precipitous, and we scrambled up. It was waymarked with red and white circles painted on trees and lengths of red and white plastic tape tied onto branches. After a last push up a steep slope of irregular bare rock we reached a little plateau where we could stand and admire the views. Directly above us about fifty feet up, the Fortress of Soko Grad. The path up looked like a goat track. Some younger walkers climbed past us and explored the ruins but we were already thinking about the scramble down and didn't need to discuss it. Spent a few minutes recovering our breath and then set off downhill.

After the walk went out to eat. Ordered trout, chips and a tomato salad. Red wine then quince brandy and pancakes with jam to share. The brandy arrived in tiny broad-bottomed glass test tubes with narrow necks, each placed into an ordinary glass which held water and ice to cool it. L thought the narrow-necked little flask was a stirrer, and after stirring it around her glass lifted it out and enthusiastically cast it backwards – 2/3 of the brandy flew out! L & I laughed, and so did the slightly bemused waiter. A couple a few tables away from us had asked for the menu in English so L went over to see if they'd like to chat. We talked for an hour. They were travelling in an old camper van they'd done up themselves, had lived in the Netherlands for a few years, before driving through France, Albania, Bosnia and Macedonia, parking up by the side of the road or at camping sites. They were blogging about their travels, due to fly home to Australia in October. The conversation turned to war, how they'd been babies when the war in Serbia had been fought. They asked if we remembered it. We said we did and that we were old enough to remember back to Vietnam. L told them about her travels in Yugoslavia forty years ago and in Berlin before the wall came down.

We said our goodbyes and went back to the room, packed all our stuff for the morning, set the alarm for eight.

Sunday 30th September 2018: Sokobanja

Reflected this morning about the young people we met yesterday. I remembered that they said they'd driven from Sofia that day.

George had wanted to go through the pass of Sofia but had been told it was far too dangerous as travellers had been attacked there and local guards killed by robbers. Our campervan friends told us that they'd found it unwise to travel at night as they'd been stopped several times by police who'd said they were 'speeding'; police who had asked for a bribe to make the 'speeding' ticket go away...

Got up this morning at half eight and finished packing. Went to our last breakfast here – a new item on the breakfast menu: macaroni cheese.

Sunday 21ˢᵗ June 1846 Great disappointment no letters from home. Bathed, strolled, dined, smoked, as usual.

Monday 22ⁿᵈ June Doctor of Quarantine came up in evening to smoke a pipe (Basilius Tandorocovitch) Thunderstorm.

Tuesday 23ʳᵈ June The Doctor, Mr Gutch and I breakfasted and started at 6 o'clock for Nissa [Niš] – lovely morning – our suite consisted of our attendant and dragoman Rhisto splendidly accoutered – crimson robe, pistols in his belt & Turkish scimitar suspended across his shoulders. Osmond the Stambul Tatar, Serojee and baggage horse. When we reached the Turkish frontier, 9 miles, we had to wait nearly an hour for the change of horses – which we occupied very satisfactorily with pipes & draughts of delicious cold spring water – here our suite was augmented by the addition of one of the Servian soldiers from the frontier. Reached Nissa about 11. Tatar went on to announce our arrival. Took up our quarters in the Palace of the Greek Archivescobole (Niskifor) – large wooden building brick floors – red tiled roof – ushered into Reception Room – large square room, folding doors, little square windows opposite side – ottomans round three sides – Turkey carpet on the floor – tray of sweetmeat handed round – liquor [   ]¹⁰¹ spirits of wine & aniseed & cold water – then Pipes with magnificent amber heads – then thick sweet coffee in small china cups placed in open work silver egg cups – after this we were asked (the question came to me bye the bye 4ᵗʰ hand – to the Dragoman in Greek – to the Doctor in Servian – who again interpreted to Mr G in Italian¹⁰² and he to me in English – when Rhisto was present we could manage pretty well thro' him alone – he knowing a little English).

We were asked whether we would take some breakfast – a siesta – more pipes and coffee – or go out and see the town – we chose the latter particularly as we intended returning to Alexinitza tomorrow. Walked about and did a little shopping. Nissa [Niš] is situated in a large plain of many miles in extent watered by the Nissava [Nišava] and has like Belgrade a very picturesque appearance from the red roofs interspersed with green trees and the glittering minarets – town dirty – houses low ground floor – 3 bridges and moats – Bazaar curious. Went back to Palace abt. 2. Pipes and coffee again – sweetmeat, liquer and water – went into another room to dinner – a small tumbler of this liquer and water first, then soup and then abt. from 20 to 26 dishes placed on table one by one – of every one of which the guests are expected to taste – which our Host washed down for us with oceans of very good red wine. Dessert consisted of apricots, cherries and cucumbers, which last he peeled split into 4 & after putting salt on it handed to us to break off

> Salt preserves
> sound sheep
> & cures such as are rotten[103]

– retired to the other room – water towels etc to wash our hands as also before dinner – Pipes and coffee – while our Host took his siesta we walked out to the tower of skulls[104] a detestable memorial of Turkish Barbarity (in a battle between the Turks and Servians in 1812 in which the former were victorious they built up this memorial turning the part of the head which was wounded outmost) – climbed to the top & carried off a skull[105] – abt. 1½ miles from Nissa – returned abt. 7 – wanted us to have supper. Couldn't indeed!

30th September 2018: Niš

Arrived at the boarding house which is in the centre of Niš city. Our landlord told us that he has many guests from the UK and other places. He said Serbia has been in many wars, he added he was against Milošević[106] and regrets that Serbians are blamed as one for a war they did not all support. He talked about Kosovo and about Albanians and about the NATO bombing in the war. He said he knows we understand this.

Settled into the room and then walked out to find the Tower of Skulls which is set in a garden surrounded by iron railings by the side of a dual carriageway. A woman came out of a second building which houses films about the history of the tower and helped us buy tickets at a booth. The current tower completely encloses the old one leaving a circular corridor, between the two. Through the open doors of the new tower we were confronted by the original  grey one, which is set behind protective glass. The skulls that are left are dotted about with many empty depressions where skulls have been stolen in the past[107]. Some of the skulls are very well preserved with teeth remaining. They vary in colour and size. We imagined the living heads of the people they were. I have wanted to see this tower since I first read the description in George's journal. The story is a terrible one.

There's a visitor's book here which has entries from all over the world in many languages. Some brutal messages from nationalists, some messages of peace. It seems to me to be a monument to inhumanity – proof if it were needed of what we are capable of, and with no glory in it. After looking at the tower we went to the small museum which had some information films running continuously with images showing how the tower looked originally and explaining the battle and troop movements. We'd seen when we went in what we thought was the carcase of a pigeon on the tiled floor and wondered why it hadn't been removed by the museum keeper. Suddenly the bird fluttered on the ground – not dead but mortally injured...

We left soon after and walked on intending to go to a Roman ruin, the Mediana, but turned back as the road got more unpleasant, narrow pavements, an out-of-town look, more industrial, dirtier. We turned back but missed our turn-off, walking on to the fortress[108] – a happy accident. We sat in an open square just outside the fortress and had a beer in the sun. Watched toddlers, with their parents, playing round a shallow stone pool – walking on the little marble wall around it. The parents very patient and sweet with them. A pack of stray dogs was hanging out here. Some lay flat out on the pavement of the square, sleeping, and some trotted about busily.

They seemed in good condition and friendly. I watched a parent let their toddler stroke one.

After our beer we walked across the bridge over the river Nišava, a pretty river running fast and low past the fortress. In the distance, from the bridge, we could see the hills beyond Niš. The fortress is a great stone enclosure with an ancient gate. We strolled through, past the Roman ruins of a bath house, an ancient mosque, archaeological ruins and remains. There are many trees dotted about including carob – we saw the brown husks on the ground. There were little land trains you could ride in around the grounds. They have children's songs playing tinnily all day. I thought of the Child Catcher from 'Chitty Chitty Bang Bang'.

Earlier we'd come across a bus unloading thirty or forty police in full riot gear – we didn't know why. We saw them here and there in small groups in the shopping precinct we walked through on our way back to the hostel. Later, in our room, we could hear crowds chanting.

Monday 1st October 2018: Niš

Woke at 6.30am coughing and read for a while. L still sleeping, though later she tells me she heard me. She made chamomile tea at about 8am which I drank and then fell asleep again until 9.30 when she woke me saying my phone was ringing. I had been in the middle of a long and complicated dream – the phone call was from Ivan, Ivanka's contact in Niš, but it was a very bad line, so he texted via Viber and suggested he come round at 11.30am to meet me and talk about the reading this evening. We just had time to go out to breakfast, after which I waited for him in the sweet little courtyard of the place – it's lined on one side with huge stacks of wood, ready for winter. Ivan arrived, very friendly. I asked after his mother as he had said via text that she is very ill. She had ovarian cancer ten years ago, followed by bowel cancer which has now metastasized. She is very sick. He talked about the fact that Serbia has three times the usual cancer rate because of the NATO bombing[109] and many of the victims are young.

We part, and I go back upstairs. L has mostly packed our bags so we decide to go out straight away. First, we head for the bus station in Niš to buy coach tickets for tomorrow's journey back to Belgrade. We queue up in one of the five ticket queues. Two men in front of us have mini arguments with the ticket seller – we have no idea why. The woman behind us is so eager to get her ticket she bumps into L's back and coughs on her neck! When it's our turn we ask for the ticket and I give my card which is declined. L by now has moved away so I shout for her to come back. Luckily hers works, and the ticket seller is all smiles. The eager woman behind us has been trying to butt in all the while to buy her ticket to Sokobanja.

We walk towards the fortress along a side road that has a big green market off it. The stalls are mostly full of peppers – every shape and colour, all gleaming. Some are bagged into net bags and people are buying great carrier bags full of them. Further on the fruits, the pulses and last of all the flowers. After the market on to the fortress, familiar from yesterday. We walk around it, partly on top of the wall. Wonderful views to the hills on both sides. The din of howling dogs comes from one hillside of suburbs.

An hour's rest before Ivan arrives at 6.30pm. He stops his car outside and we slide in. It's a short journey to the room where the reading will be, organised by Niški Kulturni Centar, in the small hall of the Niš Cultural Center. The programme is introduced by the writer Velibor Petković who is Ivan's assistant at the university. Velibor, from Bosnia originally, has been a psychologist, a radio reporter and is now studying for a PhD with Ivan – his subject being the radio reporter Dušan Radović of 'Good Morning Belgrade'[110] After the reading Ivan invites us for coffee which turns into slivovitz and cheese in a cavernous and beautiful old restaurant near Tinker's Alley. We have a long discussion about aliens. Ivan is writing about them.

Tuesday 23<u>rd</u> June (continued) Introduced to a Turkish Capitain, Commandant of Nissa – told us it was not good to come to Nissa one day and go away the next – that we ought to go down and pay a visit to the Pasha at Bagnia [Niška Banja] abt. 6 miles distant – if we would go he would accompany us and have a carriage ready to take us in the morning – of course we could not refuse – during this discourse un-intermitting pipes and coffee – magnificent thunder storm, rain in torrents – splendid zig zag lightning – went abt 8 to have a Turkish bath – accompanied by a servant of the Archbishop's with lantern and umbrellas – word had been sent to the baths for everything to be ready and clean as if for the Pasha himself (indeed the attention and hospitality shown us and honour paid us in everything was most gratifying and could not have exceeded had we been of the first rank in our own country) – enjoyed the Turkish Bath amazingly – returned to the Palace abt. 9½, more pipes and coffee in his Eminence's Bed room – like the other with Ottomans round it but smaller – a sort of raised recess with curtains before it where was his Bed. Abt 10 our Host conducted us to where we were to sleep – beds being made for us on the ottomans in the Grand Reception Room.

Wednesday 24th June At 8 O'clock after a sumptuous breakfast we found the Archbishops carriage with 4 horses, at the door in which we went with the Archbishop himself, followed by the Commandant and a picturesque retinue of Turks and Greeks on horseback (Commandant Pandour Albanian) arrived at Bagnia [Niška Banja] the scene was picturesque beyond description. Bagnia or the Bath (old Roman like that at Bagnia in Servia) water tolerably warm – situated on a gentle and prettily wooded eminence backed by hills clothed with trees to the summit – in front the vast plain of the Nishava yellow with ripe grain and dotted with trees – to the left the minarets of Nissa – to the right towards Constantinople two gigantic peaks 6000 or 8000 feet high reared their craggy summits – Ruined Mosque and Minaret – baggage, wagons and attendants – tents of Pasha and his friends – sleeping apartment and kitchen – iced water – sat in Secretary's tent till Pasha came from bath (Mehemet Pasha)[111]. Pipes & coffee – Osmond late Pasha of Nissa,[   ] Bey[112] of [   ], Syrian Dervish etc – present in violet green and blue mantles lined and trimmed with fur. Had a bath. Amphibious children washing horses etc – Sat for 10 mins in Pasha's tent – returned as we came – just escaped a tremendous thunder storm – an awful dinner 26 dishes – Seignor Georgio![113] – our host wanted to keep me there & find me a wife. Capitain drunk and ill. Mr G and I went out shopping – fruit, wine & pipes in front of house – pipes and coffee upstairs then to bed, intending to start at the top of the morning but alas!

Thursday 25th June Our intentions frustrated – obliged to undergo another meal of 15 or 16 dishes and wine in proportion after sweetmeat, liquor, water, coffee, pipe & liquor & water – then pipes & coffee again & finally got under weigh abt. 9. The Archivescobole [archbishop] (a sign of great friendship & respect kissing us on the cheek – we kissing his hand. Turkish Fortress – Pasha's Palace – Seraglio [harem] Empty!

Very hot ride. Got back abt 1 (the last breakfast and the ride finished me) very seedy! Bilious! Indigestion! etc

Friday 26th June Still seedy etc did not bathe

Saturday 27th June Ditto & Ditto Wrote to my mother & part journey to Nissa

Sunday 28th June Ditto and Ditto. Did not bathe. Letter from Aunt E[114]. Ditto & Ditto

Monday 29th June Ditto & Ditto – better etc

 Tuesday 30th June Better – went for a ride after dinner & wrote a long letter to Harrison –

Wednesday July 1st Walked to the top of one of the hills after dinner – splendid panoramic view. Alexinitza embedded in the valley – serpentining Morava – gorgeous sunset etc

Thursday 2nd July Rode to meet Col. Townley – caught in thunder storm – Col. Townley did not arrive – removed to the oven[115]

Friday 3rd July Col. Townley arrived[116] just as we had done dinner – I went for a ride over the hill – beauty very!

Saturday 4th July Out shooting with Col. Townley all day. He shot 13 head. Pigeons, doves, a quail & a dog (poor old Lord)

Sunday 5th July went grouse seeking – went to the top of a hill overlooking valley towards Bagnia [Sokobanja] – beautiful! Old Castle on crag[117] – Dobra! [good] Shot at a dog & missed him, shady!!

Monday 6th July out shooting with Col. Townley & bathed in Morava

Tuesday 7th July Bathed in Morava every day with Townley & went for a ride with Mr Gutch in the evening

Wednesday 8th July began to get impatient for arrival of despatch

Thursday 9th July Called on the Dr. um zu fragen [   ] für morgen [?]¹¹⁸

Friday 10th July Went for a ride with Col. Townley & Mr Gutch towards the frontier – beautiful sunset

Saturday 11th July The dispatches arrived at 5. Bathed by myself in Moravitza [Morava] – Off at 8¼ in the same form as we came. 1st Station Thupriae¹¹⁹ [Ćuprija] 2nd Jagadina [Jagodina] At 5 O'clock dined and off again at 6. 3rd [   ] 4. Batachina [Batočina] 5. Pashapolanca [Smederevska Palanka] at 3 im morgen [*at 3 in the morning*] – a lovely night – summer lightning – curious costumes – Bulgarian etc slept an hour at Pashapolanca.

Sunday 12th July – started at 5 – lovely morning with a nice breeze. 6th Station Polak – breakfasted. 7th Grotschka [Grocka] – clouds of dust – na dobza [*Nije Dobro – it is not good*] – reached Belgrade at 2. – crossed over, sharp shower – got very wet – found Mr Grattan, messenger at Semlin. Dined at 7. Went with Grattan to Kaffee Hause. Mr G tired and went on board Steamer. I missed steamer. Grattan exceedingly kind lent me money & made arrangements for me – took Wagen to Carlovitz [Sremski Karlovci] to meet steamer – started at 12½ lovely night – delicious [*chill*] & reached

Monday 13th July Carlovitz at 6 in the morning. Pr [*proprietor*] Johann – 20fl and 2kr – Agent for J P very civil – gave me bread and melon – Steamer arrived at 10½ – delighted to see it – *Viele Studient* [*many students*] at Carlovitz – a college¹²⁰ there with 600 [children]. Banks of river very flat woody & rank vegetation – Neusatz [Novi Sad] a fine town close to river & a magnificent fortress – Peter Wardine [sic: Petrovaradin] opposite – a good dinner on board. Capt agreeable – apologised for leaving me behind! Sported champagne and told good stories – eine schöne frau [*a beautiful woman*] – guten mensch [*a good man*] – sehr gut geschlaft [*slept very well*]

Tuesday 14th July arrived at Mohach [Mohač] at 12½ dined & started with post horses towards Vienna through Stühlweisselburgh¹²¹ [Székesfehérvár] from whence Postpferde [*post horse*] thro' Raab [Győr] all large nice looking towns & arrived at Vienna particularly dirty on

Thursday 16 July at 5½ morning – had a warm bath etc. Breakfasted and sallied forth shopping. Dined went to the opera theatre.

Friday 17 July – went to have a bath – solt die zeit für die Damen [*should be the time for the ladies*][122] – took a Valet de Place & went to see the Emperors Coachhouse[123] – magnificent gilded coaches and sledges some 50, 60 and 150 years old, the Palace, the Liechtenstein Galleries[124] and the church where all the Emperors and Empresses have been buried since 1622. Bronze zinc etc splendidly embossed and carved. Had a glorious bathe abt. 2 in swimming bath at Diana Baths, Leopold Stadt[125] abt 150 ft by 40 ft. Dined at 4 and went to the Volk Gartens[126] afterwards to hear Strauss' band – statue of Theseus and the Centaur by Canova[127] – left Vienna at 9½ – posted all night – very wet & reached Braunau, the Austrian Frontier at 6 on Sunday morning the 19th then thro Bavaria from here to Munich – beautiful gentle undulations, magnificently wooded – picturesque towns and villages embedded in woods in the recesses of the hills with the curious gilded and enamelled spires of the churches and in the distance on the left the stupendous chain of the Illyrian Alps covered with snow – approaching sometimes as near as 10 or 12 miles – extensive pine forests – reached Munich at 8 a m, went to the Goldener Hirsch [*Golden Stag*] – dined – gateway and fresco painting, picture gallery. Logi etc – a pretty clean city.

Monday 20th July Started at 6. Railway to Augsburg fortifications – lose sight of the Alps – posted to Ulm reached it at 6 – new fortifications etc – dined at the Goldene Traube [*Golden Grape*]. The frontier of Würtemberg – posted on thro' the night – very wet and reached Stuttgardt[128]

Tuesday 21st July where we breakfasted at Marcquardtz – very good & Mussirender Neckarwein[129] – Sehr Gut (very good) – took a bit of railway at [   ] & reached Heidelberg at 5 o'clock – dined and started off with post horses again for Frankfurt. Heidelberg beautifully situated and a lovely town, interspersed with trees, thick hedges etc. – on the Neckar delicious looking green water – castle a splendid ruin in a fine commanding situation – posted all night and reached Frankfurt at 5 on Wednesday 22nd. July Breakfasted and started by rail for Bebric [Biebrich] on the Rhine – railroad slow and very shaky.

At Home 2020/8: Queue

a very old man/ tugs many little packets/ from the bottom of
his bag/ each one a low value transaction/ so much for rent/ so
much for gas/ so much for electricity/ water/phone/ so many/ /
each record/ must be carefully/ retrieved from its plastic case/
pulled out/unwrapped/ its old receipts unfolded/ put to one side/
for the cashier/ who reaches for each of them/ separately/ she
reassures him/ is a safe/ pair of hands/ her mouth moves behind
toughened glass/ hard to decipher/ what she says/ this caged
oracle/ against his free speech/ he digs to the bottom of the bag
for one last packet/ and a withdrawal/ he has lived/ his whole life/
in this town/ asks if she also is local/ we wait/ us others/ as she
counts out the notes/ as he rewraps/ all his small offerings

Hochheim a little village on the sunny bank of the Main from
whence comes Hock – beautiful view of Mayence [Mainz] – spires,
fortifications, cathedral etc drawn by a horse[130] on to Bebric – reached
it at 9 & embarked in the Victoria – the day unpropitious – the sail
from here to Coblentz baffles all description – high banks wooded and
covered with vine gardens in some places reaching the height of 600 or
800ft. here and there interspersed with crags nearly every one of which
crowned with dismantled fortress & picturesque ruins occurring in
such quick succession as scarcely to be counted. Picturesque villages in
recesses at the base – small castle on a rock in the middle – a magnificent
view of Ehrenbriectstein[131] just at the junction of the Moselle with
the Rhine, an impregnable fortress defended by 400 pieces of cannon
and capable of containing a garrison of 14000 men – 500 only in
place. Lower down abt 20 miles above Cologne we came to the
Leibenbergen[132] – on almost all of which their [sic] are ruins of castles
of the Archbishops of Cologne – all of volcanic origin & consisting
of Lava trychyte[133] & basalt – the highest 1453 – the Drachenfels
1056 but by far the most magnificent – an almost perpendicular rock
rising from the very margin of the river & crowned with a ruin, an
almost perfect arch facing the river – a sort of portal & magnificent
commencement to the scenery above – named from the cave of a
dragon on it said to have been killed by Siegfried – a German hero. The
Rhine varies in width from 2000 to 1200 feet widest at Geissenheim
the chateau and Vein Gartens [*vineyards*] of Johannisberg[134] – Prince

Metternich near – the best wines Johannisberg[135] & Heinbergs 2nd
Rüdesheim Markobrunner[136] & Rothenberg Hockheim on the Main
ranks with these. Of the inferior Erbach & Hattenheim the best –
reached Cologne at 5 – a dirty and dull place – did some shopping
and looked into the Cathedral – gorgeous architecture gothic & Italian
begun in 1248 beautifully gilded and groined in the interior – walked
to extremity of fortifications – smoked a weed in gardens <u>Teaed</u>[137] –
made acquaintance with some German young ladies & finally retired
to a downy – the first since leaving Vienna.

High Summer (2019)

It begins bright blue—
skylarks singing
a little wind bluster
invisible
blue songs   scratching the sky
the blue seam of the sea
I ~~am~~ was there   just now I am
just now you are   and then   have been

the future belongs to patriots[138]
to whom does the future belong?

bees at the hemp-agrimony   hoverflies
flecks of light in sun   cabbage whites
roam these gardens and a chalkhill blue
navigates the air to find wild marjoram

~~*shale gas   will be   an important   bridging fuel*~~
~~*in the transition   to renewable technologies*~~[139]

a snake of grey mullet in the Ouse
practices union
circles   gyres
thrusts at the glassy mirror
fallen over it

huge swathes of the arctic are ablaze[140]
huge tracts of the Amazon... are ablaze[141]

THE BOY

has leant his back against a tree,
has made his knees and thighs
the perfect place to rest his hands,
the papers silky as he smooths them out...

the blackbird's back in the plum tree
who has the time to listen and to watch?

~~the Amazon is not being devastated~~
~~and consumed by fire~~[142]

...fiddles the tobacco, teasing
threads together and apart
and crumbles in the weed
before he tears a rectangle of card
and rolls it up to make a roach...

under the greengage tree in deeper shade
the currant bushes hunker   netted against birds
an adder has been caught
and through the days and nights
when no one comes
his head and half his body's poised to strike
his tail end rotting   from this ligature

parable of the allotment —
a hissing head denying what's at stake?

...sweet chafing
in his thumbs and on his lips and in
his limbs which lately rode the air.
His tongue moistens the adhesive
at the edge to lay it down...

a boy could lose himself
in summer heat

up in the clear blue

        a wind
        buffets the skylarks
        scratching out their tune

<u>Thursday 23rd July 1846</u> Left Cologne by railway at a 6¼ – the carriages
very comfortable, particularly the 2nd class – a silent rebuke to us –
railroad very rough – reached Halberstadt[143] at 12 o clock where we
stopped for ¾ of an hour & got some dinner – a Custom House here.
Aix la Chapelle, Liege and Ghent the principal places we passed
through – a fine view of Liege from the top of inclined plane – arrived
at Ostende abt 8½ had some supper and posted off to Calais – gave us
a good deal of trouble at the French Custom House in the middle of
the night.

Friday 24th July A lovely morning and drove into Calais in high
spirits at 7 o clock in the morning – made ourselves clean, had a good
breakfast and moved out of Calais Harbour on board the Princess
Alice[144] at 9½ – a most delightful crossing in 2 hours – got well thro
the Custom House – Mr Birmingham the landlord of the Ship Hotel
accompanying us, had some bread and cheese and beer and started by
the 1¼ train for London & here I must not omit from notes of travel
some mention of the Dover railway which passes most grandly at the
base of the stupendous cliffs, the sea coming close up on the other
side, and I understand in rough weather breaking over the railway –
there are several tunnels some rather long (abt. 5 mins) the railway
is particularly smooth and easy and runs the whole way through a
beautifully diversified country – gentle elevations, well wooded,
luxuriant meadows, picturesque villages & in fact very similar to
the south of Devon – passed the atmospheric[145] line from London to
Croydon – reached the Bricklayers Arms Station[146] at 5¼ and thence
after calling at the Foreign Office in Downing Street found ourselves
comfortably housed at 6 o clock in 77 Gt. Portland Street at rest from
our labours, Amen [*added in pencil*]

                Sainfoin
                may be
                safely sown[147]

A page of George's Notes on nature, time, temperature, languages and politics [written on the last page of the first journal]

Storks on the continent – building on the chimney tops
Frogs at Semlin. Nightingales in the Servian forests
Tortoises at Alexinatz. Fireflies here and at Mehardia
Sunday 21st June Thermometer 89 in the shade. 140 in sun
Friday 26th Ditto   95 do.
Chateau of the Duke of Nassau at Biebrich on the Rhine facing the river an old and very handsome palace
Kirkhain Tata (illeg) Square? [*written upside down in light pencil at bottom of page*]
Language of our Hungarian Schvagers on the night Friday 1st May urging on their horses – Ge thouu thoi geshvinkt thouu –
Time at Calais different ¼ of an hour fast
Vienna 1¼, Semlin 1½, Mehardia 1.40 fast
Walachian "the daughter of the Latin tongue "
Illyrian "the sister of Russian"
Disgusting to see two great moustachioed fellows kissing one another. Germ.
Walachia as Servia subject to Turkey pays 180,000 fl annually 300,000 inhabitants
Bebesco[148] the reigning Prince of Servia – Melosh[149] the last
Patrovitch of Wallachia[150] – Güka[151] the last
Letter Mr Gutch took for the Pascha from Monsr. Lerman[152] directed à suo excelenzo [*to his excellency*]
Vègil Murad Passia[153]
Mussir[154] de Belgrad

Ich bin bei Ihnen gekommen, um mich zu erkündigen über Ihre Gesundheit [*I've dropped by, to enquire after your health.*][155]

Meanwhile in Constantinople

Buyukdery[156] July 27 1846
No. 1[157]

My Lord,
I have the honour to acquaint Your Lordship that His Excellency Sir S Canning, availing himself of his leave of absence embarked last evening on board HMSS "Hecla"[158] in his way to England by Trieste.

His Excellency has made over to me the cyphers and the Archives of the Embassy, and I have applied to the Porte for an early audience of the Sultan at which I may deliver the letter by which the Queen has been pleased to accredit me at this court as Her Majesty's Minister Plenipotentiary during the temporary absence of the Ambassador.

I have too serious a feeling of the responsibility devolving upon me not to solicit Your Lordship's kind indulgence at the same time that I beg to assure you that no efforts shall be wanting on my part to merit the approbation of Her Majesty's Government.

I have, etc
(signed) H Wellesley

Buyukdery
July 27 1846
No. 2

My Lord,
The last dispatch addressed to Your Lordship's office by Sir S. Canning is marked no. 140 of July 25th.

I take the liberty to supply an omission in His Excellency's public correspondence by forwarding herewith a copy of the joint official note addressed to Reshid Pasha by Her Majesty's Ambassador and the Austrian Envoy in reply to that Ministers' last communication on the subject of the negotiations at Erzeroom, transmitted in translation in Sir S. Canning's dispatch no. 125 of the 20th instant.

I have Etc
(signed) Wellesley

Buyukdery August 1st 1846
No. 4

My Lord,
I have the honor to inclose for Your Lordship's information copies of two despatches addressed to His Excellency Sir S Canning by the V. Consul at Trebizond, reporting that a serious revolt had broken out in the province of Adjirah in the Pashalic of Trebizond.

Upon making enquiries of Reshid Pasha he informed me that the Ottoman Govt. had received the same intelligence and that at the desire of Nabil(?) Pasha of Trebizond they were about to send reinforcements in artillery and infantry to the scene of revolt.

I ventured to express the hope that if hostilities were unavoidable the Turkish Commanders would be instructed not to strike a blow until they were sure it would be efficacious. Mr Steven's dispatch of the [missing text] instant makes me fear that they have already been too precipitate.

I have etc, (signed) H Wellesley

I go over the text again and again. Sometimes it gives up its secrets slowly. I make mistakes and correct them. I look at the same word repeatedly, weighing the possibilities. I read other texts written at the time, look at old maps of the area. Gradually over the years I crack these mysteries and once cracked they do not disappear again, but they lose the itch of the unknown.

Some words have several spellings. Alexnitza, for example, is sometimes called Alexinitza, Alexanizza, Alexinitz, Alexnitz or Alexinatz. The postboy or Surojee can also be a Soorajee or a Serojee. A salesman (or guide for Captain Spencer) is written as kiraidji or Carojee but the actual word in Serbian is kirdžija, meaning a travelling salesman. An inn is a Khan or a Han. Rhisto's new house, spelt Nova Cousche by George is, in Serbian, Nova Kuća. Reference books of the time often use alternate spellings. Serbian words and place names are spelled phonetically by both George and others, which makes it hard to work out places, people, things.

When I start transcribing, I go deeper in. The attention to each word, each phrase, opens the text so it becomes like listening to someone telling an old story, over and over. The slow pace is helpful. I've been on this journey since July 2013. There is no hurry. It becomes a gradual unpicking of knots and problems, some of which unpick as I sleep. Each solution is a little triumph and allows me to move on to the next.

When the act of transcription takes the entire attention everything else slips away. Is it a meditation? A place outside time? If I transcribe the words about Gutch and Davies resting in a post house by a fire, lying on dirty rugs and listening to the grooms chatting, I am taken there and have left the cipher of words. I can furnish the place with more than language gives me.

The transcription proceeds in layers. First the rough transcription of the handwriting, then revisiting some words that are not clear, then adding footnotes, then looking at phrases written in other languages. I do not speak or read German and George's handwriting gets unspeakably bad when he writes in German. Google Translate helps a little except where I can't work out the individual letters. I farm out some German phrases to helpful friends who are German-speaking writers and editors. I try Facebook and get some help there too. Often, it turns out, the German phrases are incidental.

Messengers criss-cross the land, they meet and part, exchanging glances. They seek each other out in towns and cities and lend stout boots to those who need them. They are safe hands in difficult times, sleep at night beside their ciphers, spend gold which is not theirs. Their secrets straggle on strange papers.

PART 2

A letter from Calais from Mr Gutch to Hertslet[159]

Calais Aug 20 1847

Dear Sir

      I leave tomorrow on my last journey from here to Paris and shall leave Paris on the 27ᵗʰ and I consequently presume my relief will arrive here on Wednesday September the first.

[*Obediently*] very truly yours
JWG Gutch

    Calais 20 August 1847
    Messr. Gutch
    Relief of Station

Journal, the second
1847 September

Diary of second Journey to Alexnitza

Monday 27ᵗʰ September 1847 Drove down to the Foreign Office with my friend Mr Gutch as we had done every day for the previous week and at last this evening the welcome sounds "to go tonight" gave us some hopes of a start. After packing in, the baggage, Despatches etc we drove to London Bridge and after about an hour, which we blew away in a cloud of smoke, we were en route for Dover comfortably ensconced nous tous deux seulement dans la Coupée [*just the two of us in the Coupé*] and were soon in the arms of Morpheus as I had ascertained from the Conducteur (who was a Frenchman!) that the boat started for Calais à deux heures matin [*two o'clock in the morning*] and consequently that we sh'd have no chance of "turning in". We were awoke at Folkestone by a great row between a passenger and a guard – the former having done something contre d[r]oit [*against the rules*] was being dragged out by the latter by the collar, threatening that he sh'd not go on to Dover and "how dared he strike him in the face" – the guard was a great fellow of abt. 6ft 2, the offender abt 5ft nothing – with all his worldly goods apparently in a basket in his hand and was after vociferating "I shant go on to Dover? Do you know who I are. I'll have you to know who I are" However he was held by someone while the train went on leaving us in ignorance of who he were

> Separate the strong from the weak
> for the former
> drive the latter from their food[160]

We reached Dover – went on board the English boat and consigned ourselves afresh to the care of the somniferous Deity enveloped in p. jackets in the cabin.

Tuesday 28th September Found ourselves after a prosperous voyage once more on the shores of France at 5½ in the morning. Landed and walked submissively to the Douane [*Customs House*] and bore more equably than last time the ruthless disembowelling of my carpet bag and knapsack, to which small allowance I had reduced my Baggage this trip. Having passed this ordeal we went on to Dessins Hotel where Mr Gutch turned in but I having had enough of that commodity made my toilet and turned out to look round. Calais streets narrow, houses irregular in height and every other respect – green shutters and decidedly French – walked to the end of the pier 1 mile & a ½ strongly built of wood. Returned to write a letter but was soon interrupted by "Monsr. est dans la voiture et a besoin de votre sac de nuit" [*Sir is in the carriage and needs your overnight bag*] came down and found monsr in the agonies of packing. Having breakfasted went to see Mr Poignon at Cillac's Hotel – lent me his boots again. Met also Capt. Johnson there. Started at 11 O'clock in Mr Gutch's carriage posting to Ostend – road flat and uninteresting. Pavé [*cobbled*]. Avenues of Poplars. Furnes [Veurne], Dunkerque, and Neuport [Nieuwpoort] large towns. Douanne at Zudcote [Zuydcoote], Belgian frontier. Statue at Dunkerque in Bronze of Jean Bart,[161] a pirate, native of the place & afterwds. an Admiral, rather disproportioned. Coming in to Neuport both our horses fell on the Pavé but were got up again without any more serious inconvenience than severing all the harness (ropes!) soon reunited. Reached Ostend abt. 9½ had coffee finished my letter. Smoked a pipe in Mr G's room and then attempted to retire to Ma Chambre [*my room*] but found I had been locked into Mr Gutch's quarter. My bedroom being in anor [*another*] – got out through the Coach house and knocked up the Porter –

Wednesday 29th September 1847 Started for Cologne from Ostend mit dem erste Eisenbahnzug [*with the first train*] 7 o'clock travelling very comfortably in Mr Gutch's carriage. Stopped at Mallines [Mechelen] = took in Provisions – Appearance of the country from thence improves. Beautiful abt Lièges and Verviers. The engines partaking somewhat of German phlegm wheezed themselves into the latter place 2 hours after time – at which everyone who was <u>not in a hurry seemed most supremely indifferent</u>

At home 2020/9:
from ICU to L via Fb Messenger 13th June 2020

'You in any pain? X'
'Was earlier but not so much now.
When I cough it hurts–
but they give you a rolled towel
to hold against the wound. Xxxxx'

but as there was no other train to Cologne, but only a short one to <u>Aix</u> [Aix la Chapelle / Aachen] we were obliged to post all night to be in time for the Dampfschiffe [*steamboat*] at five in the morning. The railroad from Verviers runs for many miles through perpetually recurring tunnels, round precipitous rocks splendidly wooded with deep valleys below, studded with pretty little villages. In the large towns the towers of the churches and public buildings which are very handsome contrasted well with the beauties of the scenery. At Aix we stopped at Neullen's Hotel and had some supper after which our hospitable landlord insisted on our drinking a bottle of Tilberg Champagne with him.

Started abt. 11. I was under the delusion in my dreams (mystified no doubt by the Champagne) that we were driving into all sorts of "impossible places" round Gentlemen's houses, gardens etc, out of the direct road, a most agreeable "airing" doubtless but decidedly unpleasant when pressed for time – after several violent efforts which some supernatural power (the ghost of the bottle of champagne which haunted me no doubt!) appeared to obstruct, I at last succeeded in intimating to my companion my fears that we should not reach the end of our journey in time and lo! my success was the spell that banished my airy visions "Awakening with a start" I found our journey was in course of consummation most quickly and satisfactorily – & ere long we reached the Quay at Cologne a ¼ of an hour before the boat sailed. (Duke of Beaufort & family at Neullens 3 weeks) [*written in middle margin*]

Thursday 30ᵗʰ September Left Cologne at 5 in the morning by the steamer up the Rhine – not the best day possible – damp and misty and cold – & towards evening rainy – reached Mayence [Mainz] at 7½ – rail to Frankfurt at 8½ – The ruins on the Rhine that most struck me were Rheinstein an extensive ruin of a castle commandingly situated on a lofty rock – Oberwesel a round tower and village at a pretty turn of the river & the Pfalz,[162] a castle in the middle of the river on a rock. The eldest son of the baron who lived in the castle on the side of the river opposite the Pfalz was always born here to insure the heir was not suppositious.[163] The Pfalz is a picturesque looking object with four small offshoots at the four corners. We reached Frankfurt at 9½ & having deposited Despatches at the Embassy drove to the Hotel de Russie – fire near – ladies frightened appearing à la robe de nuit [*in their night clothes*] with lighted candles! Fire soon extinguished. Supped and retired to our Downies as preferable to the cold desolate Speise-Saal [*dining room*] – sat up in my bedroom till abt. 1 o'clock writing to Edw.d[164] and then passed a very agitated night haunted by the ghost of a bottle of Deidesheimer[165] and indistinct and fragmentary visions and fearful apprehensions of being called every moment at 5 o'clock coupled with unpleasant dreamy anticipations of the momentary apparition of the instrument of torture, the Kellner [*waiter*].

Friday 1ˢᵗ October. Rail to Heidelberg at ¼ 7. Frankfurt a handsome clean and exceedingly picturesque town very much in the suburbs in accordance with Prout's style of drawings[166] – country thro. which the railroad passes continues flat and unpicturesque until near Heidelberg. A beautiful new station building but yet quite unfinished – town & castle not within sight. Waited one hour till 10½ at Heidelberg and on by rail to Durlach[167] the country flat but more wooded than before and on the whole prettier. Nearly parallel with the Bergstrasse – arrived at Durlach at 12 and after nearly an hour's delay in getting horses, and thro. the breaking of the rotten material supposed to be leather, with which the horses were attempted to be guided, nearly run off the platform down a fall of 12 feet into the meadow below – we succeeded in making a start and posted thro Würtemberg (nothing very remarkable) to Stuttgardt – drove to the Hotel and post house Marcquardt's where we had supper – a young married couple sat opposite at tea – found them to be English – entered into conversation with them – they were on their way home from Venice – we started again abt. a quarter past 10 and tho. for description here, you all the world would grant Both night and balmy sleep forbid me to discount[168] at five o'clock in the morning just after changing horses at Geislingen[169] awoke by Mr G. exclaiming he had lost his keys – turned back to Geislingen and left me there while he drove back a stage 16 miles – found them at the door of the Posthouse. [*added in pencil: Mr Gutches Keys Geislingen / at 5½ awoke by his exclamation that he had lost his keys soon after changing horses – tho' he had dropped them at the stage before. Left me here & went back in a trap 16 miles & found them on the ground*]

I whiled away the time filling up some of my neglected diary [*written in middle margin*]

Saturday 2nd October Arrived at Ulm at 1½ a.m. and betook myself immediately while dinner was preparing to look at the cathedral which I must say is well worth seeing. The interior is not unlike Redcliffe Church,[170] Bristol but on a much larger scale. The splendid lofty columns, gothic arches and groined roof – the gilded glittering monuments – beautifully carved oak of the choir representing figures of saints and martyrs with its very handsome painted window facing a curious old organ of the very blackest oak and mosaic work at the very furthest extremity of the church has certainly a most magnificent and impressive effect. The exterior is very antique and venerable in appearance. The tower of a sort of magnesian limestone blackened by age and the rest of red brick also very dark – much stone carving in figures etc. Chief entrance under the tower very striking. Left at 3 and posted on to Augsburg which we reached about 12 o'clock at night. Got beds at Die drei Murren [*The Three Moors*] – rolled into the same and were plunged into oblivion augenblicklich [*immediately*]. I omitted to mention the fortifications which are in progress at Ulm of a very extensive nature – it is on the frontier of Bavaria & Würtemburg separated by the Danube and consequently important. The division is the centre of the bridge & a rapidly increasing town is building on the other side by the neu Ulm.[171] Old town curious and antique like all the towns in Würtemburg with lofty overhanging houses and narrow streets –

Sunday 3rd October Left Augsburg by rail at 8½ for Munich. Railroad flat over a wide plain for 60 miles – no scenery worthy of notice except the Tyrolean Alps – magnificent irregular chain covered with snow in the distance – the day was clear and bright so that they looked in their misty softness more like dark clouds fringed and relieved by edges of opaque white – and after leaving Munich (stopped for an hour only at the Golden Hirsch[e] [*Golden Stag*] to dine at 12 o'clock) as the day became more advanced were seen towering behind the dark pine forests of Bavaria tinged with a roseate hue surpassing all description. Fortifications at Augsburg very strong tho' now unused – moats turned to promenades. Dead houses near the cemeteries where the dead lay 48 hours.

At Home 2020/ 10: A chant for chemotherapy
– August to November 2020

Vinorelbine (capsule) and Cisplatin (by IV)
Dexamethasone
Akynzeo, Movicol and once a day Lansoprizole

refrain: blood tests and covid tests
          at their proper time etc

G-CSF injections (on days five to nine)
Pinch your tummy fat together
ease the needle in

refrain: blood tests and covid tests
          at their proper time etc

Munich a handsome city – streets broad and clean – the public buildings fine domes and cupolas – curious fresco paintings on the outside of some of the buildings. Ein Grosse Feste [*a big festival*] (October 3ʳᵈ)[172] today in Munich. Dancing music and no end of fun. Lots of people from Augsburg – sorry we could not stay – New railroad station building further into the town – old one temporarily erected of wood burned to the ground last year just between Mr Gutch passing to Vienna staying there a week and returning[173] – Bavarian Schwagers and horses – the latter good, the former slow but play the horn beautifully – one always slung across their shoulders.

Monday 4ᵗʰ October At 4 o'clock this morning was roused into consciousness by a most awful knocking & horn blowing "which would awake the dead if they had never been awoke before"[174] – this proved to be our arrival at the gates of Braunau,[175] the Austrian Frontier – were detained an hour for examination of passports etc treated very civilly at the custom house – nothing examined. When it was light enough to see we found the character of the country quite changed – much more hilly and beautifully wooded with dark firs to the summits – the cottages of wood with broad eaves and in fact bearing a very strong stamp of Switzerland. Reached Linz at 6 o'clock – situated on the Danube – strong fortifications in progress – Dined and ordered beds but nearly obliged to go on and post all night to Vienna as the steam boat could not take the carriage – but ultimately resolved to take our baggage and leave the vehicle to come on Thursday – unpacked it and put the luggage in readiness accordingly with considerable alacrity – sitting up till 11½ writing this journal almost from the beginning – and now as steam goes at 7 suppose I was to have a few hours of pleasing forgetfulness! I'll act on the supposition blowed if I don't!!!

Tuesday 5ᵗʰ October Left Linz mit dem Dampfschiffe [*with the steamer*] at 7 o'clock – Linz beautifully situated on the Danube – banks rocky and precipitous – boat crowded – three carriages on board – some great Count and a Daughter of Prince Metternich etc. the Capitan with his dirk by his side – about two hours below Linz the usual character of the Danube (low muddy banks) were succeeded by the most beautiful scenery something like that between Semlin and Orsova but not so wild and like the Avon near Bristol but on twice as grand a scale – the hills on each side rose in magnificent sweeps from the brink of the river, clothed to the summits with pines and Beech except where stupendous crags towered above them – and jutting out in every direction rearing their broken crests from among the woods – on the tops of many are perched the blackened and time worn ruins of the strongholds of the robber knights – in the recesses of the hills below, picturesque villages with their curious Austrian spired churches – on perpendicular rocks whose bases are washed by the Danube's "rushing tide" are placed convents with their red, green and gorgeously gilded domes and cupolaed towers or spires surmounted by glittering crosses & stars. On the left bank on the very summit of a broken crag stood Dürenstein[176] (the prison of Richard Cœur de Lion) a black gloomy looking mouldering ruin surrounded by fragments of rock hurled together in wild confusion from the brink of the river to the foot of the castle and a more wild and inaccessible place & desolate prison I never saw. Several English in the boat. Passed the Custom House at the Outer lines[177] on Mr Gutch showing his passport without the least trouble, leaving all the other passengers less fortunate mortals! to their unhappy fate. Drove to the Wilden Mann[178] abt. 6. Dined & sat up till abt two writing letters.

Wednesday 6th October Went down to the Diana Bade – die schwimmend bade war geschlossen [the swimming pool was closed]. After breakfast went shopping as soon as Mr Gutch had ret.d from the Embassy[179]. Uncertain as to our starting, so obliged to forgo our projected drive to Schönbrun. The streets of Vienna narrow – houses lofty – 5 or 6 stories – no pavement. The Platz handsome – fine monument, figures of the Gods on the clouds carved in alto relievo and much gilded – Cathedral glorious with a profusion of stone sculpture – a lofty pointed symmetrical spire of florid architecture. Most of the private residences like hotels of vast extent and massive but plain architecture with wide doorways and great folding gates. Too late to see any sights. Mr Levezy[180] dined with us at 6 o'clock – understood there was music at Sperls[181] Garttens from 8 to 12 went down there with Mr Gutch abt. 10 – Strauss' Band being too great an attraction to lose. The gardens were not much being little more than a courtyard studded with small trees on every one of which was hung a lamp which had a pretty effect, on two sides of this yard was a sort of conservatory looking room, the side towards the garden all glass, 150 or 200 ft from end to end in which were a multitude of small tables at which some hundreds of people many of them ladies in a pretty tolerably dense atmosphere of smoke were having supper and refreshment in various shapes, and almost every man smoking his Meerschaum or cigar. At the upper end of the room was an orchestra in which was the band abt. 30 or 40 performers and Strauss[182] himself leading. Stayed there abt. an hour and heard 4 or 5 pieces of music (for which see pocket book[183]) and was altogether excessively delighted, returned to the Inn & turned in abt. 12. Messr [*messenger*] from the Embassy with Despatches waiting since 10. Shall go however to Dampfschiffe. Morgen. [*steamship [in the] morning*]

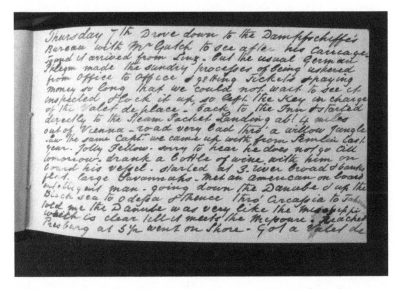

Thursday 7th October Drove down to the Dampfschiffe's Bureau with Mr Gutch to see after his carriage. Found it arrived from Linz – but the usual German phlegm made the sundry processes of being ushered from office to office and getting tickets and paying money so long that we could not wait to see it inspected and lock it up, so left the key in charge of the Valet de place – back to the Inn and started directly to the Steam Packet Landing abt. 4 miles out of Vienna – road very bad thro' a willow jungle – saw the same Captn. we came up with from Semlin last year. Jolly fellow – sorry to hear he does not go till tomorrow. Drank a bottle of wine with him on board his vessel. Started at 3. River broad and banks flat, large savannahs. Met an American on board – intelligent man. Going down the Danube & up the Black Sea to Odessa[184] & thence thro' Circassia[185] to Taheran[186] Told me the Danube was very like the Mississippi which is clear till it meets the Missouri.

'thence thro' Circassia to T[J]akiror[?]'. The place begins with a T, or a J, George's handwriting has Ts that are written like Js and vice versa – the name falls gracefully down the page in a jumble of indecipherable letters which are squeezed and flattened by the approach of the margin. I could write the word 'illegible' in a square bracket and be done with it. But it pulls at me and instead I highlight it in yellow. It stays yellow for five or six years until finally I ask for help on Facebook with a photograph of the relevant piece of text and poets respond with suggestions –Tabriz? Trabzon? Trebizon? Jahira? Tahir? Taher? And so to 'Teheran' then 'Taheran', a misspelling or alternate form of Teheran (Tehran), the old name for that city, and a possibility which suddenly seems right, the journey sensible on 19th Century maps. The handwriting unpicks. The word is legible again and plain. This bright American can travel on.

Reached Pressburg [Bratislava] at 5½ went on shore. Got a Valet de Place & perambulated the town – to see all we could. I interpreted[187] – asked questions etc. Saw the Church Dom Kirche[188] where the Emperor of Mustica is crowned King of Hungary – Palace of the Primate[189] – the committal or Prison – a monument[190] erected over the place where those who died of the plague 50 years ago were buried in the Klöster Platz. The Klöster & the Nunner.[191] Went to the Theatre (the Italian Opera House[192]) saw 2 short German plays & Dissolving View[193] – the latter capital. Views on the Rhine, Danube & in the Tyrol (falling snow etc) & heard some good singing – paid 1½ zwanz [zwanziger]

Dissolving Views 1: falling snow etc[194]

The year she caught pneumonia
was the year he called for an ambulance
was the year she wrote, *a nurse made me a jam sandwich*
the year we weren't allowed to visit
the year we lay in little beds under the thatched eaves
was the year we lay in the room with the sloping floor

and a *blackbird* sang through an open window
was the year the bed collapsed in the spare room with Penny in it
the year we spun and spun and spun on the office chair
the year the *sick brown calf* was moved to the orchard
and I hid behind the staircase door
was the year the snow fell six foot deep
the year she told me don't lie down in snow
was the year the neighbour's tiny baby died
and she said, *you mustn't ask about it*
the year snow drifted into curious ridges
was the year the doctor put a stick in my mouth. *Say Ah*, he said
the year the toad on the path leaked milk from its mottled skin
was the year we lay in bed with measles
and went out looking for *orchids* with Uncle Fred
the year we discovered the shady stands of *foxgloves*
the year bees hung in the mouths of flowers
and insects lit up like shooting stars in our headlights
the year it glittered in still cold air
was the year a wasp crawled up my sister's sleeve
the year Christopher got lost in the woods and was brought home
     by a *stranger*
the year the cows came home alone in the middle of the night
the year they stood in the yard lowing at midnight
and we took them back to their field in the middle of the night
was the year she explained that socks go on either foot
the year the *runner beans* lay down in salt
was the year we walked to the end of the lane when snow
     was falling
the year we held hands and walked in the falling snow
the year I discovered the *figure of eight*
was the year she stayed with Joyce to convalesce
the year the teacher slapped me for crying
the year she ran after me and slapped me for crying
lost her temper because the child *just wouldn't stop*
the year we sang *k k k katy* around the school piano
and swallowed long and slippery sounds. *Say Ah*, they said
was the year I coloured in
the year of *balaclavas, anoraks and snow blindness*
the year snowdrifts made curves of fences and hedgerows

and we moved from one farm to another
the year our cups and plates were wrapped in words
and kale grew taller than the cows
was the year she told her sister *I'm unsteady*
the year before the countless years of falling
when she told me *never sleep in snow*
the year we walked to the end of the lane while snow was falling

dɪˈzɒlvɪŋ vjuːz 11[195]

juː hæv kʌm tuː ðɪs ˌʌnɪksˈpɛktɪd pleɪs
ə trækt əv snəʊ weə snəʊ kiːps ˈfɔːlɪŋ
ˈəʊnli ə θrɛd əv saʊnd
jɔː brɛθ
jɔː brɛθ

– came to Der Schwann [*The Swan*] had coffee and slept there. Mr G stayed on Board in his carriage[196] – no one allowed to do so but him & me if I had liked. Steamboat leaves um 6 uhr morgens [*at 6 a.m.*]. All the talk at Vienna & here of three men who had started to swim down the Danube from Vienna to this place – one did it in 9 hours. Abt. 66 miles.

Friday 8th October Came on board again at 5½. Off soon after 6. Some part of the scenery on the river from here to Pesth [Pest] very pretty like that from Leinz to Vienna. Hills sweeping back from the river in graceful outlines clothed [*in*] wood to the summits and now and then at their base pretty towns with spired churches or at their tops ruined castles. Here also the mills formed by two boats are more frequent making sometimes quite villages as many as 16 or 18 together. Vissegraid [Visegrád],[197] of the old ruins, chiefly attracted my notice. A very extensive one crowning the summit of an almost perpendicular rock with the remains of a strong fortification running down the side of the rock and along near the base having Bastions abt 60 or 80 yrds apart & at the angle, where the wall down the side and along near the base of the upper precipice meet, stands on the top of another rock jutting out a gloomy looking prison 6 stories high. The whole is supposed to be of Hunnish architecture & is somewhat in the style we call the old Norman, gloomy substantial & unornamented.

Monday 10th September 2018: Budapest

...we wandered towards the Margaret Bridge, stopping to buy boat trip tickets to Visegrád. All the tickets were gone for Visegrád so we bought tickets for Szentendre instead, a return trip for tomorrow. We stopped to look at the memorial to the Jewish people who were shot by the side of the Danube in the Second World War. The memorial sign says only 'To the memory of the victims shot into the Danube by Arrow Cross Militiamen in 1944–45. Erected 16th April 2005'. The memorial is of shoes, made of iron: women's, men's and children's shoes left seemingly as they were taken off, before their owners were shot into the water.

Later we passed by a new monument in Liberty Square[198] which attempts to rewrite the history of the Horthy regime's actions during the Second World War. The new monument is of Archangel Gabriel, the national symbol of Hungary, dropping the orb of Hungary, while the imperial Eagle of Germany, with extended claws, prepares to strike from above, suggesting that the State of Hungary bears no responsibility for the genocide following the German occupation (nearly half a million Hungarian citizens, mostly Jews but also gypsies, gay people and dissidents were deported to Nazi extermination camps). The sculpture is set into a neoclassical background of artistically broken columns. It was ordered to be erected by Viktor Orbán, covertly, on the night of July 20/21, 2014.[199]

Across the cobbled street from the new monument is a community protest to this statue and what it represents – a single line of barbed wire hung like a washing line at just below waist height attached to which are photos, descriptions and recollections of those deported and murdered. Below the wire are small, raised beds of plants and stones (some of them painted with messages), in front of these are other mementos such as shoes, paintings, a suitcase. A sign says 'Did you know? Between 1920–1945 600,000 Hungarian people were outlawed, robbed and sent to death by the Horthy authorities. Not the Germans! This statue is a lie!' A water-damaged image of Raoul Wallenberg[200] hangs from the wire with the word Schutz-Pass[201] in the top right corner. Further along is a photo labelled 'Arrival of Hungarian Jews into Auschwitz Spring 1944'. In the photo each person has a star sewn on their left breast, the women with head scarves, old women looking ahead and the young looking to the camera, dazed, exhausted. There are three black banners attached to the wire with the words Truth, Beauty, Josag (Kindliness/Virtue) and a cloth doll, attached to the barbed wire by its wrists. It wears a pink pearl necklace, and has wings sewn to the back of its dress. The shadow of the barbed wire has fallen across its face, a cruel barbed shadow where its eyes should have been...

Afterwards we found the street, Deak Firenc, where Great-Great-Grandfather, George, had stayed at the Königin von England Hotel in 1846 – the Hotel is no more, the street now full of modern shops.

Tuesday 11th September 2018: Szentendre

Nearly overslept since we had forgotten to change the hour on the little alarm clock we brought with us. I was woken instead by a man shouting outside the hotel. Went down to breakfast. Met a lesbian couple at next-door table, health workers from Sheffield, and had a chat about the political situation in the UK – Brexit, May, Johnson etc.

After breakfast walked to Vigardo Ter Pier, no 5, to take the boat to Szentendre. Sat in two of the rattan chairs at the back of the boat. The banks showing Buda on the one side and Pest on our side. The roofs on the Buda side sublimely beautiful with their coloured and patterned tiles. Later, the banks, past Margaret Island, became more wooded. A mix of trees including many willows and poplars with some expensive-looking houses set back and boat clubs with their slipways here and there. Two single sculled canoes passed by. People and dogs passing the time on the banks – some of which were rocky and some beach-like. Parts manicured; parts as wild as I imagine it was when George was here.

In Szentendre we visited an exhibition of local Jewish history which was erected to commemorate the 70th anniversary of the Holocaust. Above the sign which explained the exhibition was a ceramic tile in grey with a raised star on it, the tile bears the words

'SZOMSZÉDAINK VOLTAK' (THEY WERE OUR NEIGHBOURS). The exhibit starts with the names of 958 Jewish people who lived here from 1781 to 1944 and shows family photographs alongside new works in ceramic.

Back on the boat at 4.30pm, the Danube exceedingly calm, the water cycling through different greens according to the ripples running across the surface. Both of us tired now and L still suffering from her cold.

12th September 2018: Budapest – Petőfi Museum

...at ¼ to 9 walked to the Petőfi Museum of Literature for my appointment with the two Annas, Anna Czékmány and Anna Kádár, which I'd arranged before leaving home. Told them about GGG and Mr Gutch and showed them the 1847 journal. I was taken on a tour of the palace the museum is housed in – the grand rooms and elegant staircases, the winter garden bow-window (an early example of ironwork used in this way). In the ballroom what I'd thought was red-flowered wallpaper turned out to be a specially made flowered silk. They had discovered the original pattern under some cornicing and had it copied when the room was renovated. In another room Anna Kádár opened a corner cupboard to show me the old hand-painted wallpaper inside – a silvery grey with gold fine stripes between fleur-de-lys. Saw all the exhibits on the life of Petőfi and they both recommended that I should start by reading John the Valiant...[202]

Later L & I walked to the huge old market where I bought paprika, hot and sweet, and some saffron to take home. Crossed Liberty Bridge and climbed up to the Liberty Monument[203]. It was hot – stopped several times on benches along the way to cool down and look at the views of the Danube, Pest and Buda spread out below us. The sky was clear and we could see for miles. The paths up to the monument are sinuous, full of steps. Many others climbed with us. Some fit, some puffing and panting. We walked on past the fort and then down paths which plunged through woodland. At river level, an underpass and a footway alongside the Danube, cycle paths, benches, so to the National Gallery for the Frida Kahlo exhibition at 4pm. Tallied up our spending so far and I filled up this journal.

13th September 2018: Hungary:
Budapest to Debrecen and back

I woke with L's cold, streaming and sniffling and feeling grumpy. Packed rucksacks for the day and walked to Keleti Station where we caught the 11.10 to Debrecen. Had to run between platforms because on approaching platform 5 where we'd been told to go, a porter told us, no, no, no – with gestures, and to go to platform 11. Back to the ticket office to double check and were told – yes, platform 5! So back we ran with just a few minutes to spare.

Very flat landscape through the Hungarian plains, the train going through the middle of small hamlets and villages. Stands of birch and willow. Fields of sunflowers, almost all gone over and dark brown; on some the lower leaves were still an unhealthy-looking yellow. Much had been ploughed with pale stalks scattered on the surface, the soil a darkish brown. We passed small crossing places where one or two cars lined up waiting. The train stopped at Szolnok where we got out to change trains – five minutes allowed for this but the Debrecen train was late so there was plenty of time to find the right platform. Finally arrived forty minutes late to Debrecen.

We had arranged to meet Imre at 4pm outside the Deri Museum so had only half an hour for a very speedy visit there. We took many photos as we trotted through the exhibits so we could look later. Unfortunately, we were not allowed to take pictures of the 19th Century fine art, of which there were three or four galleries. We noted one picture by Lotz Károly, which reminded me of George's descriptions of Hungarian travel, but we had both forgotten the details of the painting by the end of the evening![204] At 4pm met Imre outside the building. He is very friendly, a PhD student at the University of Debrecen studying the work of Thom Gunn. He is gay and has been with his partner for eight years. He tells us 'My first and only ever'. His early written English, he says, he learnt by playing *The Sims* computer game when he was a child. We went to a bar in the centre of town. Debrecen is built in the grand style with wide avenues and massive public buildings. Imre pointed out, with derision, the glass pyramid beside one building aping the one at the Louvre. After a while we went to have some food and discussed education in Hungary and my project. His friend Petra arrived, a new PhD student who had recently broken her glasses, so said she had a headache and needed wine. We went to another bar. More talk, then we made a move for the university and took a tram, 400 HUF each – the tickets must be validated in a slot machine after purchase.

The university is housed in a very grand old building with a row of fountains out front. Petra said students are allowed to go in the water at graduation. Imre added – 'who would want to go in if it's allowed?' There was an old sofa on the stage in the reading room, where I sat with Imre. He started by welcoming everyone – English and humanities students – there were about forty – and then he asked me to read the Bone Monkey poem on memory. Then we talked a bit and I read some more poems. Then the audience asked questions. They asked many and it was very friendly – when did I start writing, how do I start a poem and so on... One of the audience members was a 16-year-old on a year's exchange at a local high school – Canadian – Imre and Petra wondered how she had found out about the event. Another came up and said she was brought up in England, in Warwickshire, until she was nine, then her mother wanted to return home. Her English father, she said, was bewildered in Hungary and my reading had made her feel homesick. At the end the students presented me with two copies of *The Hungarian Literary Review*, and we got the tram back to the centre and said goodbye to Petra. Imre, L and I repaired to a bar where we drank beer. The bar was playing his kind of music – he was a Goth back in the day.[205] We talked about Gay Pride in the UK and what it is like to be gay in Hungary. He told us the students who organised the English Majors' Night that year had put on a show with a drag act in it and were worried they would be in trouble because of it. He had initiated the first 'Queer Theory' course at the department, he said, had talked to people about it and found a teacher and asked her to teach it. He tries to include LGBTQ+ in everything he does as there are always gay students who need to know they are validated.

After a while he took us to the address for the telecar he has ordered for us, so we did not have to leave Debrecen early as the last train leaves at 7.27pm. It's a system of cheaper travel by paid car-sharing. We paid 7,000 HUF (about £17). Imre introduced us and explained to the driver, who spoke no English, where we needed to go. A former professional footballer for the Czech Republic, who had played in France and now worked and played in Debrecen, also travelled with us. He said he spoke five languages but it had taken three years of listening to learn Hungarian. He wore new red boots which I complemented him on. He was going for the weekend to Paris, he said. He got out of the car at 'Westend' – a shopping mall in Budapest. We arrived at our hotel at 12.30 and went straight to bed.

Saturday 9th October 1847 at 6 o clock in the morning we left Pesth – it poured in torrents and to add to our comforts – they could not take Mr Gutch's carriage on board so he was again obliged to unpack all his luggage and convey it on board – leaving me to follow which I did by going ¼ of a mile in the contrary direction till I fortunately asked someone Wo die Dampfschiffn bis Semlin war [*where the steamers for Semlin were*] and on discovering my mistake broke like lightening thro' the darkness & rain back again & got on board in time – a miserable cold damp day & very little to be seen – did little else but smoke & dine comfortable in our crib which bye the bye was small quarters for two and a cart load of luggage, and occupied as a bed room and dining room. It was eight feet square – our beds on the two sides – the table in the middle & the luggage filling up the space between that and the third – on the 4th just room enough to open the door & come in. Our beds (sofas in the day) formed our seats at dinner but it was very jolly for all that! –

Sunday 10th October Still on board the steamer. ~~Left Carlovitz~~ At abt. 5½ (fast asleep) we left Mohatz [Mohács] stopped for 10 minutes at Nisatz [Novi Sad] and came on to Carlovitz [Sremski Karlovci] & anchored for the night – amused myself with writing letters till a late hour.

Monday 17th September 2018: Sremski Karlovci to Belgrade

I woke early at just after 7am having slept poorly because of the cough and spent some time quietly reading while L slept. We went to breakfast – table by the open window on to the Danube – stunningly beautiful with swans, a white egret, calm as anything.

Breakfast was enormous – huge omelette with cheese, thick slices of mozzarella on the side, tomatoes sliced, sliced green hot pepper and coffee (two cups). Then back to the room to pack and to pay. The taxi came and took us to the station,300 dinar, and after a bit the train arrived. The female station master comes out for each train that stops. Red hat with one gold stripe. L saw a hatstand in her office with five or six hats on it. We got on the train – intercity, plush, and bought a ticket – the guard handwrote it on a form, and we got the carbon copy. Very pretty, slightly hilly country with small villages and towns along the way. Farmland with maize, a football stadium, industrial architecture. Lots of graffiti along the walls by some of the stations. Met a little girl and her mother at the station. We have very little common language, but I showed pictures of our cat, Squirrel, (on my phone) and she showed me her bracelet. On the train we exchange names. She is called Mia (and is about five I'd say) she talks and engages everyone in conversation and says to me in English 'I love you'. We exit the train at Beograd Centar[206] – the new Belgrade train station. It was supposedly finished in July but there is no lift to get off the platform with heavy bags, there are steps to the ticket office, a couple of un-signposted slopes at the end of very long platforms, and only steps out of the station. A man with a broken arm in plaster, seeing me hesitate, lifted my case for me up the steps out of the station.

Monday 11th October 1847 Left Carlovitz at 5½ & at abt 8½ reached Semlin. Fonblanque & Tatar came over. Went back with Fonblanque to dinner. He went to pay his respects to the Prince [*Aleksandar Karadordević*] – his birthday – we went shopping. Servian shops closed. When we came back to Fonblanque's – found Moore arrived from Alexnitza – climate much warmer – sun really hot.

Meanwhile from the British summer embassy in Constantinople

Therapia Oct 11
To Mr Timoui
No. 5

Sir

I have brought to the knowledge of the Ottoman Minister for F. A [*Foreign Affairs*]. the complaints made by the Jewish Community at Damascus[207] against the unequal institution of the tax called "Ferdi"[208] by which they (the Jews) are called upon to pay more heavily than either Christian or Mahomidan subjects of the Porte. I cannot obtain any other promise from Aali Effendi than that he will direct the Pasha of Damascus to enquire into and report to him upon the validity of the complaints.
(signed) Cowley

To Mr [Timoui]
No. 6
Therapia Oct 11
Sir,

I have the satisfaction to acquaint you that your humane exertions in favour of the girl Borval have at length been brought to a successful termination. She was restored to her mother on Saturday last.

I must however observe as perhaps some justification to the Turkish Authorities at Damascus that the girl prevaricated to the last. Before her arrival she declared herself to be Mahomidan and it was only when she saw her mother that she finally determined on remaining a Christian.[209]

(signed), Cowley

Therapia Oct 12
To Aali Effendi

The undersigned etc has had the honor to draw the attention of His Excellency, the Ottoman Minister of Foreign Affairs, to the great injury inflicted on Ionian commerce[210] by the blockade of the coast of Albania. The Und^d. [undersigned] is far from denying the right & even the necessity of the Porte's acting as it has done in order to put down the revolt that has existed in that province nor upon such urgent occasions can it be expected that the interests of other countries can be taken into consideration in determining the measures that are necessary to vindicate the authority of the Sultan, and re-establish order and tranquillity.

But it must be remembered that this is not the first outbreak of the kind that has occurred in Albania. On the contrary, hardly is one insurrection quelled in that unhappy province, before another bursts forth, nor can it be expected that without a complete change of system it will be otherwise for the future. People do not rebel and place their lives, their families and properties in jeopardy for the mere pleasure of rebelling, whenever there is a continual uneasiness among a people, the [*foreign office minister*] may be assured, that there is something fatally wrong in the system by which they are governed, and its first duty is to direct a strict and searching enquiry to be made into their wants and grievances. That such is the case in Albania no one who has any knowledge of the affairs of that province can deny. By a long continued system of mal-administration the inhabitants have been goaded into what may be almost called a state of permanent rebellion.

The Und$^{d.}$ might have hesitated in stating these home truths to His Excellency Aali Effendi, were the present enlightened ministers of the Sultan in any way responsible for the mal-administration. While it has been his duty to signalise it was hardly to be expected that during the short time they have been in power and occupied as they have been by other matters of equal importance, that they should have been enabled to turn their thoughts to the state of Albania with that seriousness and attention which its importance merits. But now that they also have been obliged to vindicate the Sultan's authority by force of arms the Und$^{d.}$ confidently hopes that they will see the necessity of preventing a recurrence of these scenes of desolation and bloodshed, and that they will set themselves fairly to work in order to introduce into that country a system of administration more in harmony with the policys, habits and prejudices of the inhabitants.

It has been the duty of the Und$^{d.}$ on more than one occasion to convey to the knowledge of the Ottoman Ministers the opinions of her majesties Consuls and others as to the grievances under which the Albanians suffer, and the remedies that ought to be applied. It is for Your Lordship to weigh the value of the suggestions offered. Nevertheless the Und$^{d.}$ cannot abstain from pressing more particularly on Aali Effendi's notice the valuable hints contained in the despatch of the Lord High Commissioner of the Ionian Islands of the 24th Sept. of which His Excellency has been furnished with a translation. The Und^{d.} would from the friendly feelings which animate his govt. in regard to this Empire, consider himself at all times justified in offering amicable advice to the Porte', when he conceived that circumstances required it, even as to the internal affairs of the country. But he is induced on the present occasion to put his advice in this official form, because he cannot in duty conceal from Aali Effendi the bad effect which a persistence in the determination to [*suppress*] the Albanian Provinces by the sword and not by just and equitable laws would have upon H M Govt. Admitting, as the Und^{d.} has done, the right of the Porte to take any measures it pleases to reduce the insurrection in Albania without reference to the interests of any foreign power, still H M Govt. could not view with indifference a blockade established year after year on the coast of Albania to the serious detriment of the commerce of H M's Ionian subjects. And that the Porte will be necessitated to recur constantly to such coercive measures, cannot be doubted, unless gathering wisdom from the errors of the past, it employs consideration instead of force, and endeavours to inspire confidence and affection in the place of terror and hatred.

It will give the Und^{d.} unfeigned pleasure if His Excellency Aali Effendi will authorise him to convey assurances to his Govt. that this subject shall receive the most serious attention of the Ottoman Ministers.

(signed) Cowley

I stare at the text of a letter in the archives at Kew. The Ambassador's scribe has used an old abbreviation multiple times and I can't get it. That lack makes a nonsense of the text but finally it dawns on me, the letters just abbreviate 'the undersigned'.

George continues:

Tuesday 12th October 1847 Up this morning at 6 o'clock & all our luggage being Packed into saddlebags for putting on to horses[211] we walked down to the river with Mr Fonblanque – the Tatar is carting the baggage in a cart & crossed over in one of the government boats

– went up to the residence of the Consul where we waited an hour for the horses. These at last arrived and the baggage bound on two of them – we mounted into the saddle & rode out of Belgrade. The day was splendid bright & warm – the sun indeed so hot that I almost repented having put on the warm clothing which the season of the year wld. seem to warrant – the motley appearance presented by travellers thus journeying is most picturesque & as seen winding over the plains (the sunlight upon the bright colours of their dress adds much to the beauty of the scenery) – the Surojee (or postboy[212]) rides first, dressed in a coloured jacket & trousers of a different colour and very full, embroidered with braid – he leads by a rope the baggage horse – the other if (as in our case) there are two, being tied to the tail of the first – he wears on his head a red Fez, & on his feet red boots or slippers & embroidered leggens. Our Tatar or Guide wore a red Fez with a shawl bound round & falling down his back something after the manner of an Arab Sheik – a scarlet embroidered jacket & vest – loose chocolate coloured Turkish trousers with a Persian shawl round his waist in which were his pistols, & red boots. Mr Gutch's costume was a cap with an oilskin cover – Spanish jacket & waistcoat of black lambswool & scarlet shawl. English leathers – jack boots & huge brass spurs. My own was a Jim Crow hat[213]. A p. jacket & crimson shawl bound round my waist – red jack boots & spurs. Our ride was most beautiful. The country is very undulating & the acclivities covered with huge Forests or the underwood of those which have been cut down. At Grotschka [Grocka] we caught a glorious view of the Danube & soon after leaving this lost sight of it to be seen no more till our return. From here to the next post it is almost one continued forest – & from thence to the next pretty nearly the same. The trees are Oaks of a large size & the road has merely been formed by cutting down the trees, so as to form a ride – & this is all the attempt that has been made at a road. The stumps of the trees remaining in many places

On horseback in all weathers

Sometimes in winter
when snow lies two yards deep
in a country without roads
wolves   pressed with hunger
circle the sheepfolds

Sometimes the rider
tested to the limit of patience
must frequently alight
to open clumsy gates
and their clumsier fastenings

Or a canopy of foliage
impervious to light
harbours   loneliness
only the creaking of the saddle
allays desolation

Deep forest abounds
with immense tracts of oak
wild plums and cherries
then pieces of ground
just brought into use

Five or six feet
of each tree stands up straight
partially burnt—
brigades of lost soldiers
quartered in corn fields

…& the way being left to be trodden down by passengers to and fro, giving it in wet weather the appearance of a plowed field with cart ruts of from half a foot to a foot deep. At about 8½ we reached Palanka[214] [Smederevska Palanka] the third post abt. 85 English miles[215] & here Mr G, feeling tired & seedy, proposed to sleep for an hour or two. It was a mere attempt for tho we staid here nearly four hours – the activity of those little insects which are more peculiarly the detestation of the fair sex, & which here swarmed in myriads, rendered it quite abortive. The post house was a huge building containing 30 or 40 horses & at one end a blazing fire round which were mats, the beds of 3 or 4 Servians (the Ostlers) stretched thereon. We started again abt. 12 & in about 2 hours reached Ratscha [Rača] where we got some bread, eggs, coffee and milk and having smoked a chibouque which we did indeed whenever we stopped we were off again & ere we reached the next station Battofschina [Batočina], morning broke the 13<u>th</u> October

<u>Wednesday</u> & from here was the most beautiful part of the ride. The hills became higher & more irregular & after leaving the next halting place a town called [   ] we passed thro' a Gypsy village – huts all of mud in a narrow valley bordering on a little stream – from this we wound up thro' thick underwood to the top of the hill & then the scenery was magnificent near irregular chains of hills thickly wooded. A broad plain beneath extending perhaps 150 miles thro' which the Morava serpentined.

Wednesday 26th September 2018: Belgrade to Sokobanja

During the trip the taxi driver told us, in pretty good English, having asked where we were headed, that he knew Sokobanja well and Niš and had been stationed in Aleksinac for six months in the army in 1989. He talked about weddings, when I told him about the journal, and that George had attended a traditional wedding. He said he, himself, had also married traditionally in church but that all marriages, now, had also to be certificated civilly in the Town Hall.

When we got near the Belgrade bus station there were people gathered under the trees in the park. We noticed a man spraying the park paving and thought he was spraying for weeds, but the taxi driver said, 'he's spraying disinfectant because of the Syrians in the park. They are dirty, that's why they do it'. He seemed to have no idea of his racism or of what the refugees in the park would have gone through to get here. We arrived at the bus station just then, got out, paid the fare.

We went into the bus station café and ordered beer, salad and bread which was all very good and cheap, 360 dinar (about £2.50) for everything. Then walked through the bus station to the entrance to the stands. We passed our *jetons* to the man – these are tokens needed to enter the stands – and went to Stand 6 where our bus would leave from. (L told me about a man who had, in error, left his *jeton* as a tip on a table after a meal, and arriving at the bus station had no end of trouble getting his bus. The ticket on its own is not enough).

We drew out of Belgrade and shortly onto the motorway – the same toll road as before. The country becomes a great plain, very agricultural with fields of maize, straw gold in the light – much of it still to be harvested. The fields are planted in patches, rectangles of crops. Every so often plantations of fruit trees or bushes, under an acre or so of black netting held up by poles and wires to keep off the birds.

> Threshers will be
> constantly
> at work[216]

The light today is marvellous, everything glows. We pass small villages, near and far, and little towns, roofs tiled traditionally, and with the same kind of dishevelled barns and outhouses I grew up with on the farm. In the distance, after an hour or so, the line of hills seen from the left hand side of the bus comes closer than the faint blue outlines they were to begin with. Trees, fields and crags become visible. Many electric pylons dot the landscape, great double legged iron beasts. I see a buzzard circling. The poplars raise silver spurs in the wind. There are acres of low brush, farmers working the fields with their cars parked near them. Motels and truck stops, several large cemeteries with dark stones. Tiles on the town roofs a dark orange, the church towers are minaret-like. There are also grey concrete chimneys, chutes, rectangular heavy run-down industrial buildings. Then more farms and mountains on the right. Each time the coach stops at a coach station it must leave the motorway – each time it leaves, there's a small toll booth to stop at. The mountains on the right go back in layers, grey on grey, each layer lighter than the last. The coach stops in Aleksinac for its last major stop.

We sight the Bosphorus Hotel where for months we'd planned to stay. It is the only one in Aleksinac, a motel about a mile out of town on the main road. Ivanka had mentioned that Sokobanja would be better, more picturesque with thermal springs and many, better hotels. The bus continues on to Sokobanja – it stops frequently on this last section for local people. The outskirts of Aleksinac trail through beautiful wooded hills. The houses are a mix of traditional and modern, with many new houses half built – the bricks untidily mortared and sometimes placed irregularly or on their sides.

You get a sense of the people who live here. Tables left outside with empty chairs around them, dogs on chains looped to run along a wire, as Dad used to tie up Tip or Tim at home. Washing hung out to dry on a balcony or in a garden and, further out of town, chickens or geese with the run of the garden. The road runs on past these urban/suburban houses into country – maize fields, rough scrub, wooded hills. The quality of the light intense, golden in the afternoon. The hills still grey further back. Soon there are farm buildings, barns with bricks spaced in patterns for ventilation, or wattle without daub. Outside many houses are piles of wood stacked ready for winter. As in my childhood, children get off the bus when they reach their stop, shouting goodbyes and disappearing along side roads or into their isolated houses. Small lanes lead off to villages. Our road descends into a gorge with crags on either side. The rocks covered with wire netting. And then the sudden lake, Lake Bovan, lying in its valley and spreading towards flatter land at one end with a beach and houses scattered here and there in the distance. After the lake the bus slowly draws into Sokobanja.

The room is good with a kitchenette area and balcony, a nice bathroom with shower. L has arranged to spend two nights at another B&B because of my all-night coughing. She phones the guy and we wait outside. There is a comedy of errors then as there are several entrances to our hotel and we spend at least twenty minutes moving between them before we finally find him. He is very friendly and drives us to the flat which is after all only about 200 yards away! L's flatlet is good too. Kitchenette, divan and bathroom and bedroom. We spend some time talking to him. He says his ex-girlfriend is half Hungarian, half Serbian and lives in the same area of Belgrade as we were in and likes it there. He, personally, likes New Belgrade better. We tell him about the project and GGG. He says Aleksinac is not a good place. It is poor, the kids from there are rough – he was at school with some of them. It used to be an industrial area and after the dissolution of Yugoslavia and the war, it was bombed, it lost its industry and became poor. He said be careful there.

Later I read this:[217]

April 6, 1999

"NATO planes bombed the center of Aleksinac in southern Serbia early Tuesday, killing at least 12 civilians and injuring dozens more, some of them seriously". CNN's Brent Sadler told viewers, "I think what I'm seeing here is the largest civilian casualty toll since the beginning of NATO air strikes... I saw quite clearly that these were civilian homes... I saw body parts inside these buildings."

13th October 1847

Close under us the town of Jagodina & away on every side interminable blue outlines of distant hills among which was conspicuous the point of a mountain [Rtanj] near Bagnia [Sokobanja] like the sugar loaf in shape & 5,000ft high. On the right the lofty range of irregular hills[218] to the S. W of Alexnitza separating Servia from Albania. Our road from Jagodina lay for 40 miles over a flat plain when we reached Schupria [Ćuprija] – the last post. We then mounted another hill & on descending this the view was glorious. The valley of the Morava. The magnificent great hills behind which just before reaching Alexnitza the sun set shedding over their dark blue a gorgeous roseate hue & when at last it sunk leaving their stupendous form with the wavy outline relieved against the brilliant orange of

Airstrikes hit home in a small Serbian town

April 6, 1999
Web posted at: 5:48 a.m. EDT (0948 GMT)

From Correspondent Brent Sadler

ALEKSINAC, Yugoslavia (CNN) -- It was a night of unrelenting bombardment in the Serbian town of Aleksinac. It was a night that Serbs felt suffering and pain, anger and bewilderment.

Two blasts early Tuesday ripped through apartment blocks and apparent civilian homes in Aleksinac as NATO missiles pounded targets in Serbia.

At least four civilians were killed, 30 were injured and a medical clinic used by civilians was hit in the town, about 100 miles south of Belgrade. It appeared to be the largest civilian casualty toll since the beginning of NATO airstrikes..

"This is completely inhuman. I can't describe it," a teacher said. "I saved my children and I can only hope we'll be OK."

The point of detonation was sandwiched between a block of apartments on one side and the clinic on the other.

Confusion and panic was reported as explosions hit and fires broke out. Windows and corridors were strewn with shattered glass and splintered wood.

People wandered around in shock. Survivors said they scrambled through debris. Firefighters doused the flames of Serbian homes. The direct hits caused almost unrecognizable ruin.

The citizens of Aleksinac asked why the bombing occurred.

"There is a military barracks about half a mile away, maybe more," one man said. "But why hit us?

"We're not a target."

Images, shown on Serbian TV, of damaged buildings in Aleksinac

RELATED VIDEO
CNN's Brent Sadler reports from a small town hit during NATO airstrikes, Tuesday, April 6
Windows Media   28K   80K

ALSO
Diplomatic efforts continue despite cease-fire rejection

Airstrikes hit home in a small Serbian town

More Kosovo refugees flown out of Macedonia

Pentagon: Yugoslavia considers captured soldiers POWs

the sky, of the darkest indigo & Prussian blue – we reached Alexnitza about 6 o clock in 31 hours. Had some supper & went to bed.

Various Foreign Measures of Length reduced to the English Measure.

Foreign Measure.	English Measure.			Observations.
	Miles.	Furl.	Yds.	
1 Bohemian Mile =	5	6	· 17	Some people make a
1 Danish Mile =	4	5	104	German geographical
1 French Post =	4	6	186	mile = 8071 yards
1 Flanders Mile =	3	7	50	English, or 4 miles 4
1 German Geographical Mile =	4	4	183	furlongs 151 yards,
1 —— long Mile =	5	6	7	Some = 8101 yards
1 —— short Mile =	3	7	39	English, or 4 miles
1 Hamburg Mile =	4	5	104	4 furlongs 181 yards.
1 Dutch Mile · =	3	5	16	Some = 8106 yards
1 Italian Mile =	1	1	45	English, or 4 miles 4
1 Prussian Mile =	4	6	108	furlongs 186 yards.
1 Russian Werst · =		5	67	
1 Saxon Mile =	5	5	5	
1 Swiss Mile =	5	1	133	
1 Westphalian Mile =	6	6	208	

14 Dresden feet = 13 English feet.
1 Dresden Ell = 2 Dresden feet = 1⅔ English feet.
21 Dresden Ells = 13 English yards.
  1 Dresden Ruthe or Perch = 8 Dresden Ells = 4⁴⁸⁄₅₁ English yards, or 4·9523
    English yards.
A Saxon mile has been fixed at 2000 Ruthen = 9905 English yards = 5 miles
    5 furlongs 5 yards English.
1 French League (lieue commune) = 4444 mètres (25 = 1 degree of latitude).
1 Lieue de poste = 3898 mètres = 4263 English yards or = 2·413 English
    miles.

Austrian Measures.

Land . . . 1 Joch	= 1⅔ English acre.
Corn . . . 1 Metzen	= 12₁₀⁷ „ bushels.
Liquids . . 1 Eimer	= 12½ „ gallons.
Solids . . Centner	= 123 lbs.
Timber . . Klafter	= 216 cubic feet.

Alexnitza 2

Thursday 14th October Did not get up till 10½. Found a gun here in pretty good preservation, powder, shot & all the other appurtenances. Went out with the gun abt 2 o clock – saw a splendid hare which I missed with both barrels & a quail which I did not fire at being too far.

Tuesday 12th October Continued [added as afterthought here, to original journal entry] Met on the road between Polak & Palanka[219] abt. 5 in the evening an Austrian courier who gave us a Salaam which we returned & our Tatar stopped to talk with him for a few minutes. He had a Surojee & baggage horse & was armed to the teeth as I have since understood is very necessary in crossing the Balkans – he was from Constantinople. He had a brace of huge pistols & Yataghan in the shawl round his waist & a long Turkish gun slung across his shoulders.

Friday 15 October. Went out shooting. Mr Gutch with me butterfly hunting. Saw a fine covy of partridges but all sport marred by the brutes of dogs who rushed into the middle of them barking wildly in the most undisciplined & ill conditioned manner. Having marked the greater part down & thinking I had got rid of the confounded dogs who were in chase of one or two in another direction I stole quietly down but was again disappointed of a shot by the devils coming helter-skelter back & flushing the birds again on one side of the break while I was on the other. Mr G then went home with the whole pack of my tormentors and I beat the ground backwards & forwards for more than two hours but I could not find them again. I had plenty of time however for admiring the beauty of the scenery which as the day was bright & clear was seen to great advantage. I stood on the top of one of the small hills surrounding Alexnitza – most of them covered thickly with dwarf oak, and in the open spaces, vineyards. The town, which we shd. call a village so scattered & irregular is it, tho occupying a large extent of ground lay beneath, picturesque with its red roofed houses & tall minaret shaped church spire. Encircled on three sides by these wooded hills which are relieved by successive heights of mountain ridges from behind glittering with their white rocks like unmelted snow. Onwards towards the Turkish frontier lies a broad plain thro which glides the Morava girt on its right by the lofty & irregular chain of the Raschna[220] & in front & on the left apparently terminated by stupendous ridges of the Balkans rearing the[ir] lofty heads ridge on ridge into the clouds.

Saturday 16th October: went out for a ride – passed thro' Alexnitza – market day – lots of cattle & plenty of poultry, turkeys etc – called on the Doctor at Quarantine – he recommended us not to go out towards the frontier as if any of the numerous <u>pack</u> of canines by which we were attended happened to come in contact with any of the unfortunates who were being escorted into quarantine, the miserable canine would instantly be shot. <u>Lest he should carry infection!</u> We rode over the beautifully wooded acclivities towards St Stephano & a more singularly wooded country it is scarcely possible to conceive. An unbroken mass of dwarf oak shrubs of not more than 6 or 8 feet high – though there is another kind which attains the height of 20 or 25 feet. The same beautiful mountain scenery that I have before mentioned & which is always in sight go which way you will. Close before us a beautiful mountain[221] near St. Stephano its snow white rocks glittering in the sun. Behind the zigzag frowning dark blue ridge which separates Albania from Servia & from East to South (some of their white crests & precipices receiving the beams of the midday sun with dazzling brightness. [*Soft*] blue mountains reared their lofty heads ridge on ridge & outline after outline backed by the nearer summits of the Balkan range, till their receding forms mingled with the misty haze of the sky. Returning early I went for a gallop by myself along the plain towards Bagnia [Sokobanja] & indulged in pleasing reveries.

No letters – great disappointment! [*written along edge of page*]

Sunday 17th October Delighted when I got up to find Rhisto returned who had been obliged in consequence of our being so late to escort Moore to Belgrade. Went out for a walk with Mr G. – beetle hunting – shaking the trees over an open umbrella!

Mr G Considers the Wing Folding Patterns of the Coleoptera

Beetles bounce about in this umbrella –
their tough exteriors yield
to a creamy butter if I pin them down.
Which should I measure, classify and carry home?
Whether they live in water or on land, whether
they dive or flightless walk the stones, still
they are winged as I should like to be.
Their wing-veins – paths I'd love to travel on –
pleated in secret like a folded map,
a footloose chart for wandering at will –
but how uncertainly they rise – that weight
they carry seems so much like mine.

Diversified the <u>portering</u> of such a pursuit by a couple of chases after butterflies which I caught with my hat. Made a multitude of enquiries of Rhisto, while smoking our pipes after dinner, as to various trips & their practicability. But some of the places were too far (the Sophia Pass, Widin [Vidin], Bourgas) & the first very dangerous. When he accompanied an English traveller to Constantinople 3 or 4 months before, requested by a Tatar of the Sultan to be allowed to join his party with his Surojee & baggage horses, & on going out of Phillopopli[222] [Plovdiv] were attacked by a band of robbers & eight guns discharged at them at once from a wood near the bridge as they were crossing. 4 horses fell, one Surojee shot dead & another wounded & afterwards received the blow of a Yataghan which gave him a wound from the crown of the head to the chin & down the hand which he put up to save his head. Rhisto, following with the Englishman, put his hand on his rein & held him back. The robbers got off with the baggage. He told us you go Albania, stop at Kaffee house, eat, drink Kaffee so. Say you go on – you not stop here the night – you go away two, tree hours so, you shoot – conveying very forcibly to our imaginations the pleasing probability of our having a bullet thro' us – 32 hours to Sophia – 15 into Albania –

Doctor called – told there was an English Traveller in Quarantine – Mr Gutch sent him an invitation to come & see us when he came out the following morning. After 36 hours incarceration[223].

Quarantine

I was quartered with a wild and motley crew:
Turks, and Arnouts, Greeks and Zinzars, Jews, Armenians
and Gipsies. All habited in the costume of their tribe
and speaking tongues as might have rivalled Babel.

Our four-footed companions were doomed
to quarantine with us and made their own concert
braying, lowing and barking. Of all the wayfarers'
annoyances, quarantine's most prejudicial to health.

The quarantine establishment is large, strong palisades
and a guard of pandours. Sheds for merchandise,

stables, a han, and huts for wealthier travellers.
But most were kiraidjis, swineherds, and drovers

who preferred the night air to the expenses of a han,
and who bivouacked in a large space in the centre,
around a blazing fire. I saw three to four hundred persons
drink gallon after gallon of wine and raki

but here was no quarrelling nor fighting. They sang
smoked, danced and cooked, performed on the bagpipe,
reed and gousla and harkened to storytellers and bards
who asked but just a few pari from their listeners.

Our clothes, bedding and papers were fumigated
although there's been no case of plague for several years.
Every little item swells the travellers' bill of costs,
the guard of honour demands their own bakschisch.[224]

Monday 18th October The first thing that greeted my eyes when I came
out of my room this morning was our fellow countryman in question
seated in our Divan & quietly smoking a chibouque. He apologised for
his early visit & travelling costume. He introduced himself as Captn
Spencer & I, having lighted my chibouque, we were soon conversing
most pleasantly. Mr Gutch soon appeared & asked him to breakfast,
to which we adjourned tout de suite & subsequently to dinner. We
found him a most agreeable companion. Full of conversation and
anecdotes of his travels which he had published (n. page 1)[225] – he was
just returning from a tour thro' the Ionian Isles, Greece & European
Turkey, had been in the Turkish Camp (Ali Pascha) & had been
hospitably entertained by Gialico, Chief of the insurgents. In Bitolia[226]
[Bitola] he found a man just shot by robbers (heard the report) life but
just extinct. His vest smoking round the wound having caught fire
from the discharge of the pistol. I walked with him down to his Khan
to see his small amount [of] worldly goods two small saddle bags & a
diminutive carpet bag containing his linen & a seedy old suit of Black,
his coffee & smoking utensils

Making the Acquaintance of Captain Spencer

Of all the travellers he was the one
who journeyed lightest: a carpet bag
and two small saddlebags contained his linen
and an old black suit, a scimitar given him

by a Tartar Chief in Bokhara[227], a gun broken
in a skirmish with Arnaut bandits, a brace
of pistols and a remnant of a Regenschirm,
a Scotch plaid & mackintosh for blanket

& counterpane and an old piece of carpet
for sleeping on. With these he had passed
days and nights on the sands of the desert,
in the snows of the Caucasus. He showed me

his Firman from the Vizier Raschid Pascha
and a pass from Gialico, Chief of the Insurgents.
At Bitolia, he told us, he had found a man
just shot by robbers, the report still in his ears

as he turned a corner. The man's vest
smoking round the wound. Thus we rode
together, agreeably, discussing Metempsychosis
and the souls of fallen angels bound to earth.

A footnote to Bukhara

In Khorasan there's no other city
with so many names.
They arrived and departed
on the tongues of traders
who wandered the silk roads.
In Arabic it was known as
Copper City, City of Merchants
and in Tang Chinese was styled

Place of Good Fortune.
Here Tajik is spoken—
stolen from Persian;
the name of the language
meaning foreigner, stranger.

a gun broken in a skirmish with Arnaut Bandits, two brace of pistols,
a remnant of a <u>Regenschirm</u> [*umbrella*], a carpet for sleeping on & a
Scotch Plaid & Mackintosh for blanket & counterpane – with these
he had passed days & nights on the sands of the desert & the snows
of the Caucasus & the Balkan. Went out shooting with him & found
him very amusing. He pointed out the pass of the Balkan. Found a
covy of partridges which were scattered as usual by the dogs. I bagged
one. His gun (the Doctors – loaded 4 or 5 mos. [*months*]) missed fire/
both barrels)

Tuesday 19th October, I offered him a sofa in my room last night as
more comfortable than the Khan which he gratefully accepted. We
talked for more than an hour before we went to sleep. His wife living
at Heidelberg a native of Caerleon (a Pritchard) – said he knew Lord
Palmerston well & would interest himself with him for me & would
certainly mention me most favourably in his forthcoming work...

In Alexnitza (Captain Spencer's account)

A drummer is sent forth
to announce new laws
or call the people to arms.
He also announces, rat-a-tat-tat,
the exact hour of nightfall.

Then gaudily painted
transparent paper lanterns
folded so they fit in a pocket
are brought out and lit
there being no streetlamps.

To walk without a lantern
is a punishable offence.
They float in all directions
small obedient glow-worms
in the vastness of the night.

Captain Spencer –
on friendship, manners, culture and excursions

'My detention in the quarantine proved the means of introducing
me, through the German doctor of the establishment, to two
English gentlemen at Alexinitz, that town having been selected by
Her Majesty's corps of messengers as their principal station in these
provinces of European Turkey; and I must ever remember, with
grateful recollections, the pleasant days I spent with Mr. Gutch,
who, with true English hospitality, insisted upon my removing to his
residence, as soon as the period of my detention was over. This was,
in truth, an unexpected, an unlooked for invitation, in a country so
far removed from the great world, and can only be appreciated by the
man who has been for any length of time shut out from all intellectual
society; for however much we may feel inclined to render all due
homage to beautiful Nature, in her most romantic and picturesque
forms, and to rate at their full value the agreeable excitement of change
and novel incident, yet after a time these become stale, and we pine
for a companion, with ideas more enlarged than that of a kiraidji, a
swineherd, or an Haiduc. On entering the sitting-room of Mr. Gutch,
how great was my pleasure to see my old friend the "Times" lying
on the table, with the venerable "Christopher North"[228] in all the
majesty of age and honour reposing by his side, and how gladly did I
welcome the Quaker-coloured "Quarterly" and the gay blue and buff
"Edinburgh" – nay, I thought the merry face of Master "Punch" wore
an expression of greater archness now that he had arrived in Servia.
None but the traveller, who has been long cut off from enjoying the
rich treasures of England's mind, can fully appreciate the gratification
with which I devoured the contents of these and several other first-
rate English publications.[229] I was also received in the most friendly
manner by Mr. Davies, of Crickhowell, South Wales, who had
been for some time peering into the pathways and byways of poor

Servia. Our mornings were devoted to riding excursions among the mountains, or shooting-parties, and, as may be supposed in a country like this, abounding with game, we had excellent sport. At present, Her Majesty's messengers are but indifferently quartered, but when their new house is finished, the station at Alexinitz will be a most agreeable séjour; there is capital fishing in the Morawitz, the country abounds with game, and the vicinity of the vast mountain range of the Balkan, and the romantic Bosnia and Upper Moesia,[230] afford a variety of pleasant excursions which would even repay a journey from England.' *Captain Spencer, Travels in European Turkey, in 1850: Through Bosnia, Servia, Bulgaria, Macedonia, Thrace, Albania, and Epirus; with a Visit to Greece and the Ionian Isles...* Colburn & Company, 1851, pp72-74.

George continues:

Tuesday 19th October 1847 (cont) ...& allude to the very pleasant day he had spent with us at Alexnitza & hoped that our acquaintance thus begun would not end here & that if I had time I would look in upon him at Heidelberg – I got up early & went shooting leaving him the use of my bath of which he was very glad not having enjoyed so great a luxury for many a day – had been on horseback three weeks since leaving Athens. Showed me his Firman from the Vizier Raschid Pascha & a pass from Gialico. We had ordered our horses to ride with him part of the way for a ride towards Belgrade, but his <u>Carojee</u> was unable to start today having broken his saddle – so he accepted Mr Gutch's invitation to dinner & we went out for a ride about 3. Had a beautiful ride & agreeable – discussed Metempsychosis, Ampsychosis (Greek Doctrine) a probationary state on earth of the souls of the fallen angels & German Philosophy – the Bitolian Pass of the Balkan by far the finest. Magnificent mountain scenery on Circassia. He had fought with the Circassians in their war against Russia[231]

Who now remembers the Circassian tribes? Of the Cherchenay, the Guaye, the Khatuq and the Khegayk – none survived. Of the Zhaney – three families, and of the Makhosh, one. It is written that 'The Chebsins are now only a memory, giving their name to one of the valleys adjacent to the Black Sea.' It is written that the language of the

Hatuqway was 'like a magpie's shout'. Who remembers the songs of the people? They who are bones in the forests, char in the topsoil.

Who now remembers the Russian General, Zass? – he spiked Circassian heads on spears, on a small hill near his headquarters. Who saw their beards blown about by the wind? Who remembers the trunk he kept under his bed – that unbearable smell?

– mountains 15,000 & 20,000Ft high – he had penetrated thro' Tartary nearly to the frontier of China. Tribes at war – we returned to dinner at 6 & spent another very intellectual & pleasant evening over our chibouques. Walked down with him & smoked in Khan.

Captain Spencer – on dressing up and dressing down

'On leaving Alexinitz, my kind hosts, Mr. Gutch and Mr. Davies, accompanied me for several miles on my route, both capitally mounted, and appeared to great advantage, with English saddles and bridles. Mr. Davies exhibited a most imposing exterior to the astonished Servians; his costume being the English hunting dress – scarlet jacket, top-boots and cap; profound indeed was the respect they exhibited to a Frank so habited, concluding him, no doubt, to be in his own country at least a Pacha with three tails[232], as they bowed to the earth when we passed. My friends amused themselves at the expense of Georgy and myself, maliciously wishing us transported to Hyde Park, or Regent Street, in our present dress, not forgetting to picture the wonder and laughter our travelling apparatus would excite. In compliance with the advice of Georgy, who acted not only as my kiraidji, but in these matters as my preceptor, I had added an additional number of little bags with provender, especially dried fruits, and filled my leathern bottles with a fresh supply of wine and raki; as Georgy exerted all his eloquence to convince me that, as we were now about to enter the country of the infidels, we ran a fair chance of being either starved or murdered. To guard against the latter most undesirable contingency, I placed an additional pair of large Turkish pistols in the holsters of my saddle; these, with my sabre, a formidable hanjiar, my English pistols stuck in my girdle, and my long gun slung across my shoulder, sufficed to prove to any Arnout desperado, or marauding Haiduc, we might chance to meet on the Sultan's pathways and byways, that the English Frank was not a man to be robbed or maltreated with impunity. We had a pleasant ride over a beautiful country abounding in tiny glades and ravines sufficiently elevated to render it picturesque and romantic. At Drugevatz[233] [Draževac], with sincere regret, I bade adieu to my two friends, and crossing a small river of the same name, behold I was within the Turkish frontier.' (Spencer, 1851, pp. 119-121)

The Horses of the Kiraidjis
'The spot was a favourite halting place, had a fine spring
gushing from the rock, ornamented by a fountain, erected
by a pious Mussulman with an inscription'. —Captain Spencer

The caravan had halted at an elevated plateau
shaded by the foliage of a giant linden tree,
the way was impassable because of the storm.

Forty to fifty men with the produce of Macedonia,
Thessaly and Albania had camped around fires,
cooked, boiled coffee and smoked. A scooped-out

trunk of a tree made a trough for the horses
with a wooden drinking cup for travellers.
A cloudless sky and bracing wind came later.

Then they all yelped a guttural phrase and each
of the horses, freed in the woods to forage,
ran to his owner who held a little pouch of corn.

One impenetrable cry; but a horse knows well
his master's voice and grasped by the mane submits
to the labour of the packsaddle, the burden of the road.

Small change (Captain Spencer's account)

En route we'd seen wolves and wild-cats,
and near to the villages, hares.
The deer were called Jir[234] and Sirna,[235]

hart and roebuck, skittish leapers.
Eagles and hawks soared above
while ortolan swarmed like larks
on a stubble field in England.

Ascending Mount Lepar[236] we startled a bear,
aimed for the heart and head,
although we'd no need of the flesh.
We dyed the earth red with his blood
and gave him to Georgy, our Kiraidji,
who slouga pokorni[237]'d and dobro s'dravie[238]'d
as he fastened the corpse to his horse.

When we quit the next town on our route
Georgy's purse bulged at its seams;
twenty piastres from the state
for harvesting vermin, thirty for the hide,
to say nothing of the inn keeper's coin
for the quarters he salted and dried
to cook on the hearth of his han.

The Ortolan Bunting[239]

Fragile bird of scrubland and field, weighing
less than an ounce in the hand. The song
of the male's like that of a yellowhammer,
the head olive-grey, instead of bright yellow.

Size of a sparrow, but netted in flight;
caged up for weeks and fattened on millet,
gorging in darkness to double its weight,
then drowned in a vat, pickled in Armagnac.

Roasted eight minutes, and plucked for the table,
the feet go in first, one mouthful, one bird.
Molars come down, a wet crunch through the rib cage,
the whole thing at once.   Cover your head

out of pleasure or shame. A rush of hot fat scalds
the throat; slight bones prickle the roof of your mouth.
The yellowhammer's song from the tree is still just:
Chit, chit...... little-bit-of-bread-and-no-cheese.

Spencer's[240] Cock and Bull Story
(with two penn'orth from the cockerel, the good housewife and an old friend of the family)

There was once a cockerel, a fine fellow, who slept each night with his many hens in the wide-spreading branches of a mighty oak. Each evening in this vast resting place they settled down, the cockerel taking the topmost branch. A good housewife looked after them, an honest woman, who kept them safe.

TGH: Good House wife, hah! That's what they call an 'independent business-woman', around these parts!

We had unfortunately set out on our tour during one of the interminable fasts of the Oriental Church and as the stock of provisions, with which we had furnished ourselves at Belgrade, was now exhausted, we could get nothing in the town better than stale carp and tench from the Danube and the Morava – poor fare for hungry travellers. In vain we despatched Georgy in quest of a fowl, or even eggs – it was of no avail; the fanatic inhabitants would neither sell, nor even cook, an article of food forbidden by their church.

The cockerel scratched each day in sweet dark leaf mould... his talons sharp and his eyes beady, his comb and wattle blood-red banners, always ready to ride his hens. Stab, stab went his beak for a husk of corn and a silky earthworm.

TGH: I keep to my faith and that's a very private thing. My soup of Danube river-fish is always very tasty.[241]

Determined to provide ourselves with a more substantial meal than the mess of soup, composed of fish, garlic and beans, the hanji was disposed to set before us, we sallied forth towards the environs of the town on a foraging expedition. We had not proceeded far when our eyes were gladdened by the sight of a goodly array of barn-door fowls, preparing to take up their quarters for the night in the wide-spreading branches of a mighty oak; but, alas! No offer of ours could prevail upon the good housewife to sell us one of her cackling charges, and so become accessory to our breaking the commandments of her Church.

The cockerel ruffled his hackle and sickle feathers, flapped briskly up to find his usual perch.

TGH: I kept repeating, "No, they're not for sale!"

Thus balked in our endeavours to procure a supper, like two hungry men we determined to carry off by force the first fat fowl we could lay hands on, even at the risk of paying an exorbitant price, but we soon found that we did not give our feathered friends credit for half the agility they possessed, as they one after the other, eluding our endeavours to catch them, took refuge among the branches of their vast roosting-place; so that our promised supper began to assume the doubtful aspect, if not of a castle, at least of a bird in the air; and as we stood panting and wearied with our fruitless chase at the bottom of the tree, we could not help feeling that, in our case, a bird in the hand was worth a score in the bush.

He watched the crafty hens run rings around them, squinted at little panting-puffing-men, at his own good housewife berating them, and then let out a yell, cock-cock-cock-a-doodle-doo! What's the cost, the cost, the cost?

TGH: How dare they take by force what wasn't theirs! I swore at them!

Coûte que coûte [*no matter the cost*], determined not to be conquered by a chicken, I resolved as a dernier resort to have recourse to the loaded pistols I carried in my belt, and drawing one forth, took deliberate aim at an insulting chanticleer, who in imagined safety, at the top of the tree was clapping his wings, and crowing defiance at our futile efforts to entrap him; when, lo! A bullet through the head laid him struggling at our feet,

The branches of the tree kept falling past him, his nerves and sinews trembled. Where does the blame lie? the cockerel coughed, as the sky dived

past him and he met with Death.

TGH: I couldn't speak. My breath was taken from me.

Death (takes a deep breath): an opening they slide through

and throwing a dollar to the astounded and horror-stricken owner, we hoped to escape in peace to our han. Vain delusion! The uproar which followed could not have exceeded if the Arnouts had stormed Hassan-a-Palanka [Smederevska Palanka]; and we were followed to our inn by an angry, vociferating crowd of men, women and children who heaped upon our devoted heads every abusive epithet which their voluminous, and not over choice vocabulary furnished them; we were in the same breath called dogs of heretics! Latin hounds! And unbelieving flesh-eating Franks! All uniting in clamorously demanding justice on the transgressors.

His body softened, his feathers draggled. A red brown stain dripped from his lolling head. Where does the blame lie? His shadow fretted as he went forwards cradled in the good wife's hands.

TGH: This dead weight in my hands and, in my heart, this rage.

Death: no barriers to this crossing

Fortunately, in the midst of the uproar, the kapitan and the judge made their appearance, with several civil officers of distinction in the town. As soon as anything like silence could be obtained, I stated my case at full length, to which the judge listened with the most profound attention, evidently treating it as a matter of the highest importance,

I was never allowed an opinion, the ghost of the cockerel muttered.

TGH: I was never allowed an opinion, never allowed a voice.

Death: their sentences unfinished

and finally, much to our satisfaction, pronounced a verdict in our favour. "Were we not Franks?" said he; "and was it not a manifest violation of the laws of hospitality to refuse to furnish strangers with such articles of food as their Church, like an indulgent mother, permitted them to enjoy? How," as this light of the law most logically argued, "could the same laws be expected to hold good for all creeds? Here we have two distinguished Frank travellers come to visit you from the Far West, who after a long and fatiguing day's journey, have been unable to procure, in the whole town of Hassan-Pasha-Palanka such an ordinary article of food as a fowl – for shame, Servians! For shame! Blinded by your fanaticism, you have violated the laws of hospitality, and by forcing these strangers to an act of violence, you have brought down disgrace on the name of a Servian."

Where does the blame lie? the cockerel wondered. One rule for them, and one for us, he marvelled.

TGH (*sings bitterly*):   *Thieves and bullies never listen,*
                        politicians make things up.
                        Vile pretence is all around us,
                        we can see they're ALL corrupt!

Death (sighs, rubs his head): nothing is permanent

The piece of money we had thrown to the good housewife was now demanded, and with some reluctance produced; upon viewing it, our Aristides gravely declared it to be ten times the worth of the fowl, and after estimating its true value, the residue to the amount of several piastres was presented to us, which we however added to the prime cost, as an indemnity to the rest of the feathered troop for the loss of their gallant leader

The ghost of the cockerel still lives in the ghost of the tree, sleeping each night with the ghosts of his many hens. The ghost of the good housewife still watches over them. What's changed, he croodles. Nothing much! That arrogance of men; those who travel, those who rule and those who deny the rights of good women.

TGH: The cockerel knows the truth; I won't deny it, though he's a little light on Feminist theory, gender inequality, discrimination, object-ification, oppression, stereotyping, cultural imperialism and patriarchy.

Death (smiles enigmatically): and so we go onwards

148

George continues:

Wednesday 20th October 1847 Went out shooting after a fashionably late breakfast – our usual hour 10½ or 11 & 6 or half past our dinner hour – As usual the infernal curs of dogs by which I was accompanied marred all my sport – saw two fine hares & some wild pigeons which we started before I could get a shot – made a mental resolve to be a host in myself next time dass ich auf dem Jagd gehe [*that I go hunting*]. I subsequently got amongst a cloud of starlings & killed 10 at one shot. Saw a quail also which the dogs flushed & then went barking in its wake as they had done with the hares much to my annoyance. Returned home having expended my small stock of shot & was surprised to find Mr G just going out for a ride – he having promised to meet me on the hill – sat down & smoked a chibouque & read German. Received a visit from the Illyrische Lehrer [*Illyrian teacher*] whose acquaintance I had made a day or two before by walking into his Schule hause [*school house*] in mistake for Rhisto's <u>nova cousche</u> [*Serbian: Nova Kuća trans: new house*] sat & smoked chibouques & talked in German which he spoke pretty well & slowly & deliberately so that I could understand the greater part of what he said. Showed my German books. Read a Fytte of the Cid which he said he could understand perfectly – had seen Undine in Servish – asked if I would lend it him to read & when he brought it back another – das werd' ich gern tragen; Sie sorgen aber für es, und nicht schmutzig machen. Ich bin ein Lehrer sagte er darum nöthigt es nicht mir zu sagen, es nicht zu schmutzig machen [*I'll gladly bring it, [but] take care not to get it dirty. I'm a schoolteacher, he said, so there's no need to tell me not to get it dirty.*] I was much amused at dinner by Rhisto's calling his waggon drawn by Oxen his <u>Beef-carriage</u>. He told me the names of several things in Servia which I wrote down.

No letters. Disappointment. 2 [n d]. severe [*written in inner margin*]

> *And what of love? – it is never spoken of – but if it is expressed it is conveyed as longing – 'No letters. Disappointment. 2 [n d]. severe'.*

Thursday 21st October Mr Gutch having an attack of the Doldrums our proposed ride to the convent of St Stephano was deferred – but I being equipped, booted & spurred was determined to have a ride so ordered my horse – meanwhile walked with Mr G to see Rhisto's new house for the English Messengers – the largest house in the place, quite a palace. Entrance hall & offices etc on the ground floor & a capital underground cellar – above, up a magnificent stone staircase a large corridor, Divan at one end in a Bow window with raised floor & curtains across – balcony at the other end with a beautiful view of the mountains, plain, river & town – dining & drawing rooms & three bedrooms. Sand under all the floors to keep away the fleas. Started for my ride abt 12½ promising to return abt 3 for Mr Gutch – had a beautiful ride to the Turkish frontier – passing first over an undulating mountain common, studded here & there with the dwarf oak then winding round hills thickly wooded but wearing the brown livery of autumn with the Morava at their base 100ft below. Its glittering bends visible for many miles along the vast plain bounded on the S W by the irregular chain of the Reschna & on the S E towards Stamboul by the ghost like points of the two rocks which rear their soft forms arrayed in bluish white drapery on either side of the Pass of Sophia – the Captain of the guard house at the frontier (a Servian) who recollected me again since last year when I went to Nisch [Niš] with the Doctor, Rhisto & Courier asked me to dismount – gave me chibouque & capital water – smoked a couple of pipes & carried on a sort of guerrilla conversation not understanding a word & answering "Dobra"[*good*] to everything – came back & persuaded Mr G to go for an hour's ride before dinner down by Morava. I was perfectly astonished at the immense <u>clouds</u> of starlings I here saw together which altho' they did not absolutely darken the air as I have been informed by a friend once came under his observation (I think in Belgium) might by a little stretch of the imagination be almost thought for a moment to obscure the sun as they passed before it. I certainly never saw them in such myriads before – my horse was a lazy devil (dear to <u>buy</u> at a zwanziger) whose sides I could not keep my spurs out of all the way.

Friday 22nd October Went out shooting & walked out over an immense deal of ground from 1½ till 5 o clock – saw a hare which whether from the distance the smallness of the shot or other good excuses! or from the <u>incompetency of the workman</u>, escaped my murderous designs. I understand there are lots of hares tho' they do not honor my levges [*leverages*] with a very numerous attendance for fear I suppose of my levying a contribution to our table of a <u>leveret</u> or two from amongst them.

They drove the hare from its form
'When it be cas'd... cut it into little pieces, lard them here and there'[242]
Hannah Glasse

shy brown hare
tucked into earth

by blackthorn
brake

where trembling
grasses surge

heart-stung
to startled g|race

Shot a few larks – which however Mr G seemed rather to despise
and did not look upon as so good a <u>lark</u> for breakfast the following
morning as the starlings, which certainly were excellent – not unlike
Quails – walked down to the Kaffeehouse [*coffee shop*] after dinner
& found mine Host [*the coffee-shop keeper*] entertaining his friends &
relations preparatory to his taking unto himself a wife on Sunday – he
gave me coffee, chibouque & wine which I drank to his health thro'
the medium of a man who spoke German & interpreted – they were
all at high supper, ornamented with gilded balls, as the old custom
was to decorate laurels & potatoes at Xtmas. On the opposite side of
the room were 4 or 5 female singers chanting the most extraordinarily
barbaric strains I ever heard & from time to time came round to the
guests kissing their hand & depositing with them an embroidered
kerchief in which they were expected to put a piece of money when
it was again fetched. On my expressing a wish to make a donation
the same ceremony was gone thro' with me – & they were evidently
gratified at the, to them, liberal deposit of ½ zwanziger, the sum being
usually 2 or 3 paras (abt. a 20th part). Before I left the bridegroom
elect requested I would come there on Sunday – when they should
have feasting & dancing and I should see his Bride & on my making
the request charged me with an invitation to the Herr Courier [*Mr
Gutch*].

Saturday 23rd October Today rather cloudy, colder & seemed blowing up for rain. The weather hitherto having been warm, bright, cloudless & in the sun exceedingly hot – almost as much so as any day last summer in England. Paid the schoolmaster a visit & took him a German book I had promised to lend him – sat & talked & smoked with him for ½ an hour.

Es war ihm sehr beliebt mit mir zu sprechen, weil sehr wenige Leute in Alexnitza Deutsch sprechen. Er spricht nicht viel Deutsch und wenn er ist in Wien gewesen, er spricht immer [angekommen], da spricht man so [verfeinert] dass er koennte nicht gut sprechen so geschwind, dass er könnte nicht gut verstehen. Weil ich aber so sorgsam und so gut spreche, dann kann er mich richtig verstehen. [*He really enjoyed speaking with me, because very few people in Alexnitza speak German. He doesn't speak much German, and if he went to Vienna, they speak [in such a refined manner] that he can't understand them well. Because I speak so carefully and clearly he can understand me properly.*][243]

Out shooting again the whole day till dinnertime or rather attempting to shoot for 1 hare the only thing I saw to shoot made her escape – took only the little spaniel, Catty, with me who hunted capitally & behaved uncommonly well to do her justice – at dinner Rhisto told us the marriage would take place in the church tomorrow at 9 o clock & he would let me know – the husband elect sends today as a present to the Lady's father a sheep decked with gold accompanied by a band of music & for the two or three previous days he keeps open house for his friends – "tomorrow go in Father's house, so go in church & come out go from Kaffeehause & eat yez, drink yez, six, seven o clock"

Two most welcome letters! [*written in the inner margin*]

Sunday 24th October Drums, Bagpipes etc from an early hour disturbed me from my slumbers – no end of processions parading the town backwards & forwards, at last abt. 10½ Rhisto informed me "Now Mister, they going in church" – so to the church I went & soon after a grand procession appeared – the bridegroom (my friend the Kaffeehouse keeper) in full Servian costume walking in front in the midst of the male relations of both parties – then followed the bride surrounded by the women – she had a wreath of flowers round her head & long silver strings from the crown of the head falling all round her and forming almost a veil – on arriving at the church the other wedding party which was that of the Hauptschullehrer [*secondary school teacher*] & [*was*] already there took precedence as being <u>in high life</u>. The other being of the lower orders.

The bride and bridegroom stood side by side at the table – two large pieces of coloured muslin being thrown over them both – & boys standing round with lighted tapers – the marriage service was the[*n*] performed by three priests in Servian (at least I conclude so as I did not understand a word of it. They, (the Brautpaar [*newlyweds*]), received the bread and wine. The ring was put on. Incense was wafted round them from a bronze burner by the priest who crowned them over the muslin with two gaudy looking things like Bishop's mitres and <u>trotted</u> them thrice round the table & they then became <u>one</u>, but slunk out of the church as much like <u>two</u> as ever I saw. They then adjourned to the Bridegrooms (one room), his sitting room parlour and bed room, & Mr Gutch & self being invited to follow did so, where preserve sweetmeats, cold water & rakee were handed round & chibouques furnished – we were asked to stay and dine in ½ an hour but having just breakfasted we declined. I promised to look in again in the evening – & then went for a <u>short</u> walk with Mr Gutch before dinner – came back & manufactured some apple dumplings for today & an apple tart for tomorrow (*both turned out very good!).

After dinner, feeling it incumbent on me to keep faith with mine host of the Kaffee, went down there & the scene beggars all description – on a dark dirty brickfloored room, filled with smoke & human beings as full as it could hold, & smelling of everything, from the supper with fragments of which a table at the side was covered, up to the wild, dirty & strange-looking collection of humans with which the room was filled – was the party collected & dancing like wild Indians with an immense degree of hallooing & stamping of feet round a Moorish visaged Gypsy who was playing the Tambour & a Servian who played the bagpipe, called in the language of the country of which it is a national instrument, – Guildar (they have also a one stringed lute which they call Gusle). Wine & chibouque were brought to me & having danced one round & made a donation to the bride of a couple of zwannzigers I stealthily made my escape from a scene with which I was rather disgusted.

From thence I adjourned to the schoolmaster's where I was considerably better pleased. Rhisto was there & the Director & Doctor of Quarantine & the under schoolmaster whom I have before mentioned, all three of whom spoke German so that I got on pretty well – a seat was offered me directly & wine & a chibouque – we had no end of dancing in a circle round the musician (the national dance) and sometimes the musician (a bagpipe player) would vacate the centre and his place was filled by two of the dancers in a sort of waltz – the lady having challenged her partner by striking him on the back with a twisted handkerchief – they each put their right and left arms round each other's waist alternately – turning first in one direction & then changing to the other – I danced a turn or two with the Bride & was then seized by another lady & turned round with surprising velocity. The ladies were all dressed very nicely some in velvet jackets embroidered with gold & some in watered silk trimmed round with fur – the Bride wore a pink flowered silk skirt & over it a brown silk robe trimmed with fur – a red fez cap with a blue silk & gold tassel – & her dyed hair twisted round in one large plat & a wreath of flowers – Mein Freund, der Schullehrer hat mir gesagt – es freut die Gesellschaft sehr Ihnen zu sehen – sie glaubte, daß die Engländer hoch und übermüthig waren – es ist sehr angenehm aber die junge Herrn so freundlich & so gastlich zu sehen [*My friend, the schoolteacher told me – the gathering is so happy to see you – they believed that the English were proud, and arrogant – it is pleasant however to see the young gentlemen [being] so friendly and hospitable.*]

On leaving at 10½ shook hands with the Bride leaving 3 or 4 zwanziger behind & she kissed my hand – [*written in the inner margin*]

Three years after first transcribing the story of the school-teacher's wedding I discovered two pages had turned together when I originally photographed the journal. My habit had been to transcribe from the photographs with both texts open on the screen. I'd enlarge the photograph where it was hard to transcribe. Puzzle it out word by word, working for a few hours at a time. I'd check that the dates ran consecutively. Here George wrote a lot, so I missed that this day spread over several pages. When I had that journal to hand, I began using my father's magnifying glass, to recheck words I wasn't sure about. Suddenly I turned a page and discovered a second invitation, a raucous dance, the disgust of ggg at the kaffee keeper's wedding feast.

Sunday 16th September 2018: Novi Sad to Sremski Karlovci

Spent a quiet morning reading, catching up on social media and the news at home, then packing the bags and making ready to leave the apartment in Novi Sad. We asked the Airbnb owner to order us a taxi for Sremski Karlovci for 12 noon.

At Hotel Dunav the receptionist took our passports and handed us key 117. The room basic and plain. One double bed and one single. Old fashioned huge TV and a notice saying any broken furniture must be paid for. Enormous old bath and toilet in adjoining room. But all clean and comfortable enough. We settled then walked out and into town.

Much blowing of car horns and a wedding party passed with young men waving Serbian flags from the windows of their cars and shouting and laughing. One was sitting on the window-ledge, his body outside the car. They all parked up where they could and went into the church. After lunch we wandered off around the town. Saw the fountain with four lion heads[244] Ivanka had told us about. One is supposed to drink from one side of the fountain or the other for love.

It was very hot, 30+ degrees C so we tried to stay in the shade. Saw wineries and the old grammar school, 1791 (current building 1891). Still in use as a secondary school. Gardens were shady and pleasant with roses, yew trees etc. The houses here are old, traditional, beautiful but often faded and in need of repair. We walked back to hotel Dunav for a beer on the terrace overlooking the Danube. It was stunning. The further bank lined with mixed deciduous woodland on the point of turning. Three swans in a row swimming near the further bank, small boats drawn up over there, a narrow shore, then the wide Danube, dark green in the distance, then grey-blue under a blue sky. We watched a couple of boats go past, silent in the hubbub of voices from the terrace, their outboard motors making a white wake which soon vanished in darkened and widened trails. Across the way two or three bathers were wading in the shallows. There were oaks, poplar, birch, willow and others I couldn't make out. A wagtail popped down and picked about on the pavement below us.

At 7pm we went out for a walk to find the railway station. It was almost derelict at the front. L started walking up some steps, but the wood was rickety and rotten and we soon decided that the steps, however unstable, led to someone's house. Then we walked round the back of the building and it was clear that this was the station and platform. A woman in the office wrote down the times of the trains to Belgrade for us which go at 11.10am and 14.05pm. We decided to get the morning train and to taxi to the station because, although it's only seven minutes' walk, the bags are very heavy.

Then to supper at the restaurant next door to Hotel Dunav – Restaurant Passent. A wedding party there was in full swing with a group of musicians singing and playing for two long tables of wedding guests inside the restaurant. We were taken to the far end of the garden next to the Danube to a table lit by a single candle. The couple at the next table used the torch from their phone to illuminate their meal. Old songs drifted over from the wedding party and we ate then left for our hotel room next door. The singing went on for hours – male voices, in song after song, which seemed to settle into our dreams as we gradually drifted off to sleep.

Monday 25th October 1847 As the weather seemed threatening to break & Mr Gutch more lazy every day & evinced progressively more & more disinclination to any superfluous exertion I ordered my horse & determined to take this "long ride" of 12 English miles! Accompanied only by my own special & agreeable attendants happy Reminiscences & pleasing reveries – found them very cheerful & unremitting in their attendance – after a delightful gallop on a little grey, well worth a zwanziger, over hills & thro' valleys & woods along a beautiful glen a few yards above a dashing rivulet with cottages prettily dotted here & there having in sight nearly all the way on the right the stupendous ridges & crests of the Balkan – & before me the rocky mountain beneath whose shadow overhung by its frowning shattered crags on every side but the one by which the gorge is entered stands the little convent & chapel of St. Stephano. The monks I had seen when there before were nowhere visible – I put my horse in a stable myself & strolled towards the chapel which a peasant came & opened for me – it would hold I should think about 12 persons – the screen, painted with likenesses of our saviour & the virgin behind where women are not allowed to enter, is a table with a curious old silver gilt bible & prayer book (I conclude) in Servian characters – necklaces of small coins are hung round the necks of the paintings – came out & filled my chibouque when the same peasant brought me a bit of charcoal to light it. Adjourned to a beautiful spring where I had a draught of most delicious water & threatenings of more than I wanted, from heaven, in the shape of large drops, which however, considerately seeing I was well supplied, did not persevere – spent a delightful half hour in smoke & the perusal of my just received English letters & having then had a climb up the rocks to look for a view, which the hard hearts of the Eminences denied me, mounted my steed & rode home as pleasantly as I came – saw a young Bulgarian like a younger Robinson Crusoe clothed in goatskin trousers & cap – Horse fell with me just before reaching home in Alexnitza & pitched me over his head but saved myself Harlequin fashion by 'lighting on my hands & then on my feet. Mr G just returned having come to meet me & got tired.

Begun a letter for post on Thursday [*written in inner margin*]

Tuesday 26th October Very heavy rain in the night & the atmosphere considerably colder but the morning very fine again & bright tho' still very cold. Went out shooting abt. 1 & walked all day without getting a shot or indeed seeing anything to shoot at. Observed that the rain on the previous night had been snow on the hills, those in the distance towards the frontier of Albania having their summits covered & contrasting very prettily with the smalt blue of the nearer ones

A footnote to Smalt Blue

To molten glass add cobalt oxide
for colour which is never strong—
if ground too fine the pigment weakens
so grind by hand and not for long

– had a very pleasant walk tho' no sport & returned to dinner about 5 & found Mr G had walked as far as Rhisto's new house about 300 or 400 yds – sat up till 12 o clock filling up & inking over the pencil part of my diary[245] – smoking sundry chibouques. Reading, musing etc.

Wednesday 27th October Surprised this morning by a disagreeable visitant from heaven in the shape of a large heap of snow lying in the broad fire place of my bedroom & which had thus intruded on my privacy down the low straight chimney – I could hardly believe my eyes at first, but on jumping out of bed & rushing to the window I was soon convinced of the fact that there had been a heavy fall of snow in the night & that it was still falling in the most indefatigable manner – how the face of the country was changed & how bleak & desolate it appeared in its winter garb thus suddenly donned after the bright sunny landscape with the varied tints & brilliant hues of autumn, its bright blue sky & its soft blue hills. It snowed nearly all day which I spent in finishing my letter to England, smoking a little, reading a little & about 4 as it had done snowing went out for a "Buster" but stopped for a quarter of an hour um Deutsch zu sprechen mit meinem Freund dem Schullehrer [*In order to speak German with my friend the schoolteacher*] – waded 3 or 4 miles thro' the snow & returned to dinner after finished my letter & gave it to Mr G to inclose to Fonblanque as he thought they would go quicker by that means – wrote <u>some</u>, read some, thought some & smoked some.

Thursday 28th October Grievously disappointed at not receiving any letters which was aggravated by Mr Gutch's enjoyment of that luxury. The snow having partially disappeared, ich setzte auf dem Jagd fort [*I continued with the hunt*], & had to undergo the oft told tale of seeing a fine hare started & chased by the yelping cur miscalled a spaniel – returned at 3 wearied dirty & thoroughly disgusted. Went out for a short ride with Mr Gutch – indescribably filthy slippery & cold & the snow clad Balkan looked bleak & drear in his wintry uniform & yet as "Slow sinks more lovely ere his race be run along"[246] Albania's "Hills the setting sun" a beautiful roseate hue gleamed warmly o'er their white summits & made them look lovely even in their coldness. I was glad to have seen Alexnitza in its winter as well as its summer garb – perhaps for the last time.

Old Stone Mountains

distance still lays down
complicated hues

you might ask

if anything alters
is it us

the question

our hidden
bones

how did we get here?

layer on layer
utterly and completely blue

Friday 29ᵗʰ October: Caught a great cold & staid indoors the greater part of the day writing letters, reading etc. Our domicile just the sort of place for catching colds – with windows, most of the panes, in which paper supplies the place of glass – the sitting room has brick floor (as indeed have all the rooms) & no carpet – it has one window & is a passage room with 3 doors shutting in a rough way like that of a beast house & fastening with a hitch. The fire place is like a little brick oven before which you may bake your feet with the accommodation of a free amount of cold air round your head & body – the house is chiefly built of mud & wattling with red tiles put loosely on the top – an old Turkish Guard House stands by built on piles forming a sort of arched gateway to this Ambassadorial Residence. Took a short meditative stroll before dinner.

Saturday 30ᵗʰ October A good deal of rain last night. Spent today much the same as yesterday in polite literature. Noch sehr krank mit dem Schnupfen [*Still very sick with a cold*] but went out for an hour and a half's walk before dinner. Mr Gutch accompanying me for about ¼ of a mile & then turning back – the snow almost entirely gone affording a more pleasing anticipation of our approaching Ride homewards.

A journey is not a journey without boredom, those days of waiting for despatches, those brief entries in which nothing much happens – that is a journey. I feel it in the ennui, tedium, day-dreaming, homesickness that seeps out of George's briefest entries. I feel the depression of Mr Gutch, how he finds it hard to stir himself, his fits of the doldrums. I wonder about his feelings, his grief, his anxiety about his wife, the malaise that creeps over him the longer he stays away from home. I begin to see the more difficult emotions these men carry with them.

Sunday 31ˢᵗ October: Another severe disappointment in not getting any letters which one looks out for in such a monotonous life with anxious expectation & of course is proportionately disappointed. Wrote & read all the morning. Went down about 3 to pay the doctor a visit, sat & smoked a pipe with him & talked in German – explained why English was not so very difficult as he imagined it to be – that we did not read it & write it differently but that we called the letters of our alphabet different to that of other nations. Had a short rush up the mountain & home at 5. Two or three more weddings at which I was not present – it appears this is a favourite month for being married here – Rhisto says more marry this month I think.

Loneliness

He wonders why the mountains look blue –
not until 1861 will it become clear
that complex equations govern the colour

Until then it will seem that the mountains fade
like fabric worn for too many winters
like ink on paper which confines the heart

Land that is insubstantial in many torn layers
offers itself to the sky and seems to become it,
but when you arrive, is stony and problematic

Monday 1ˢᵗ November 1847 Staid in doors writing & reading till 3. Went out for a ride on Messengers horse – very pleasant horse – leads beautifully walking close beside you – a characteristic of the Turkish horses – walked the greater part of the way home from the fountain on the Belgrade road finding it very cold – having crossed the hill from the Bagnia road.

Drawing of "Messenger's House Alexnitza" 2nd Nov 1847

<u>Tuesday 2nd November</u> Took a sketch of the Den of Eolus in which the Messengers at present freeze & of the house in which they are to live eventually. Went out for a walk carrying my gun but did not see anything except a beautiful view from the top of one of the small hills which enclose Alexnitza on three sides & which one I had never been to the top of before. Beneath lay the town in peaceful repose the most conspicuous objects the church with its glittering <u>tin</u> spire, Rhisto's new house & the new Council House – away for

Rhisto's new house – Alexnitza 2nd Nov 1847
built expressly for Queen's Messengers

20 miles beyond extended a wide plain thro' which meandered the broad waters of the Morava with upwards of twenty glittering bends visible to the eye – on the right the undulating dark blue mountains of Albania, while in front the misty soft blue hills melted in the distance with the two lofty points of the Balkan at the Sophia Pass rearing their heads above them all still covered with snow & blushing a soft crimson in the rays of the setting sun. Alexnitza is a third rate struggling town & mean & dirty when you are in it with but one chief street & the houses chiefly of wood & mud & watling [sic].

A scattering of light in molecules of air

Our eyes are more endeared to blue than violet
and blue is scattered almost as much as violet

when you look at mountains in the distance
blue light is scattered inside the invisible

Wednesday 3ʳᵈ November Writing letter for tomorrow's post after which went out with my gun for an hour or two to look for a hare over the old ground but saw nothing notwithstanding I walked most zealously & enthusiastically thro' a multitude of Black thorn brakes with the greatest indifference to the severe laceration they inflicted – came back & persuaded Mr G to release himself from his drawing for a short period & have a ride towards Shapillac[247] to meet the coming Messenger – had a splendid ride & a glorious gallop along the plain the whole way for 6 or 8 miles flat & turfy – the day was bright & clear & the fresh air very exhilarating and we enjoyed our ride excessively – the country looks glorious – black clouds continually coursing over the sky & casting the most beautiful contrast of light & shade upon the hills – over the Albanian hills hung a black cloud enveloping them all in a dim & gloomy shade while on their summits the sun poured a flood of light from behind the dark cloud like "yon dark Caloyer"[248] with a halo of celestial glory round his head. Messenger (Grattan) arrived with his friend Mr Heneage about 11 o clock – half an hour after I had been in bed – got up to see Grattan – received a letter from my mother very welcome – the 3ʳᵈ letter only since leaving London.

Thursday 4th November Walked down to quarantine before breakfast & paid the Doctor a visit as I suspected we should not be violently early after the hard work of two of the party of the day before. Very much disappointed at not getting any letters as my mother's letter received [*via*] messenger the day ~~before~~ yesterday had led me to expect. Can't conceive what has become of them – got breakfast about 12 & went out shooting with Grattan & Heneage about 1½ – found 4 birds in a covey which after pursuing them backwards & forwards for some time thro' the vineyards we succeeded in bagging three – killing one bird each – we afterwards beat over my old ground & saw one cock & a couple of ducks but did not get another shot. Both Mr Heneage & Mr Grattan very agreeable & very conversable & we made a very nice little sociable party of four. We dined & talked and smoked & smoked & talked till abt. 12 o'clock.

Friday 5th November: Having breakfasted at a rather more reasonable hour we managed to get off for our shooting this morning about 12½. Beat an immense deal of capital Black thorn cover well adapted for holding game but anything but capital for walking thro' – walked till about 3½ without having seen a feather or a <u>hare</u> but enjoying a most agreeable chaffy walk – the sun continuing very hot & the weather bright & clear. Returning home, the dogs hunting wildly thro' cover, a fine covey of partridges got up & as I was walking well up to the dogs (my two companions strolling lazily behind) I got a shot & dropped one – we marked them down & walked up to them again, but the dogs hunting wide flushed them with only one long shot being fired which failed to take effect, they crossed the Morawitza & we had to return to a bridge abt a ¼ of a mile up to get at them but when we did get among them we committed great havoc in abt ½ an hour – Grattan killing a brace, Heneage 1 bird & I one more out of about 8 or 9 which had got up originally. Returned abt. 5½ to dinner. Got a pack of cards & after having had an immense deal of talk & argumentative eloquence on politics, theology & the social systems of nations (Grattan very radical & republican) we varied our proceedings with a few rounds of Van John at which I was a winner of [f]11.1 Zw.

Saturday 6th November: Went with Grattan & Heneage again auf der Jagd [*on the hunt*] & walked over an immense deal of ground for four hours but saw nothing except one hare which Grattan fired at &

missed. Scraped ourselves through a wide extent of Dwarf Oak copse which clothes the surrounding hills & Heneage said he saw a woodcock which however we failed to flush again – very hard & difficult shooting & very little return except a very pretty & agreeable walk. We had an immense deal of chaff & argument especially Grattan & self on various topics, theology, politics etc. Every observation or assertion was sure to produce some objection on Grattan's part & consequently terminate in an argument – he is very warm, very talented & loquacious & I think very agreeable – a compound of my Uncle Capt. G. Cox[249] & Capt. Allen. In the evening after dinner more chaff over our chibouques & a rubber of Dummy Whist[250] (as Mr G would not play) ½ zwanziger points & eins on the rubber[251]. I took Dummy & lost 1 point.

Sunday 7th November – a very welcome letter from post this morning – strolled out in the bright clear air & warm sun to peruse it. Hills looked as if seen thro' a veil of white gauze & the blush on the distant Balkan in its snow white garb like that on the cheek of a Bride softened by her drapery of lace.

In sight of Mountains [252]

Nothing can now be more simple than the monetary system *white crests & precipices* Circular Exchange Notes (paid unless ground for suspicion), Bills of Exchange calculated some**time**s in guilders sometimes in florins and stivers *[Soft] blue mountains* At Cologne (via packet) obtain Prussian money *dark indigo, Prussian blue* the 10 guilder piece is the best gold for Belgium, Holland and Germany. The gold coins are the Napoleon (20 francs), the new Louis (20 francs), the double Napoleon *the ghost like points of the rocks* (40 francs). Sovereigns are the best **to** take to France and Napoleons, the best for Switzerland *still covered with snow & blushing a soft crimson* For the ordinary purposes in **travel**ling through Belgium, Prussia, Frankfort, the Duchies of Nassau, Darmstadt, and Baden it is useful to know that florins and kreutzers *surmounted by old Castles* are given **in** exchange for the various coins current in Germany and 1 Prussian dollar (thaler) is 30 silver Groschen, 1 silver groschen is 12 pfenning, 1 florin is 60 kreutzers. The Prussian pieces of 10, 5, 2 ½ silver groschen are marked *interminable outlines* 3 ein thaler, 6 ein thaler and 12 ein thaler. Gold *overhung by frowning shattered crags &* is measured in

French Napoleons, Ducats and Frederics. The complicated tables of coins published in works relating to Switzerland can be only embarrassing *a zig zag path through a most delicious wood* Although each *almost perpendicular* canton has its own coin: florins, batzen, rappen *eagles soaring overhead* angsters, deniers *stupendous crags at every break,* hallars *in dense foliage* and schillings and although the people of one canton will not take the coin of their neighbour yet there is never anyone whose eyes did not glisten at the **sight of** a five franc piece. Bankers in Switzerland issue notes *in the distance* which are readily taken in the canton, better than carrying a bag full of silver across the **mountains** *seen thro' a veil of white gauze* Foreign money is not legal tender in Belgium *a drapery of lace* or Germany *a bluish white drapery* but is received at the railway offices at the following rates of exchange 1 Prussian *smalt blue* Frederic = 21 francs, 1 Pistole, 1 Ducat = 11 franc and 50 centimes, 1 French Crown = 5 francs and 50 centimes, 1 Brabant thaler (originally struck by the Emperor of Austria *in sight of the Danube*) = 5 francs and 68 centimes, 1 Prussian thaler = 3 francs and 70 centimes. In Austria a 20 kreuzer coin is called a zwanziger after *zwanzig*, the German word for "20", the 1/2 zwanziger or zehner passes *the Morava* for 10 kreuzer; The zwanziger *in a flood of light* is the most convenient coin and most easy to reckon *meandering* by. Gold ducats are the best coins to take out of Austria *serpentining* into Turkey; In Hungary, the monetary system is the same as in Austria. In Servia *its glittering bends* and Turkey, accounts are kept in Piastres and paras, 3 aspers make a para, 40 paras make a piastre. The asper *upwards of twenty glittering bends* is only imaginary *pouring* 1 Zwanziger = 3 piastres 10 paras. **We shall find** one Piastre (silver or base metal) = 2 ½ d English money *a dazzling brightness* There are also 2 ½, 3, 5 and 6 piastre pieces, Rubiah and Beschlik, **the**se two **last** are also in **gold**. A purse in which large sums are calculated is 500 piastres *shattered crags on every side* At Scutari in Albania money is bought at a loss and changed at an advantage. The word backsheesh *crowned with dismantled fortresses* is familiar to the traveller in Turkey, w**here** it means **a** gratuitous **gift** of money, in return **for** any trifling service. This magic *the moon just sinking* word allows any door to fly open which causes considerable confusion to **strangers** It may be of use to recollect the following in passing *thro a chasm in the mountain* from the Austrian Dominions into

Turkey *a narrow & precipitous gorge* that nothing can now be more simple than the *black clouds coursing* monetary system *& rain in such torrents as I never saw before.*[253]

George continues:

Sunday 7th November (cont) Mr G having extolled my talents in cookery, I was assailed by the most earnest solicitations to concoct ein Englischer mehlspeise [*an English cake/pastry*] to which my good nature was not proof, so passed an hour in the fabrication of an apple pudding which was pronounced at dinner to be sehr gut [*very good*]. I then went to pay some farewell visits – first to the Schullehrer who went with me to his camarad [*comrade*] and interpreted for me – they were all most friendly & expressed their regret at my going so soon – Der Hauptschullehrer [*the secondary-school teacher*], at whose wedding I was, said he was anxious to make me a present to remember him by & as I had given his wife one on her marriage – gave me a pair of socks of her work. The doctor who I went to visit & gave a powder flask & shot belt I had brt for him from England – expressed his regret he had nothing better mir zu geschenkt zu geben [*to give as a present*] & presented me with an Albanian pipe & a pair of Serbische Strümpfe [*Serbian socks*]. At both of these places I was obliged to drink wine & coffee & smoke chiboukes. On my way home I was waylaid by the Herr Director of Quarantine & carried to his house to undergo the same process. His house – Patron's day St. Demetrious. Candles to church und unendliche Wirtschaftlichkeit [*and unlimited hospitality*]. Argt [*argument*] abt the fair sex after dinner.

> All ewes, wethers
> and lambs
> should now be well kept[254]

Monday 8th November: No Despatches. Went out shooting with Heneage – he killed two ducks. I did not get a shot – had a pleasant walk along the banks of the Morava – saw a good many ducks but found them very wild. Had a rubber of Dummy Whist & lost two zwannzigers to each of my adversaries.

Tuesday 9th November: Again no despatches. Grattan, Heneage & I went the same way as yesterday to look for the ducks – the dogs put some up which went off without our getting a shot but as the Dog still gave tongue I neared the bank of the river just in time to get a shot at a teal which I <u>knocked over</u>. Heneage then went home & Grattan & I continued our walk when I was fortunate enough to get a shot at a duck which I killed – made another mehlspeise – very good! Played a little Van John – lost 4 florins.

Wednesday 10th November: Depechen not I think so morgen [*no rush this morning*]. Mister! Said Rhisto – so we went out shooting in the contrary direction today but did not get a shot. Heneage got one but too far to do any good – a pleasant walk & plenty of chaff – was reading an amusing book, Henrietta Temple,[255] which I wanted to finish so did not play cards. Did a pipe or two.

Thursday 11th November Still no dispatches – went out shooting up the river again towards the frontier. Heneage and I got a shot at two quail, which, being in a hurry we of course missed. Grattan who was some distance behind going home "wiped my eye" – Heneage and I walked on for some distance but did not get another shot. No cards – Grattan seedy and went to bed early. This morning betrothal of Judge's daughter – at home to receive visitors. Coffee etc. handed [*round*]. Made me a present of a silk handkerchief. To be married next week – ugly and old – a pretty little girl there.

> Sheep should close-feed the grass
> no bent
> be suffered to rise[256]

Friday 12th November. Dispatches arrived at last about 10 o'clock this morning and I having been dressed some time was obliged to go thro' the agreeable occupation of making my toilet again for riding – got off about 1. Habited as when we came except that I had exchanged my Hungarian "Tile" for a Tatar Turban. The day was cold and frosty and a thick fog which contracted our view and obstructed the prospect of the splendid scenery we had enjoyed on our way to Alexnitza: yet even this weather had its beauties and the white hoar frost which thickly clothed every spray of tree and herbage and hung in rich and glittering festoons and contrasted prettily with the dark brown garb with which approaching winter had endued the foliage.

> 'The white hoar frost' on 'every spray of tree and herbage' becomes a souvenir for these departing messengers, a hard-wired memory of place and time. My notes on Serbian folk-lore[257] say that trees, stones and animals have a secret language, the knowledge of which is sometimes gifted by a snake:
>
> > 'Don't ask for silver', says the snake,
> > 'Request a wilderness festooned in ice'.

We arrived at Jagodina in great force (about 50 English miles) Mr G confessing to being a little tired, but feeling myself as if I had scarcely ridden at all. It was then 8 o'clock and quite dark but we agreed to go on another post (4 hours) before we halted to rest. It is anything but pleasant riding thro' this country in the dark to say nothing of the danger – obliged from the unevenness of the roads to keep the tracks of the waggon wheels which one cannot see. Over hills – down into ravines – across bridges formed only by roughly hewn timber placed cross-ways, half of them loose. Thro' dark forests obstructed by felled trees, half burnt stumps and roots, with horses wearied by the length of the journey, renders the ride very perilous.

Saturday 13th November After having laid down to rest for 3 or 4 hours on some old and dirty rugs, the only beds of the Servian stallknechts [grooms], spread round a blazing wood fire in the centre of the post house (an enormous barn the domicile of both men and horses, perhaps 50 or 60 of the latter)

Staling

At places where horses are in the habit
              of staling[258]
a stoppage
            of half a quarter of an hour
is permitted

where, by the same token, I did not get a wink of sleep and had the satisfaction of listening to the sonorous sounds that the nasal organs of Mr G & the Tatar produced, we were in the saddle again about 4 in the morning having arrived at Battottschina [Batočina], the name of this station, about 12 at night. I must confess I felt rather tired and not much refreshed by the attempt to sleep. The morning foggy and cold & still very dark. The roads much like what we had come over. Got on to Ratscha [Rača] by about 6 or 6½ and rested for about half an hour and got some coffee bread and eggs and on to Palanka [Smederevska Palanka] the fourth change by about 8. It was then quite light and we got on quicker and with less danger. Mr Gutch had a tumble with his horse, between this Kolap [*collapse*] and a kick on the leg in getting up, but nothing of consequence[259]. Came down from the mountain in sight of the Danube just before reaching Grosschka [Grocka] at nightfall. Fog very thick. Trees on the island gloomy and dim. Met the Austrian Courier. The last stage seemed interminable in the dark but reached Belgrade eventually at about 7 o'clock in 30 hours[260]. Had a capital dinner at the Consul's who was in Semlin & sat up till 10 o'clock reading 4 letters I found waiting me and smoking. Mr G faint and seedy and went to bed without any dinner.

Sunday 14th November Went over to Semlin early quite refreshed by a good night's rest – got well thro' quarantine. Did a little shopping packed my traps.

Wednesday 26th September 2018: Belgrade

Fresh bright day. Coffee in bed and then washing/dressing/ breakfast and final packing. After which we walked to the Green Market[261] for a look round. L had been before, but I hadn't had a chance. The market is something like Ridley Road Market in Dalston but set out in a square behind a façade of little shops. The stalls sell locally-produced food – whatever is in season. One sold herbal teas including Greek mountain tea, chamomile tea, and selections to cure ailments such as bronchitis[262] – I should have bought some! We bought nothing as we are moving on today.

Fonblanque dined with us at 2 o'clock. Killed an hour or two at Kaffee (Billardspielen [*playing Billiards*]). After many pros and cons decided to start with post horses tomorrow in der früh [*early in the morning*]. Supped with Fonblanque at der Goldene Löwe [*The Golden Lion*], came back to bed and cut my hand confoundedly mit eine verflüchtige Turkishe Pistole [*with a cursed Turkish pistol*] loading it just before going to bed as Fonblanque had been entertaining us with stories of Hungarian robberies and I thought I might just as well carry them loaded in our journey. Mr G kindly bound up my fist.[263]

At Home 2020/ 11: Killing strays – August to November 2020

> an odd metallic taste in my mouth
> I am the grey woman
> who desires sauerkraut
> sharp clean and strong

Monday 15th November Started about 9½ on the most disagreeable journey I ever made in my life. The morning foggy and cold. The roads at first pretty good but soon muddy and rough beyond any conception or description. Got to Metrovatz [Sremska Mitrovica] about 6. Horses apparently very tired. Dined while they rested and started again about 9½ as they were to go as far as they could. The jolting from here was awful and the road desperately morastig [*marshy*]. I was amused by the cries of our Kutscher [*coachman*] who got down to belabour his horses 'Anzuhe, Anzuhe, ne' and at last in the middle of a village about 3 or 4 miles from Metrovatz, came to the carriage window and declared 'Sie können nicht weiter' [*you cannot continue*] and took the horses off leaving us stuck half way to the axle in mud. All that night.

Tuesday 16th November Our Kutscher returned about 4 this morning with two additional horses, in all 5, and with these after some vain attempts by dint of our getting out and pushing at the wheels we were extricated having been left to our solitary reflections and quiet slumbers about 6 hours. Thinking of the stories of robberies and murders with which Fonblanque had regaled us. Got thro' swamps and jolts to the next station where we got fresh horses and reached

Essek [Osijek], a strongly fortified town, about 11 o'clock at night. Got something to eat and drink, pork & Somlauer wine at the post before. Old fellow very jolly and hospitable and the whole of this stage expecting every moment to be overturned. Such roads I could not have conceived. Passports etc to be shown.

Wednesday 17th November Roads much better. Had a splendid team of 4 grey horses from Essek to Thukshardt[264] [Szekszárd].

Thursday 18th November Roads still tolerably good except just before reaching Raab [Győr]. A fine town where we got a pretty clean dinner almost the first meal that one would not at after times have looked at with repugnance from the extreme dirt. For a few miles before Raab, road very sandy, could not go out of a walk and jolted sometimes with ones hand against the roof of the carriage. Left Raab about 4½ and from the next station took the Bauernpferde [farm horses], 4 in hand, and [at] full gallop reached Parndorf the last station from Vienna about 12 o'clock.

Friday 19th November Very glad to find ourselves this morning about 4½ at the Barrier of Vienna.[265] Nothing searched. Delighted at this portion of the journey being done. No description can convey an idea of it. I only wonder the carriage held together and that we had a sound bone in our skin. Hungary is a dreary flat bounded on every side only by the horizon and the drivers, frequently for a short cut, drive right across country over ploughed fields, ditches etc. We did during the night.

Turned in for an hour or 2 and went and did a deal of shopping etc, – a splendid day. Packed, dined and at the Embassy for dispatches at 10 at night, en route for Old England.

Saturday 20th November After anything but a comfortable night (bright and a sharp frost and Mr Gutch perpetually opening the window with the idea that the Postillion was drunk and once to prevent him changing horses with a carriage we met thus forcing me one moment and freezing me the next). Woke after a short restless sleep at Molk, remarkable for its stately convent with towers, domes and pinnacles, purple and gold. Leave the Danube here – road all the way from Vien through rows of poplars, passed through Amstetten, Strengberg, road beautiful but very hilly – the country prettily undulating and clothed with pine woods and forests and dotted with Swiss looking towns and villages with Austrian churches with their lofty and gay looking cupolaed towers. The latter part of the way before reaching Enns (a large strongly fortified town finely situated on an eminence above the Enn whose walls are said to have been built from part of Richard Cœur de Lyon's ransom). The distant view of the Noric[266] Alps bounding this picturesque country was extremely splendid – the sun was just setting behind this rugged and irregular chain and pouring down its sides a flood of golden light. We stopped at Enns to dine at the Adler – the prettiest little girl waited on us that I have seen since I left England. The Austrians generally plain. The road good tonight and had a better snooze tho' Mr G was again restless and the night was cold, foggy and frosty. Kept on towards Salzburg instead of turning to Braunau [Braunau am Inn] after leaving Lambach.

Sunday 21st November Arrived at Salzburg about 9 o'clock and stopped to breakfast. The morning very frosty and a thick fog insomuch we were quite deprived of the beautiful scenery which surrounds this place (much to our disappointment). The alps were never once visible and we were obliged to content ourselves with the beauty of country thro' which we passed – as all this part of Austria and Bavaria near the alps, its character is very Swiss – undulating knolls rising around clothed with magnificent pine woods and dotted with Swiss cottages and villages. The coachmen very slow but play the horn nicely. Just about dusk saw a deer trot across the fields which on seeing us quickened his pace cleared the rails into the road and from thence disappeared in the forest. Stopped to dine at a small village and post Traubartstein[267] – at night postillion drunk – no sleep.

'Just about dusk saw a deer trot across the fields which on seeing us quickened his pace cleared the rails into the road and from thence disappeared in the forest'. I'm driving through Suffolk on a country road and ahead of the car a herd of deer crosses over. That wild and tentative grace is set as a permanent image, revisited the instant I read George's sentence. At dusk, deer in the shadows, cross quietly from one time to another.

Monday 22nd November Reached Munich about 2½pm and after some little delay in finding the Englische Gesandte [*English Messenger*] drove to the Golden Hirsche [*Golden Stag*] and enjoyed the luxury of 4 or 5 hours in bed. Up at eight. Beautiful morning, strolled out, bought a view of Munich. Breakfasted and started by railroad to Donauwörth. Slow but sure, arrived at Augsburg about 1 and stopped there ½ an hour. The station is a little distance from the town which however looks well with its Bavarian capped towers and spheres and strong fortifications. Immediately on leaving Augsburg found a good deal of snow had fallen. Country flat. Reached Donauwörth (a new route to me) by 2½. A fine old town once strongly fortified and very Bavarian in character, narrow streets lofty houses 5, 6 & 7 stories with black roofs and gable ends in the Elizabethan style. Left Donauwörth at 3. The drive exceedingly pretty along the rich and fertile valley of the Ries. Haarbourg[268] [Harburg] – first post a curious old town. Lofty houses with gable ends (which Indeed prevail thro'out Bavaria and Wurtemberg and Baden) and very narrow streets beautifully situated at the foot of a perpendicular Rock on the summit of which is an extensive ruin of a castle. You pass along the base of these frowning rocks for a mile before reaching Haarbourg. The town is almost entirely inhabited by Jews and consequently has the appearance of being very dirty and poverty stricken. The drive still very pretty and diversified with hill and valley, we reached Nördlingen about 6½ and stopped to dine at the Krone (Posthouse). Very attentive and gave us a most excellent dinner. Mr G was frightened from the Goldener Ochs [*Golden Ox*] [*where*] we stopped first by the dirt and cool indifference displayed. Summoned by a pretty tune on our Schwager's Bugle we made a start again at 7½ – a beautiful night, I again very wakeful, with a bright moon which showed off to great advantage the curious old towns we passed thro' – the country too appeared beautiful and caused me to regret the absence of daylight.

At Home 2020/ 12: Travel

a walk is prescribed to maintain core body strength
so we wander the industrial estate
(foam blows like sea spume
over the fire station forecourt)
where pavements are empty

Tuesday 23rd November Awoke out of a pretty sound sleep at the last change before Stuttgardt. Country highly cultivated undulating and very little wooded. A long hill down to Stuttgardt which is prettily situated on the Neckar surrounded by hills. Capital limestone roads. Handsome new barracks. Curious richly painted and gilded covered promenade near the entrance to the King's Palace. Drove to the Embassy about 8½ and from thence to Marquardts Hotel (good but expensive). Breakfasted and put the steam on in hopes of reaching Bruchsall in time for the 3 o'clock Eisenbahnzug [*railway train*] to Frankfort – road heavy and very hilly, postillions slow and not to be hurried, country not very remarkable for beauty except with regard to the curious old towns with their picturesque towers and spires. Passed thro' Bruchsall before reaching the station. A fair day – it was almost dark but it seemed to have some fine old buildings and curious spires and was a much larger town than any we had passed since leaving Stuttgardt. We passed thro' 3 or 4 handsome old arched gateways in traversing the town and at last reached the station about ½ a mile out at 5 o'clock and having occupied an hour and ½ as we best could left at 6½ quite dark and reached Heidelberg about 8. Got some supper (very acceptable having had nothing since breakfast at Stuttgardt) a bottle of excellent Moussierender Hocheimer [*sparkling Hochheimer wine*], sundry pipes and went to bed about 11 as we had to get up pretty early for Der erster Eisenbahnzug [*the first train*] to Frankfurt – the only thing I noticed particularly (daylight not being necessary for that) were the lamps for lighting the streets hung across from house to house on ropes or chains. It is still very general on the continent. I noticed at Mayence, Bruchsall and I understand exists in some parts of Paris still.

Wednesday 24th November Up at ½ 4 heavy rain in the night, a warm muggy morning – too dark to see anything – left Heidelberg by the 6 o'clock train. Handsome bridge building over the Neckar (quite close to the temporary one we passed over)[269] and very substantial as far as the darkness would allow it to be visible. The grey dawn gradually displayed the rich fertile and highly cultivated plain thro' which we were passing, indeed it had quite the appearance of a garden, on the right, low undulating hills clothed with vines to the summit and picturesque towns situated here and there in embrasures at their base, while from above, solitary towers as at Weinheim and Heppenheim crowning the highest solitary point near looked down upon them. The railroad is very steady and the fastest I have been on on the continent. The stations are very handsome, and the names conspicuously blazoned on each end in large gilt raised German characters. At the station at Darmstadt Mr G was nearly left behind. He was asleep and as we entered a handsome station and not having seen the name and taking it for granted it must be Frankfurt exclaimed "here we are".

At Home 2020/13: The Kingfisher

gold coins by an edge of the river/ the water slabbed/
a weight of mercury/ then this/ this blue-green arrow

Mr G immediately got down and went to order horses and had it not been for the timely hint of his error casually given him by someone would have inevitably had the satisfaction of seeing his carriage go off with me as its only inmate. Reached Frankfurt at 9. Drove to the embassy then to Rothschilds[270] to deposit a bag of gold. Thence to the Hotel de Russie, a handsome and good hotel. Breakfasted at 10 and went out lionizing. Went to see the celebrated Ariadne[271] by Danecker among a collection of statuary in marble and plaster in a small gallery in the grounds of Mr Pittman.[272] Very beautiful and enhanced by a pink silk curtain before the window giving the colour of life to the beautiful form and lovely Grecian features. From thence we went to the Picture Gallery which is quite modern and contains nothing very good. Three or four pictures pleased me which I have noted at the beginning of this book,[273] especially the wise and foolish virgins by Schadow. This is nicely painted and the idea prettily carried out. In the centre our Saviour is entering a chamber by large folding doors at the top of a flight of steps and on the right hand in the foreground are the wise virgins in attitudes of hope, humility and prayer holding out their lighted lamps, while on the left among the foolish virgins reigns sleep, confusion, surprise, terror and despair, one a lovely face, lies stretched in sleep, clasping her lamp in her extended hand, the light of which is being extinguished by a deluge of water from an earthen jug – one with frowning brow and hand encircling her lamp is trying to blow it into a blaze and another trying to wake a fourth who is just opening her eyes to a consciousness of her misery.

Went next to the town house where the kings dine after their coronation in [a] large chamber spoiled by its shape (failing of an oblong at the window end) but gorgeously painted and gilded as to its convex roof and with full length paintings in niches of the Emperors of Germany from Charlemagne up to the father of the present Emperor of Austria, Francis II. There is also a council chamber where the kings were formerly elected, now used as a Senate house. Passed thro' the exchange which has a curious painted ceiling which appears to descend in the form of a wine funnel to the numerous pillars on which it is supported, something after the manner of groining. Saw the house where Charlemagne lived, but somewhat renovated. A curious old tower to the cathedral[274] with 4 flanking spiral pinnacles the one from the summit has fallen down, giving it an unfinished look. Returned to the hotel at two. Found Mr Ridgeway there on his way to Alexnitza. Mr G had to go to the embassy and I amused myself by writing up some of my diary. Sent to the post but no letters. Disappointed! Left Frankfurt by the 5½ o'clock train for Mayence. Drove to the Hotel de l'Europe (where the queen stayed) Elegant and good hotel. Too dark to see anything of the town. Moon over the broad waters of the Rhine. Dined "baccoed" and went to bed at 11 o'clock.

Thursday 25th November On getting up there was a tremendously thick fog so as there was little or no chance of a boat[275]. Determined to post to Cologne. Started at 9am road beautiful by the side of the Rhine from the first post (Burgen) where it crosses another smaller river – the road is smooth and level along the base of the magnificent precipices which bound the Rhine about 30 or 40 feet above the water. The rocks basaltic, vines occupying every space between. Pass thro' several picturesque old towns. Basaltic pillars Mr Gutch said the same as at Staffa used for mile stones and rails to the side of the road. Beautiful old ruin [Rheinfels Castle] on an eminence overhanging St Goar. Reached Coblentz about 6. Almost dark. But it appeared a handsome and comparatively modern town built in very large squares. Stopped at the post house to dinner. Very comfortable. Had a bottle of Rheinwein – exceedingly good. Awoke out of a sound sleep by arriving at Cologne 1½am turned in.

Friday 26th November Up at 5 and drove to the railroad station by about 6 o'clock. Quite dark. Town as at Heidelberg and Mayence lighted by lamps suspended across the streets. Old with narrow streets and lofty antique gable-ended houses. Well off and rail for Ostende by ¼ 7. Soon after starting we had a beautiful view of Cologne with its spires and dark and antique looking old cathedral in the dawning light of the rising sun which spread behind it a curtain of the most beautiful rose colour streaked with black throwing out most conspicuously the dark forms of the buildings. Reached Aix at 9. It has some handsome buildings and looks well from the railroad. From here tho' is an inclined plain of about 1½ mile up which we are drawn by steam. Ropes made of twisted wire and perfectly round.[276] From here, as before, country one wide plain as far as the eye can reach but rich and well cultivated. Reached Halbestadt[277] the Belgian frontier about 11. Got some dinner at a very good restaurant. Started again about 11½ and from here to Lieges the line is most picturesque thro' a rocky and beautifully wooded district, entering tunnels every 5 minutes and crossing little green secluded plains between. Then winding round hills with precipices above and valleys below, abounding with pretty villages and murmuring streams. A long inclined plain from Lieges for 3 miles. A very powerful engine in a <u>sort of conservatory</u>. The country again flat. Got to Mallines (Mechlin) about 4. Lace[278] manufactured here. Halted ¾ of an hour. Quite dark. Heavy rain. Arrived at Ostende at 9½ had coffee at Hotel d'Allemagne and off about 10 posting for Calais[279]. Posting very bad. Done up Lisle Railroad. Detained for horses at nearly every post ½ or ¾ of an hour. Very little trouble at the Custom House at Zudcote [Zuydcoote] this time –

Tuesday October 2nd, 2018: Niš to Lewes via Belgrade

Got up early to be ready for a taxi at 8.45am. Our last morning in Serbia. Packed up the last bits and pieces, showered, ate the breakfast we'd bought in the supermarket yesterday – rice cakes and banana with a cup of chamomile tea. Met and paid the owner who told us he knew Russian and his wife English. Took a taxi to the bus station, we were early for the bus. I had a headache, feeling decidedly seedy. The coach came in at 9.15 am and we boarded – suitcases below an extra 50 dinars each. The journey was very smooth. L watched a film on her phone – she had propped it in the magazine holder in front of her and looked very comfortable. I slept on and off, lolling forwards and sideways, jerking awake. Near to Belgrade it started raining – only the second time since we've been away, I think. Whole journey was grey. We came into the bus station on time, retrieved bags.

There were about five or six taxi drivers by the bus stop touting for trade and asking if we wanted 'taxi to airport'. We shook our heads and rolled the bags round to the bus-station café and had lunch. L scouted out where the airport buses go from while I sat with the bags and wrote this. She came back saying the information office in the old station had been helpful (the woman there lounging back in her chair and on the phone) had said the stop was just round the corner. Weather grey and cold, everyone is now bundled up – I am wearing jacket and scarf – and glad of them. The tablecloths are red-check gingham with many cigarette burns scattered across them. My headache has almost gone. Groups of men, here and there, drinking, talking, gesticulating, smoking. Looking forward now to walking into the house at home.

Trundled the bags round, luckily an airport bus was waiting, with us as the only passengers. The driver heaved on our bags and we set off straight away for only 600 dinars, a fraction of the price of a taxi. We were set down by the airport door. Inside crowded – people using phones, iPads, watching programmes. Lots of noise, many different languages. Groups, families drowsy from waiting, sorting through bags, singing, chatting, or just looking into the middle distance. We have several hours to wait as our boarding gate has not yet been listed.

Moved to a quieter area and had a snack, the woman selling it said it was not chicken, but the brother of chicken (Turkey!). Waited then went through passport control, a very bored guard looked at our passports, and finally through the security checks to the room where we waited for the flight. I read and L watched a film on her phone. We walked onto the plane easily, seats 4E and 4F. 4D was taken by an ex-ballet dancer originally from the UK – an intense woman who talked to us for quite a while. Her husband, she said, was a dance/ballet choreographer – she told us about some of the ballets he'd choreographed, and her family history although I cannot now remember the details. I read for most of the flight, and dozed a couple of times.

Landed on time at 8.35pm and then commenced the mad dash to get a train which would get us home at a reasonable hour. Off the plane quickly and to passport control and customs – a quick walk through, then baggage reclaim... our bags came out mercifully quickly at which point we sprinted with them out of the airport down a slope to wait for a shuttle bus to Luton Parkway Railway Station. The bus took ten minutes to get to the station. We dashed into the station and up SIX escalators and ONE lift to platform 1. The train we needed was just drawing in. We were soon in Lewes where we got off wearily and straight into a taxi which took us home by 11.40pm and so to bed.

Saturday 27th November 1847 Awoke at the last change from a short but sound snooze to find the morning decidedly moist and that we ought to have been in Calais about an hour before, however as Mr G felt convinced that the boat sailed for Dover at 12 we did not much mind and solaced ourselves as we gazed on the distant spires with the bright anticipations of speedily setting foot again on English ground, but alas! The vanity of human foresight we arrived at Dessin's Hotel at 8½ to learn to our extreme disgust and mortification that the boat had sailed about 10 minutes. Not very philosophically I fear we resigned ourselves to the hard fate which compelled us to quell our impatience and cool that and our heels at the same time for a whole day at Calais but our good genius prevailed and sent us help when least expected. I was occupying myself with my arrangements most deliberately when Mr G who had told me ½ an hour before that he should not be ready for breakfast for an hour and a half knocked violently at my door and said "We shall be off in ½ an hour". I "put the steam on" finished my toilet, crammed my traps into my trunk and jumped in after them and nearly locked myself in, but eventually escaped time enough to nearly choke myself with a morsel of bread and a gulp of coffee and follow Mr G and our baggage to the packet. Went ½ way down the pier, met Mr Macdonald[280] coming on the Paris station and went out in a boat to the packet. We had a gloriously rough passage and as we rode over the dark green waves which reared their snowy crests around, above the rail against which I leant. I felt that "exulting sense" that "pulses maddening play"[281] which "thrills the wanderer of that trackless way" and particularly when the wanderer has added to his other feelings of delight the prospect of a near approach to home after a two months experience of the dirt and barbarism of Germany, Hungary and Servia. We had a Government Steamer specially to convey us across on the authority of the Consul[282] and in about two hours and a half from weighing anchor we were entering the harbour at Dover and a magnificent sight it was as we approached the picturesque town lying below and flanked on both sides by the white cliffs of old England while the castle crowned the height above it, as we approached the mouth of the harbour the packet which seemed whirled about like a walnut shell was brought sharp up to the windward side and shot diagonally in a most grand and awful way right into the harbour on the crest of a great wave. I felt a momentary shudder for I could not help reflecting what utter annihilation it would be to miss. Passed thro' the Custom House with little or no trouble. They were very civil. Went to the Ship Hotel got some luncheon and off for London on the Express Train at 1½. Reached London in about 3 hours and having called at Rothschild with a bag of gold from Frankfurt and deposited despatches at Foreign Office were once more snuggly domesticated at 77 Great Portland Street by about 7 o'clock – the very day two months and to within half an hour of our leaving it.

8th February 2020:
77 Great Portland Street and Downing Street, London

We turn to walk down Great Portland Street where George lodged with Mr and Mrs Gutch in 1846 and 1847. Son, J, messages us to ask us to turn on location tracking so he can find us more easily. Then we see him, in among the crowd of passers-by, smiling and waving, jogging towards us.

We hug, so lovely to hold him – it's been more than a month since we saw each other over Christmas. Immediately we set out trying to find no. 77 – more complicated than it seems because in the intervening years the numbering on the houses has changed several times. We're not sure if the current no. 77 we find, which has a bicycle shop called Velorution underneath a modern façade, is in fact where Mr G's no. 77 used to be. The shop has scaffolding over the ground and first few floors – it looks like a 60s façade – blocky and plain with rows of windows – quite run down. On the opposite side of the street, though, 70-74 Great Portland Street, looks much more like where they might have lived back in the 1840s. This remnant of a terrace, too, is in the process of being done up. The lowest floor is hidden by hoardings but, above it, three floors of brick-built facades rise impressively and look like they might be of the right era. Above those are attic rooms set back in what were probably servants' quarters – these have scaffolding too. The windows have all been taken out preparatory to the refurbishment. The construction firm, Knightbuild, have pasted building regs. on the hoardings. The street is now a hotch-potch of houses and shops of many different periods. We walk up and down for a bit imagining Mr Gutch and Mr Davies setting out in a carriage from here for Downing Street in 1846 and 1847.

We stroll towards Downing Street (where the Foreign Office was at that time) without bothering with a map, wandering and talking. Crossing over Oxford Street, along Horse Guards Road and into Parliament Street. Both ends of Downing Street are completely barred to prevent terrorism. At the front end strong steel barricades and a revolving barred gate let in only those who have passes. There are four or five police with automatic weapons behind the bars and crowds of tourists taking pictures clustered in front.

Later to Charing Cross Station (opened 1864) – having mis-remembered, thinking it was the station they set off from – although it wasn't built by 1846 and, in fact, they went from the station of the Dover Railway over London Bridge[283].

We walk all in all about twelve miles, stopping for a beer at the 'Nell of Old Drury' pub, in an upstairs room, just the three of us. Then on to the legal district, Carey Street, the Knights Templar, Chancery Lane, Smithfield Market, Farringdon – where Lesley remembered all the Saturday nights she'd spent at the London Lesbian and Gay Centre [67-69 Cowcross Street]. We tried to recall which building it had been in – long gone.

This night the moon was full, a Super Moon called Snow Moon or Hunger Moon. It was large and bright, the shadows on it very clear. I took a photo of it when we were near Smithfield market. How small it looked in the picture, how very far away.

At Home 2020/14: Six monthly CT scan result July 2021

A letter arrives with the latest summary
– no recurrence noted –

the final sentence promises
survival surveillance
which provokes unexpected hilarity
in our odd and beautiful household

Letters concerning Mr Gutch's fall from his horse

From Mr Gutch to Hertslet
No 77 Great Portland Street
November 27th 1847

Sir
    I regret to say that in consequence of my horse having fallen with
me on my homeward journey through Servia and in doing having
severely kicked me on my right leg, and the irritation consequent
on the homeward journey having caused much inflammation on
the injured leg it will not be in my power to take duty for some few
weeks – you will therefore have the goodness to place my name on
the sick list.
        I am Sir
                Very obediently yours
HWG Gutch

Messr. Gutch
27 Nov 1847

Messr. Gutch Laming from accident in Turkey. Unfit for Duty
[*note from Hertslet appended to letter*]

To Louis Hertslett Esq
Foreign Office
Downing Street

No 77 Great Portland Street
Nov 28 1847

Dear Sir

I last night on my arrival in London wrote a letter to Mr Lewis Hertslett informing him that I shall not be able to take duty in consequence of an accident I met with on my return home; my horse having fallen with me on my return journey, through Servia, and in rising kicked me in the leg, this is now so inflamed from travelling that I must reluctantly lay up; I have today been to my medical man, who says it will be the height of folly my attempting a journey for a week or two – I write this in case your [illeg.] should not be in London. I shall if necessary be very happy to forward you a medical certificate to verify what I have asserted as I imagine there are very few of my colleagues in London – my certificate and passport shall be sent you in a day or two – I brought a box for Mrs Hertslet from Mr Adamburger[284] of Vienna the contents of which are I hope uninjured.

Obediently very truly yours
JWG Gutch
Mr Gutch
28 Nov 1847
[note from Hertslet appended to letter]
Injury from his horse falling upon him in Servia

Messr Gutch
28 Nov 1847
Medical Certificate

Nov 28 1847
Great Portland Street

Dear Sir

I herewith beg to enclose a certificate from Dr Ashburner who has at my solicitation seen me today and which will I trust prove sufficiently confirmatory of the statement I forwarded to you yesterday evening on my reaching London. I regret exceedingly my inability to immediately again take duty and the more so as I fear that few of my colleagues are in London.

77 Great Portland Street
London
29th November 1847

I certify; that Mr John W.G. Gutch having, during his late journey to Servia, met with a severe accident on his right leg, from the kick of a horse, is for the present unable to take another journey without the risqué of serious injury to his health. Mr Gutch has, besides the results of this accident, a cutaneous disorder that would render some repose and a course of alternative medicines of great importance to him.

John Ashburner, MD

George's Notes

Post from Belgrade to Alexnitza
Grotschka [Grocka][285] 1st 3 hours
Rest at a small house half way
Kolak [Kolari] [286] – 2nd 3 hours
Rest at a small khan ½ way
Hassan Palanka [Smederevska Palanka] [287] 3rd 5 hours
Ratsha [Rača][288] at town where we stop to rest
Battotochina [Batočina][289] 4th 5 hours
Bagaradan [Bagrdan][290] small town
Jagodina[291] 5th 5 hours
Paracgn [Paraćin] [292] Palanka   halt
Tochupria [Ćuprija] [293]
Schupilliac 6th   5 hours
    A small house of halt
    Alexnitza[294] 7th   5 hours

Turkish
Bosh – nonsense
Keffe – rest
Hahi – well

Caracho – *Spanish Expletive*

Har da kan [*Turkish – all blood(?)*]
Turkish
Schildwacht hause
Germ. Guard House

A Missing Page

> A missing page
> torn out   of which a tiny scrap remains
> "rocks where"

The waters of the Danube [*noted at the top of the next page*]

Weinheim
Heimsbach
Heppenheim
Hasingenberg (?)

Words and Phrases Taught to George by Rhisto [295]

Servian

Sonsa – the sun [*sunce*]

Messetz – the moon [*mesec*]

Svera – music [*svira: the music is playing (muzika svira) or he's playing music (on svira)*]

Dobra – well, good [*Here, possibly used as an adverb Dobro – 'good' or 'It's all well'. Common in everyday language, as affirmative agreeable answer. Can also be used as an adjective, where it changes according to the noun gender: dobra žena – good life. dobar muž – good husband. dobro date – good child. Via Ivanka Radmanović*]

Kamen – a stone

Sedim – sit [*sedim (I sit)*]

Dobra Vitscha – Good evening [*dobro veče*]

Dobra Utra – Good day [*dobro jutro*]

Nova – new [*nova, nov, novo*]

Cousche – house [*kuća , nova kuća – new house*]

Vodour – water [*voda*]

Vatra – fire

Pattow – a cock [*petao*]

Gusle – musical instrument

Guitdar – Serbian bagpipe [*gajde*]

Cone – Serbian horse [*konj*]

Psetto [*pseto or pas – dog*]

Nesne Serbscke dagovoiesh – don't speak Serbian [*(Ja) ne govorim srpski – I don't speak Serbian. In Serbian there's no need to use a pronoun in front of the verb, as the ending of the verb indicates who is the subject. Literally: Ne znam da govorim Srpski*]

Yes – yes [*da*]

No – ne

Coschere – horse carriage [*kočija*]

Kohla – beef carriage [*kola. An open wooden cart or wagon, used by farmers to transport goods, usually pulled by oxen, cows, a donkey or a horse*]

Niegar – book [*Knjiga*]

Genise – marriage [*Possibly: ženi se (as in 'he is getting married'), marriage: venčanje*]

Mladogenier – husband [*mladoženja – meaning groom*].

Mladonevester – wife [*mlada or nevesta – meaning bride*]

Kniegar – book

Bogarmi – by god, certainly [*bogami*]

Heuti – on, forward [*translation not possible*]

Dobra Dusha – until arrived [*As a greeting: to a guest: dobro došli – literally: (we hope) you are well arrived/ true meaning: welcome to our home. Dobra duša also means – good soul, good person*]

Bolin Nasha – at home [*To the host: bolje vas našli – literally: we find you in better state than us or we hope you feel better than us / true meaning: thank you (for your hospitality)*]

Kakos te gospodene – how are you sir [*kako ste, gospodine*]

Tala baga dobra – well thank you [*hvala bogu, dobro – Thank God, (I feel) well*]

Kakos te vi – how are you [*kako ste vi*]

Bog – God

Brachia vodour – hot water [*vruća voda*]

Lardno vadour – cold water [*hladna voda*]

Oparli Swatschi – light the candle [*upali sveću*]

Di me – give me [*daj mi*]

Metti sedlo no mog conia – saddle my horse [*provincial: meti sedlo na mog konja. Correct: stavi sedlo na mog konja or osedlaj mi konja*]

Ochesti mog chisni – clean my boots [*očisti moje čizme*]

Alenio – coal [*uglja*]

Obesheniac – (oath) you once hung (?) [*Obećanje – meaning oath/ promise*]

Lebra – bread [*provincial: Leba or leb. Correct: hleb.*]

Emash ti – have you [*imaš ti or imaš li*]

Pilaki – fowls [*pilići – chicken*]

Messo – meat [*meso*]

Nosh – knife [*nož*]

Blagodari – thank you [*blagodarim. Now: hvala*]

Nushka – fork [*viljuška*]

Cashaka – spoon [*kašika*]

Tschasha – glass [*čaša*]

Vino – wine

Tschai – tea [*čaj*]

Kaffo – coffee [*kafa*]

Mazlo – butter [*maslo. Now: puter*]

Soli – salt [*so*]

Rest/lessness

I think this storm
may float off down the river
I lie in bed in the attic
raindrops   thunder
on roof tiles

where will this uneasiness
end?   will it loosen
from its lodging

   and settle

here   where everything's
in motion?   It can sink
in shallow water by a stand
of reeds   these reeds
with darkened tips

vibrate in any trickle
of the tide   any progress
of the air   and from a distance
blush the bank with gold
from which two swans

suddenly explode
their wings   in counterpoint
their backs   a dazzling now
to which we cling   or
in abandonment   let go

Afterword

Notes about the text and chronology:

I have followed as far as possible George's layout, punctuation, abbreviations etc. He was often, as I was while writing my journal, catching up, a few hours or days after the event described, and sometimes his memory failed and he left a blank or wrote what now seems to be a mistake. Sometimes he overwrote with pen after having made the original draft in pencil. Sometimes his pencil strokes were faint and hard to decipher. He used varied abbreviations; his punctuation was erratic. His German was not always accurate, but he littered his pages with German fragments. His Serbian, including place names, was written by ear. To make things easier for the reader I have added in the month, and sometimes the year, after each of his dates. I have put some modern place-names beside the 1840s place names in [brackets] where there is an uncomplicated alternative, but where there are multiple alternatives to place-names, as is often the case, or more detail is helpful I have also put them in the endnotes or glossary. I have put translations of the interjected French, German and Serbian phrases in [brackets] to make the text more easily readable and have used the same [brackets] for text notes. The glossary lists places, people, things that may not be familiar to the general reader. In other respects, I have kept as close as possible to his original. I have used his text without abridgement, apart from three poor pencil sketches of roof details and the cliffs at Novi Sad; having found it, I was averse to losing any of it – like a skeleton laid out in a museum its small bones seemed as important to its integrity as its larger ones.

There are three main timelines: 1846 and 1847 when the journals were written; 2018 when I visited Serbia and wrote my journals; 2020/21/22 when I visited London to find 77 Great Portland Street, wrote about my diagnosis and treatment and some notes on process. My diaries of 2018 are inserted into the 19th century journals where there is a point of connection with George's diaries, either through being in the same place or where there is a point of synchronicity, rather than following each other strictly chronologically.

Selective Timelines:

1796: Edward Jenner develops vaccination for smallpox.

1804: The First Serbian Uprising, led by Karadjordje against the Ottomans.

1815: The Second Serbian Uprising, led by Miloš Obrenović.

1816: First steamship crosses the English Channel.

1817: Establishment of the independent autonomous Principality of Serbia.

1821: First regular cross-Channel service by steam reduces crossing times to two hours and forty-five minutes (as opposed to at least three to four hours under sail).

1825: Regular steamship service between Cologne and Rotterdam on the Rhine begins.

1830: First public railway in the world built which uses only steam locomotives (The Liverpool and Manchester Railway).

1834: Slavery Abolition Act takes partial effect.

1835: Sretenjski Ustav, the first constitution of Serbia.

1837: Queen Victoria comes to the throne.

1839: Daguerreotype invented.

1840: Vaccination Act of 1840 – vaccination for smallpox free of charge in UK. The world's first adhesive stamp, used in a public postal system, the Penny Black, revolutionises sending prepaid letters cheaply.

1841: Richard Beard opens Daguerreotype Studio in London.[296] First edition of *Punch* published.[297]

1842: Nikolai Gogol publishes His novel *Myortvye Dushi (Dead Souls)*.

1843: Ada Lovelace writes world's first computer programme. Søren Kierkegaard publishes *Frygt og Baeven (Fear and Trembling)*.

1844: First electric telegraph sent. Alexandre Dumas publishes *The Three Musketeers (Les Trois Mousquetaires)*.

1845: Invention of the safety match. Edgar Allan Poe publishes his poem 'The Raven'. Between 1845 and 1849 The Irish Potato Famine,[298] kills over one million people, exacerbated by the actions and inactions of the Whig Government, headed by Lord John Russell.

1846: Ether first used as an anaesthetic.[299] Prime Minister, Robert Peel (Conservative) replaced by Lord John Russell (Whig). Charles Dickens begins publication of *Dombey and Son*. Robert Browning and Elizabeth Barrett Browning secretly marry. In continental Europe the blight on potatoes and rust on rye crops in 1846 and 1847 causes widespread famine and disease. First steam locomotive railway line opens in Hungary between Pest and Vác.

1847: Vuk Stefanović Karadžić reforms the Serbian language ('Speak as you write, write as you speak') by making it the official language, establishing the 30-letter Cyrillic alphabet in which every letter corresponds to a sound. Works supporting these language reforms are published including *Gorski Vijenac* (*The Mountain Wreath*) by Petar II Petrović Njegoš, *Pesme* (*Poems*) by Branko Radičević and *The War for Serbian Language and Grammar* by Djura Daničić. Chloroform first used for anaesthesia. Charlotte Brontë publishes *Jane Eyre*. Emily Brontë publishes *Wuthering Heights*. Anne Brontë publishes *Agnes Grey*. The Brontë sisters publish under the masculine pseudonyms Currer, Ellis, and Acton Bell. Thackeray begins serialisation of *Vanity Fair*.

1848: Paraffin extracted from coal. Anne Brontë publishes *The Tenant of Wildfell Hall*. Elizabeth Gaskell publishes *Mary Barton* anonymously. Two-year outbreak of cholera begins in England and Wales, killing 52,000.

1849: Dickens begins publication of *David Copperfield*. Deaths in England from diarrhoea are 18,887.

1853: First bicycle with pedals invented in Germany.

1856: Birth of Nikola Tesla, Serbian inventor, electrical engineer and futurist. The first rail line using only steam locomotives (begun in 1854 as horse-drawn) opens in Serbia.

1864: Remnants of the Circassian population forcefully deported to the Ottoman Empire.

1870: Franco-Prussian War begins. 500,000 deaths in Prussia, Austria and Belgium from smallpox.

1871: Smallpox epidemic kills at least 40,000 in England.

1878: Serbia is declared an independent country at the Berlin Congress.

1884: First Serbian National Railway train service from Belgrade to Niš.

1882: Elementary education (ages five to ten) in UK compulsory.

1901: Death of Queen Victoria.

1914: The assassination of the Archduke Franz Ferdinand of Austria by a Bosnian Serb Gavrilo Princip precipitates the First World War.

1918: Proclamation of Yugoslavia, the Kingdom of Serbs, Croats and Slovenians (until 1941). Limited suffrage allowed for women in the UK and in Hungary. First World War ends.

1939: Second World War begins.

1941: Rebecca West, British author and travel writer publishes *Black Lamb and Gray Falcon* about her six-week journey through Yugoslavia in 1937.

1944: First mass produced antibiotics.

1945: Proclamation of the Socialist Federal Republic of Yugoslavia (lasts until 1991). Women's suffrage in Serbia. Second World War ends.

1948: Women allowed to be awarded degrees at Cambridge.

1961: Ivo Andrić, writing about life in his native Bosnia under Ottoman rule, wins the Nobel Prize in Literature.

1971: Most Women in Switzerland gain the right to vote in federal elections after a referendum.

1980: Global Commission declared smallpox eradicated.

1990: The Federal Supreme Court of Switzerland allows women full voting rights in the final Swiss canton of Appenzell Innerrhoden.

1992: The Bosnian war begins on the 6th April. [300]

1995: The Bosnian war ends on the 14th December.

2010: Research conducted for the Office of the Prosecutors at The Hague Tribunal calculated the minimum number of victims of the Bosnian war as 89,186, with a probable figure of around 104,732.

2017: Slavery criminalised in Chad.[301]

2022: Global deaths from Covid 6.6 million as at 5th December 2022.[302] Afghanistan forbids girls' education at Secondary School and University. 24 February 2022, Russia invades Ukraine.

A Few Brief Words on Context – Political and Social

As we can see from the selective timeline above, huge strides were made in science, literature, transport, communication and industry in the 1840s. Lighting by gaslight was in use from the 1800s and was spreading through Europe in the 1840s but was not yet universal. Steamships began to cross the Atlantic in place of sailing ships and railways were developing rapidly in the UK and across parts of Europe, although not yet in Hungary and Serbia. It's clear from the journals that infrastructures were being developed at a tremendous rate; railways, railway stations, bridges and roads were being built. New and experimental technologies, such as the London Atmospheric Line were being tried. George notes the changes taking place even from one year to the next and records the use of older technologies, such as water mills on the rivers, where it interests him. Women, however, struggled in a patriarchal world. Education was limited and erratic. Health was a lottery. Wars were continuous.

The 1840s were a time of great progress in the UK and abroad in technology and construction although they were known also as the hungry forties.[303] Queen Victoria had come to the throne in 1837 and reigned until her death in January 1901. She was admired at the time for her stable government at home, and enormous expansion of the British Empire abroad. We, however, have a contextual view of the expansionism of the British Empire, the colonial attitudes of the British towards their subjects, the wealth that was based on slavery and forced labour. The Slavery Abolition Act, (1833) that abolished slavery in most British colonies, and that freed about 800,000 enslaved Africans in the Caribbean and South Africa as well as a small number in Canada, took effect on August 1st, 1834[304] but full emancipation for all was not made legal until 1st August 1838. *After Abolition: Britain and the Slave Trade Since 1807 by Marika Sherwood* (I.B. Tauris, 2007) makes clear that Britain continued to profit enormously from slavery and the slave trade as slavery only became illegal in India in 1848, on the Gold Coast in 1874, and in Nigeria in 1901 and British investment continued in places where slavery remained legal, like Cuba and Brazil. Britain relied on imports from slave-owning countries and, for example, the industrial Midlands still imported vast quantities of raw cotton from the USA and Brazil, where it was grown by slaves. My own family, I was shocked to discover while researching this book, included family members from the 18th and 19th Centuries, who profited from slavery in sugar estates in the West Indies. Sarah Corke (George's wife) writes of her ancestors: 'Some of them settled in Bristol' (she writes that they were originally French), 'but part of the family went to the West Indies and became prosperous possessors of large sugar estates, sending home the produce to their relations in Bristol, who became wealthy merchants in consequence'. Their middle-class lives, like so many others, were built on the theft of other people's lives.

Robert Peel was Prime Minister (Conservative) until 29th June 1846 and was replaced by Lord John Russell (Whig) from 30th June 1846 until 21st February 1852. Viscount Palmerston (began as a Tory, defected to the Whigs in 1830, then became the first Prime Minister of the newly formed Liberal Party in 1859), who was later to serve two periods as Prime Minister, served as Foreign Secretary from July 1846–December 1851. Historians consider Palmerston to be one the greatest Foreign Secretaries owing to his deft handling of crises although his policy towards the Ottoman Empire is thought not to have had a lasting influence. Edward Spencer, on first meeting George, tells him that he knows Lord Palmerston well '& would interest himself with him for me'.

Both of our travellers were very well-educated men with university degrees, however women in Britain were denied formal higher education, only being allowed to attend university lectures during the 1860s and were not allowed to be awarded degrees until 1878 at the University of London, 1895 at Durham, 1920 at Oxford, and a shockingly late 1948 at Cambridge. Women were barred from studying at Jesus College, Oxford, George's old college, for over four centuries (from its foundation until 1974). George's attitude to women was definitely of its time – referring to them as 'the fairer sex' and in Serbia as commodities for marriage. His considerations of women are class-based and he only records a conversation with an educated princess because he is surprised by her education and is impressed at meeting a princess. Secondary schooling for girls in Britain in the 1850s was also limited with middle and upper-class girls either being educated at home with a governess[305] or at a fashionably expensive girls' school. Education was very class-based and poor children could be in work by the age of ten both because education was not free and to supplement the family income. Many adults of the time would have been illiterate – George, for example, mocks the accent and speech of the working-class man ejected from his train on the way to Dover in 1847 who has 'all his worldly goods apparently in a basket in his hand'. Elementary education was from age five to ten. Not until 1882 was elementary education in the UK made compulsory and not until 1891 was it free. Classes, where children did attend school, could be very large – 70 to 80 children in inner-city schools – and in the middle part of the century rote learning of the three R's was enshrined in the system with payment made to schools on results. Consequently, children were often taught to memorise texts rather than be taught to actually read them.

Women in the 1840s were denied a vote. In England, Wales and Scotland they received limited suffrage in 1918 and on the same terms as men (over the age of 21) in 1928. Women's suffrage became law in 1945 in Serbia when women voted for the first time in the November parliamentary election that solidified the power of the Communist Party of Yugoslavia. In Hungary women attained limited suffrage in 1918 (voting for the first time in 1922); and full suffrage in 1945, but as in other communist states, civil rights of both men and women could be described as symbolic, as the system was a totalitarian one.

The 1840s were a time of famine and disease, although this is only hinted at by George who was protected by wealth and class. In continental Europe the blight on potatoes, like that suffered in Ireland, and rust on rye crops in 1846 and 1847, caused widespread hunger and sickness. Cholera, typhus, TB and diarrhoea were prevalent as was smallpox (an epidemic in 1871 killed 50,000 people[306]) along with the usual childhood diseases like measles, mumps, scarlet fever, whooping cough, diphtheria. In the 19th Century, TB killed about a quarter of the adult population of Europe. For those born in the first quarter of the 19th Century, as George and Mr Gutch were, it was a major achievement to survive infancy and childhood, even though they were protected to some extent by their class. Childbirth for women was extremely dangerous with puerperal fever killing many due to poor hygiene of doctors. In the second quarter of the 19th Century 30 per cent of all children in England and Wales died within their first five years. Successful treatments for diseases were embryonic and insanitary living conditions and misunderstandings about infection meant lives were often lost over minor injuries. The journeys these men undertook were hazardous and tiring. Although they stayed in good hotels when these were available, still they also roughed it and slept by firesides at waystations when necessary and rode on horseback for many hours, especially when speed was demanded. There was a pest or plague cordon between the Austrian area and the Principality of Serbia and between the Principality of Serbia and the Ottoman Empire, because of the fear of outbreaks of the plague which did erupt from time to time. From 1838, the Ottoman Empire called on Austrians to organise quarantine and the Turkish cordon which extended from the Black Sea to Niš, enlisted the support of Austrian, Italian, German or Polish doctors as we see in these journals.

Serbia in 1846 was a Principality,[307] a semi-independent state, which emerged after the Serbian Revolution of 1804–17. George notes, at the beginning of the second journal, a book he would like to read on the Serbian Revolution: *Ranke's History of Servia and the Servian Revolution translated from the German by Mrs Alexander Kerr,* 1847 (Ranke, 1847),[308] indicating his own interest in recent Serbian history. Previously the region had been under Ottoman control for three and a half centuries. The Principality was negotiated first through an unwritten agreement between Miloš Obrenović, leader of the Second Serbian Uprising, and Ottoman official Marashli Pasha, and subsequently full independence was achieved in 1867 when all Ottoman troops were expelled. Serbia was recognised internationally in 1878 by the Treaty of Berlin. Aleksandar Karađorđević (1806–1885) was the Prince of Serbia between 1842 and 1858 during the period covered by the journals. From 1841 to 1882 its capital was Belgrade. Sandwiched between the vast Austria-Hungary Empire, with its capital in Vienna, the Ottoman Empire and several other Balkan states, Serbia occupied a position of some strategic importance but came largely under the political and economic control of Austria. It was a sparsely populated area at the time.

There were many revolts and uprisings during 1848, the year after the second journal was written. It was the most widespread revolutionary wave in European history but within a year reactionary forces had regained control and the revolutions collapsed. Much has been written of this period by people far more knowledgeable than I am, but it seems important to know that our travellers were carrying despatches during the very moments before this revolutionary wave. The revolutions were led by ad-hoc coalitions of reformers, the middle classes and workers, which did not hold together for long. Many of the revolutions aimed to remove the old feudal structure and to create independent national states. They began in France and spread across Europe affecting many countries. There was widespread dissatisfaction with political leaders, demands for participation in democracy and government, demands for freedom of press, demands of the working classes. Many thousands of people were killed. The only significant lasting reforms, however, were the abolition of serfdom in Austria and Hungary, the end of absolute monarchy in Denmark, and the definitive end of the Capetian monarchy in France. The revolutions were most important in France, the Netherlands, Germany, Poland, Italy, and the Austrian Empire, but did not reach the Ottoman Empire.

We do not know exactly what was contained in the dispatches carried by Mr Gutch. Among a plethora of concerns, Sir Stratford Canning, in his fourth period in Constantinople, was devoting his chief energies to: the internal reform of the Ottoman Empire; a serious revolt had broken out in the Pashalic of Trebizond; and there was a good deal of activity to do with the second treaty of Erzurum, which was signed at the end of May 1847, and which sought to heal relations between Turkey and Persia. In 1847, Canning's replacement, Cowley was dealing with reports of trouble in Albania, which was affecting trade to the Ionian Islands[309] due to a blockade. We know that despatches Gutch carried home with him in 1847 were urgent because as Mr Davies says on 27th November 'we had a Government Steamer specially to convey us across on the authority of the Consul and in about two hours and a half from weighing anchor we were entering the harbour at Dover.'

The People

George Sydney Davies (1822–1895) was the first son of George Augustus Apreece Davies (1791–1874) and Caroline Cox (India, 1796–1880) of Crickhowell, Wales. He attended Jesus College, Oxford[310] (which drew most of its students and fellows from Wales; entrants to the college in those years were generally less than twenty young men per year) and obtained his BA in 1841. He became a solicitor, like his father (Firm, Davies and Son), a registrar of the county court and clerk to the justices, commissioners of taxes and high bailiff of the Crickhowell County Court. From 1843[311] until 1846 he was completing Articles of Clerkship at his father's practice.[312] After finishing the Articles and taking up lodgings with Mr Gutch in Great Portland Street, he set out on the first journey four months later. We do not know why he set out on the journey as that is never discussed. Edmund Spencer simply says of George, he had 'been for some time peering into the pathways and byways of poor Servia' (Spencer, 1851, p. 74). We can make some suppositions – he is going adventuring before settling down – this may be a version of the grand tour, an education in the ways of the world[313] – he has somehow, perhaps through his aunt Cordelia Cox, made the acquaintance of John Wheeley Gough Gutch, a surgeon, naturalist, and early photographer who became a Queen's Messenger and so has the ideal opportunity to travel in *relative* safety to an interesting part of the world. He is having a break after years of education before beginning his career as a solicitor, he had finished his education some years sooner than most of his contemporaries as he matriculated at the early age of 15. He is able to speak German, a language Mr Gutch doesn't appear to have, so can act as a translator for him when needed. Mr Gutch may have wanted a companion to help with the difficulties of travel especially as he often had poor health. Travel involved posting all night at times with frequent transfers from railway to horse drawn carriage to horseback to river steamer with bags containing confidential dispatches being transferred each time.[314] A companion meant that the Messenger could catch a few hours of sleep while his friend guarded the dispatches.[315]

George married Sarah Ann Corke (1818–1900) on 17th January 1849,[316] and they had seven children. Helen (1851–1940), George (1852–1940), Ethel (1854–1943), Evelyn (1856–1947), Isobel (b.1858), Richard (1859–1928) and Emily (b.1862). In the 1861 census they were living at Maes Celyn, Crickhowell together with a governess, a parlour maid, and a nurse maid. George was listed as Attorney and Solicitor. Their daughter, Evelyn Frances Caroline Davies (1856–1947), married Charles Bruce Gaskell (1833–1899) and one of their four children, Eileen Blanche Gaskell (1895–1981), was my maternal grandmother.

After a long career as a solicitor, George died on 8th June 1895 aged 73 years. The death certificate gives cause of death as 'Cancer of bowel 6 months, obstruction of bowels 1 month. Operation.'

John Wheeley Gough Gutch was an early photographer, and his details appear in several books on the subject[317] along with his photographs of the 1850s. Gutch was born at Kingsdown, Bristol on 23rd December 1808. He was born into a cultured Bristol family. The poets Coleridge, Southey and Wordsworth were friends of his father. Gutch studied to be a surgeon at the Bristol Royal Infirmary in the 1820s and was granted membership of the Royal College of Surgeons (MRCSL) in 1831, when he was 22. He left Britain for Italy in 1831 to become a private physician in Florence and in December 1832 married Elizabeth Frances Nicholson. In November 1833 they had a son. The family left Italy in 1835 and returned to Swansea in South Wales where he practised medicine. It was in Swansea in March 1838, that his son, John Frederick Lavender Gutch, died aged four. There were no more children and, it seems clear from the letters of his surgeon at the beginning of this book, that his wife had developed a severe uterine complaint which may have prevented further pregnancies.

Gutch was interested in many scientific areas – he was a member of the Meteorological Society of Great Britain and a fellow of the Linnean Society. He maintained a tide gauge at Swansea and corresponded with astronomer royal Sir George Biddell Airy. He was also interested in geological phenomena and later made many photographic studies of quarries and rock outcrops. Insects were another fascination, he had a particular interest in Coleoptera (winged beetles), which he collected on his travels[318] and he also collected many butterflies. On 18th October 1843[319] he abandoned medicine and became a Queen's Messenger, a government post which involved taking diplomatic dispatches to European cities and other parts of the world. He combined this with editing the annual *Literary and Scientific Register*. It is not known why he gave up medicine – he may have been frustrated by the limited choice of treatments that he could offer patients (Sumner, 2010, p. 32).

He left South Wales and moved to London. The census of 1841 shows him and Elizabeth living at 36 Great Portland Street with two family servants. By 1846 at the time of the first journal they were living at 77 Great Portland Street[320] and George was lodging there with them as this was the house they left from and returned to[321]in both of the journals. The duties of a Queen's Messenger were hard on the body, as we can see from these texts, requiring many hours on horseback and long days travelling on difficult routes. It was on a mission to Constantinople in 1854 that Gutch became ill and suffered a stroke which forced his retirement from diplomatic service on 9th July 1854. In retirement he pursued his passion for photography and many of his British photographs of that time and details of his life were published in 2010 (Sumner, 2010). Gutch was experimenting with photography as early as 1841 (no early work is known) but photography is not mentioned by George in these journals and early cameras would have been very heavy to carry on long difficult journeys where speed was required, luggage was restricted, and it may have been risky to be seen taking photographs in foreign countries where he could have been mistaken for a spy. Sumner records that Gutch did take a camera with him on at least one of his later overseas trips as in May 1851 he made a whole-plate paper negative of the Spanish Minister of War's Residence in Madrid (National Trust Collection, Lacock). Gutch died on 30th April 1862 at 38 Bloomsbury Square, London, aged 53. The cause of death was albuminuria (a sign of kidney disease) and an abscess in the kidneys. His wife Elizabeth Frances died in Weston-super-Mare on 27 September 1869, aged 57, from heart failure.

Captain Edmund Spencer, who appears in the 1847 journal, was a prolific British travel writer of the mid-19th Century. His books are entertaining, and his accounts colourfully describe the people and places he experienced, but we are left to fill in for ourselves how he, like Gutch and Davies, may have been experienced by the locals. His behaviour in the killing of the good wife's cockerel during a fast of the Serbian church certainly shows his arrogance, his misogyny and his condescension. He wrote many books on travel in Europe. From 1847 Spencer undertook an extensive voyage through the southern Balkans, which he described in his two-volume *Travels in European Turkey, in 1850, through Bosnia, Servia, Bulgaria, Macedonia, Thrace, Albania, and Epirus, with a visit to Greece and the Ionian Isles* (London 1851).

It is in this volume that he mentions meeting George and Mr Gutch in Servia in 1847 and describes their quarters, their outings together and their hospitality. George describes meeting him following Spencer's release from quarantine after he strayed over a border from Servia into Bosnia by mistake and was picked up by a troop of Servian pandours. About being taken into quarantine Spencer says, 'the most ludicrous part of the affair is, that a traveller can easily evade the quarantine altogether, by taking a circuitous route over some wild mountain district' (Spencer, 1851, p. 71), a note which, since Covid, strikes us suddenly as contemporaneous although the disease in Spencer's case was the plague. Spencer's account of their meeting gives us an external view of the tale told by George and allows us to see him briefly through another's eye.

The Hertslet Papers are held in The National Archives at Kew and contain the collection of accounts, vouchers, registers, regulations and other papers relating to Foreign Service Messengers and the background workings of the Foreign Office collected by *Lewis Hertslet* (1787–1870). Here we find handwritten letters sent in by Mr Gutch when he was sick, when his wife was ill, when he questioned current regulations. We find details of pay and mileage allowances of Queen's Messengers, and written responses to specific questions of the Secretaries of State; we find details of messenger travel allowances being reduced as new train lines across Europe were constructed and messenger complaints about these reductions; we find details of the horseback routes used in Serbia, and we learn that in 1843 the qualifications required for a Queen's Messenger in the Foreign Service were that no person should be appointed over the age of 35. Mr Gutch was 34 years 9 months 25 days when appointed so he had only just applied in time. Messengers were, in addition, required to 'have a competent knowledge of Foreign Languages, and be well qualified for performing Journeys on horseback.' The pay in 1843 was £60 per annum plus board wages on Foreign Service of 13s 4d per day, and at home of 7s 6d per day with a profit on foreign journeys of 6d per English Mile. Ian Sumner notes that Gutch's annual income would have been about £700 which was a good income for the times, although this sum may have included expenses (Sumner, 2010, p.33). On July 19th, 1839, Palmerston noted 'I think it proper to announce to Your Lordship, for your information and guidance, that the three Secretaries of State, who alternately appoint to the Situation of Queen's Foreign Service Messengers have, of late, appointed Military Officers to the performance of this Duty, and that it is intended that the future Vacancies in the Corps of Queens Foreign Service Messengers shall also be filled by Gentlemen.'[322] *The Hertslet Papers* fill in a great deal of detail about the life of Queen's Messengers in general and I have added letters from Mr Gutch to Hertslet and Hertslet to Mr Gutch to the text where they reflect on his particular experience and add to our understanding of his life.

The Herslet Papers show the systems that were put in place to keep the Foreign Messenger Service running smoothly and show that Gutch, and other messengers, struggled with the administrative burden at times – using the wrong paper for letters, not sending in sick notes without a reminder. The administrative staff at the Foreign Office wrote copious letters, memoranda etc to sort out queries and impose policies and filed them diligently. Much of the correspondence is fascinating. In 1853, for instance, Fonblanque wrote to Addington asking if Messengers could sometimes be sent by water to Constantinople instead of overland. You can hear the frustration in the tone of his letter written in reply to one denying his request where he is clearly explaining to office-bound people back home the realities of rough travel at the time: 'Whatever *'Murray's Handbook'* and like authorities, may say to the contrary, a tatar, – whether Turkish or Servian, despatched from hence to Constantinople, would cost (including his journey back to Belgrade) fully fifty pounds. From want of employment it is very likely the tatars here do not justify their former reputation, and perhaps, tho. some cause has rendered them inefficient elsewhere, for a despatch sent by one of them from Omar Pasha, then at Scutari, to the Ottoman Governor of Belgrade was twelve full days on the road, though the weather was favourable and no other cause of retard alleged by its bearer'.

Illustrations

Glossary of People, Places and Things

Aali Effendi, Mehmed Emin Âli Pasha, Mehmed Emin Aali: (1815–1871) a prominent reforming Ottoman statesman during the Tanzimat period.

Addington, Henry Unwin: (1790–1870) British diplomat and civil servant. Permanent Under-Secretary of State for Foreign Affairs from 1842.

Aleksandr: *see Kozhedub, Aleksandr*

Alexnitza: Aleksinac, a town and municipality located in the Nišava District of southern Serbia.

Alto relievo: a sculptural relief where forms extend from the back-ground to at least half their depth.

Amos: *see Mattio, Amos*

Amstetten: a town in Lower Austria, between Linz and Vienna.

Andrić, Ivo: Yugoslav novelist, poet, short-story writer. Nobel Prize in Literature, 1961. Wrote about life in his native Bosnia under Ottoman rule.

Andrić, Radomir: (b.1944) president of the Association of Writers of Serbia (2010–2018). Award-winning poet, lives in Belgrade, works as an editor of the Second Program of Radio Belgrade.

Archivescobole: archbishop.

Arnaut: Turkish term used to refer to Albanians.

Ashburner, John: (1793–1878) member Royal College of Surgeons. Specialist in midwifery and women's diseases. Doctor to Mr and Mrs Gutch.

Bagnia: refers to two different places both of which are spas. Sokobanja which is near Aleksinac and Niška Banja which is near Niš. The word *banja* in Serbian means spa.

Bakschisch: in the Balkans and former Ottoman Empire bakschisch means bribe, gratuity or backhander. Bakšiš (Serbian) means a gratuity.

Bane: *see Zubović, Branislav*

Batochina or Battotochina or Battottschina or Battofschina: Batočina: town and municipality in the Šumadija District of central Serbia.

Beaufort, Duke of: Major Henry Somerset, 7th Duke of Beaufort, KG (1792–1853), Earl of Glamorgan until 1803 and Marquess of Worcester between 1803 and 1835, a British peer, soldier, and politician. Duke of Beaufort from 1835–1853.

Bebric: Biebrich am Rhein, a borough of city of Wiesbaden, Germany. Incorporated into Wiesbaden in 1926. Biebrich, on the opposite bank of the Rhine from Mainz, was the embarking and landing place for passengers sailing down the Rhine.

Bitolia, Bitola: a city in the southwestern part of North Macedonia. *See also endnote 226.*

Bohémia: Kingdom of Bohemia or Czech Kingdom, part of the Habsburg Austrian Empire after the dissolution of the Holy Roman Empire in 1806, then the Austro-Hungarian Empire from 1867. A separate Kingdom until 1918, known as a crown land within the Austro-Hungarian Empire. The Czech language was called Bohemian in English until the 19th Century.

Bokhara: Bukhara is the fifth largest city in Uzbekistan. *See also endnote 227.*

Bourgas: Burgas, or Bourgas, is the second largest city on the Bulgarian Black Sea coast and the fourth largest in Bulgaria.

Bovan, Lake: reservoir created by the construction of a dam in 1978 for hydroelectric power and water supply. Located on Sokobanjska Moravica near Bovna between Sokobanja and Aleksinac.

Brindish, Rhisto, Risto: His name would probably have been Risto Brindić. Via Ivanka Radmanović. A Tatar and interpreter employed to look after the messengers at Alexnitza; a guide on journeys to Belgrade, to the Ottoman Empire border, to Niš, to Constantinople and to other places as required.

Britzka, brichka or britska: a long, spacious horse-drawn carriage with four wheels, folding top over the rear seat, rear-facing front seat, pulled by two horses. 19th Century equivalent to a motor-home – with conveniences (beds, dressing tables etc.) for the traveller.

Bruchsall, Bruchsal: (orig. Bruohselle, Bruaselle, historically known in English as Bruxhall) a city in the state of Baden-Württemberg, Germany.

Burgen: a municipality in the Bernkastel-Wittlich district in Rhineland-Palatinate, Germany.

Caerleon: Welsh: Caerllion, a town on the River Usk now incorporated into the northern outskirts of the city of Newport, Wales.

Caloyer: a monk of the Eastern Church.

Canning, Stratford: (1786–1880). British Diplomat. Ambassador in Constantinople for over fifty years.

Capitainitza, Kapetanica: the wife of a Kapetan (captain).

Carlovitz: Sremski Karlovci or Karlovci (Serbian) or Karlowitz or Carlowitz (German), a town and municipality located in the South Bačka District of Serbia, on the bank of the river Danube, five miles from Novi Sad.

Carojee: see *kiraidji*

Chaff, chaffy: banter, badinage. Also colloq. 1827 To banter, rail at, or rally, in a light manner. *OED* (1933).

Chamberstick: a short candlestick designed to be carried.

Cherne: The Cerna (Hungarian: Cserna) a river in Romania, a left tributary of the river Danube, which flows into the Danube near the town of Orşova.

Chibouque, chibouke, tchibouque: a very long-stemmed (between 4 and 5 ft) Turkish tobacco pipe.

Cillac's Hotel: See *Quillac's Hotel*

Circassia: a region in the North Caucasus and along the northeast shore of the Black Sea whose original populations were decimated by the Circassian genocide perpetrated by Russia from the 1860s.

Constantinople: formerly Byzantium, then Constantinople. Renamed Istanbul in 1930. Also referred to as Stambul, Stamboul.

Conyngham, George W. Lenox: (1796–1866) Chief Clerk of the Foreign Office From 27th July 1841.

Corke, Sarah: (1818–1900) married George Davies, the writer of these journals, in 1849. They had seven children.

Coupé, coupée: end compartment in a railway carriage seated on one side only (1853) *Shorter Oxford English Dictionary, 1933*.

Cowley, Lord: see Wellesley, Henry.

Cvetanović, Ivan: professor of Stylistics, Rhetoric, Linguistics and Literature at Faculty of Philosophy, University of Niš, Serbia. Poet, prose and play writer.

Danecker: Johann Heinrich von Dannecker, a German sculptor (1758-1841).

Danilevsky: From 1843, the Russian representative office was headed by Danilevsky, the father of the famous philosopher and pan-Slavic ideologue, Nicholas Danilevsky.

Darmstadt: a city in the state of Hesse in Germany, located in the southern part of the Rhine-Main-Area (Frankfurt Metropolitan Region).

Davies, George Sydney: (1822–1895) The author of these journals and my great-great-grandfather (ggg), later a solicitor in the family firm.

Despatches: official confidential documents sent from the Foreign Office to British diplomatic and consular posts abroad and from those posts back to the Foreign Office.

Dessins Hotel: hotel at Calais. "*Good but extravagantly dear.*" (Coghlan, 1847).

Dimitrijević, Milena: Director of the Public Library at Veliko Gradiste.

Dissolving View: a popular type of 19th Century magic lantern show showing a gradual transition from one projected image to another.

Distaff: the rod on which flax is wound preparatory to spinning. Also, of or concerning women.

Donauwörth: a town and the capital of the Donau-Ries district in Swabia, Bavaria, Germany said to have been founded by two fishermen where the rivers Danube (Donau) and Wörnitz flow.

Drachenfels: Dragon Cliff – The Drachenfels or 'Dragon's Rock', is a hill in the Siebengebirge uplands in Germany. The ruined castle Burg Drachenfels, on the summit, built between 1138 and 1167, bears the same name.

Dragoman: an interpreter, translator and official guide between Turkish, Arabic, and Persian-speaking countries and polities of the Middle East and European embassies, consulates, vice-consulates and trading posts. A dragoman spoke Arabic, Persian, Turkish, and other European languages.

Drei Mohren: (3 Moors), one of the oldest inns in Germany, good and comfortable, with great civility;' (Murray, 1873, p. 42).

Ducat: a coin used as a trade coin in Europe from the 13th to 19th Centuries. The gold ducat contained around 3.5 grams of fine gold.

Effendi or Effendy: a title of nobility meaning lord or master, especially in the Ottoman Empire lands and the Caucasus.

Ehrenbreitstein: a fortress on the east bank of the Rhine where it is joined by the Moselle, overlooking the town of Koblenz. *See also endnote 131.*

Enns: a town in the Austrian state of Upper Austria on the river Enns.

Eolus, Aiolos, Aeolus: in Greek mythology the divine keeper of the winds, king of the mythical, floating island of Aiolia, who locked storm winds inside his island and released them to ravage the world, when the gods commanded it.

Erzeroom, Erzurum, Treaties of: two treaties (1823 and 1847) that settled boundary disputes between the Ottoman Empire and Persia.

Essek, Esgek: Osijek, fourth largest city in Croatia. Due to its Habsburg and Ottoman history it had names in other languages: Hungarian: Eszék; German: Esseg or Essegg; Turkish: Ösek; Latin; Essek.

Firman: any written permission granted by an Islamic official at any level of government either for travel or to conduct scholarly investigation in the country.

Fonblanque, Thomas de Grenier de: Vicomte de Fonblanque (1793–1861), Consul General and Chargé d'Affaires in Serbia.

Frank: Eastern Orthodox and Muslim people used 'Frank' to describe Europeans from Western and Central Europe who followed the Latin rites of Christianity. The term has a complicated history.

Frogs, frogging: ornamental braid twisted on a coat.

Furnes: Veurne; French: Furnes; a city and municipality in the Belgian province of West Flanders.

Fytte: Part of a poem or song, a canto.

Ghasthause: Gasthaus, a German-style inn or tavern with rooms.

Geissenheim: Geisenheim, on the Rhine's right bank between Wiesbaden and Rüdesheim.

GGG: great-great-grandfather, Davies, George Sydney.

Gialico: referenced by Spencer as Giulika, chief of an insurrection in Albania. (Spencer, 1851, p.158).

Goldener Hirsch: Golden Stag Hotel, Munich. "*greatly improved under a new landlord, the son of the former one, and now scarcely, if at all, inferior to its rival. Table-d'Hote 1 fl 12 kr; good*". (Murray, 1844, p. 34). However, by 1850 it had deteriorated: "*Inns: None can be said to be good. Goldener Hirsch (Golden Stag), Schwäbinger Strasse, decayed and badly managed*" (Murray, 1850, p. 51)

Gousla, gusla, gusle: bowed, single-stringed musical instrument of the Balkans always accompanied by singing, with a round wooden back, a skin belly; played in a vertical position, with a deeply-curved bow.

Grattan, Henry Colley: Queen's Messenger. Appointed 10th December 1844. Retired 19th Jan 1863. (Wheeler-Holohan, 1935, p.276).

Groining: the curved edge at the junction of two intersecting vaults.

Guildar, gaida, gayda, gajde, gajdy: a bagpipe from the Balkans and Southeast Europe.

Guld., Gulden: The gulden or forint (German: *gulden*; Hungarian: *forint*; Croatian: *forinta/florin*; Czech: *zlatý*) was the currency of the lands of the House of Habsburg between 1754 and 1892.

Gutch, John Wheeley Gough: (1808–1862) Queen's Messenger, early photographer, surgeon and naturalist with whom George Davies was travelling when he wrote these journals. Often referred to as Mr G.

Haarbourg, Harburg: a town in Bavaria with a medieval castle, in the Donau-Ries district on the Wörnitz River.

Haiduc, hajduk: used in the European lands of the Ottoman Empire to describe brigands of the Balkans.

Han, khan: an inn or lodging house.

Hanji: innkeeper

Hanjiar: a large dagger with a curved blade and a large handle.

Harlequin: an agile trickster in a Harlequinade.

Heimsbach: a town on the Bergstraße.

Heneage, Dudley, Captain: served formerly in the 10th Hussars; then employed in Turkey as extra foreign service messenger (1853). The Foreign Office list for 1857. (London: Harrison, 1857).

Heppenheim: a town in South Hesse, Germany along the Bergstraße with a mediaeval Starkenburg (castle).

Hertslet, Lewis: (1787–1870) English librarian and editor of state papers. 1801, appointed sub-librarian in the Foreign Office; 1810 librarian and keeper of the papers. *The Hertslet Papers* are archived at the National Archives at Kew.

Hochheim: Hochheim am Main – a town in the Main-Taunus district of the German state of Hesse, near the right bank of the Main River, three miles above its confluence with the Rhine.

Hollandische Hof (Dutch Court): inn at Heidelberg *"with a view of the ruins of the castle."* (Coghlan, 1847, p. 165).

Holmes, George: Queen's Messenger. Appointed 10th November 1824. Retired 1st January 1859. (Wheeler-Holohan, 1935, p. 277).

Ivan: see Cvetanović, Ivan

Ivanka: see Radmanović, Ivanka

Jagodina: a city in central Serbia, on the banks of the Belica River, historically densely-forested region.

Jakšić, Đura: (1832–1878) Serbian poet, narrator, playwright, painter, teacher, bohemian. Lyricist of Serbian romanticism and Serbian painter of the 19th Century. Work includes poems, stories, plays in verse, and an unfinished historical novel about Serbian-Turkish relations.

Johnson: Captain Cecil Godschall-Johnson. Queen's Messenger. Appointed 19th March 1839. Retired 1st Jan 1876. (Wheeler-Holohan, 1935, p.275).

Karađorđević, Alexander: (1806–1885) Prince of Serbia between 1842 and 1858 and member of the House of Karađorđević.

Kinchens: Kinchin from kindchen (German) little child. OED.

Kiraidji or carojee: Kirdžija were merchants or travelling salesmen transporting salt, sugar, brandy, matches, wheat and spices. Edmund Spencer hired Georgy, a kiraidji, as a guide because as a travelling sales-man he was familiar with routes Spencer wanted to explore for his travel guides.

Kozhedub, Aleksandr: (Александр Кожедуб, b.1952). Novelist, poet, essayist. Member of the Bureau of the Creative Association of Prose of the IGO JV of Russia. Lives in Moscow. Writes in Belarusian and Russian.

Lambach: a market town in the Wels-Land district of the Austrian state of Upper Austria on the Ager and Traun Rivers. Site of Lambach Abbey, built around 1056.

Liéges: Liège, a city along the Meuse River in Belgium's French-speaking Wallonia region.

Llanwrtyd: a small settlement in Powys, mid-Wales with a gorge above it called őő's Leap.

Logi: Loggie (Italian) or loggia, a covered exterior gallery or corridor usually on an upper level, but sometimes ground level. The outer wall is open to the elements, usually supported by a series of columns or arches. In this case he describes compartments of the Pinakothek Gallery in Munich. (Murray, 1844, p. 42).

Lymouth: Lynmouth village, North Devon on the northern edge of Exmoor. The village straddles the confluence of the West Lyn and East Lyn rivers, in a gorge 210 m below the village of Lynton.

Mallines, Malines or Mechlin: Mechelen, French: Malines, traditional English name: Mechlin is a city and municipality in the province of Antwerp in the Flemish Region of Belgium.

Marcquardt's Hotel: Hotel at Stuttgardt. *"Marcquardt's Hotel, Königs Strasse; very good, but rather dear: Table-d'Hote (French Cook), 1fl 12 kr with wine; breakfast with eggs 48 kr;"* (Murray, 1844, p. 5).

Maslovarić, Vidak M: (b. 1950) poet, reviewer, member of the Board at the Association of Writers of Serbia and President of the International Literary Collaboration. Works translated into French, English, Romanian, Russian, Macedonian and Roma languages.

Mattio, Amos: (b. 1974) Italian poet, novelist and translator. He lives in Milan.

Mayennce: Mainz (French: Mayence) capital and largest city of Rhineland-Palatinate, Germany. Located on the Rhine at its confluence with the Main river, opposite Wiesbaden.

Meerschaum: a pipe made from the soft white clay mineral, sepiolite, whose name means, in German, 'sea foam'.

Mehadia: a small market town and commune in Caraş-Severin County, Romania lying in the Cerna River valley. Located on the site of the ancient Roman colony Ad Mediam, noted for its Hercules baths. *See endnotes 64 & 68.*

Metempsychosis: in philosophy, the transmigration of the soul, especially its reincarnation after death.

Metrovatz: Sremska Mitrovica. In Croatian it is called Srijemska Mitrovica, in Hungarian Szávaszentdemeter and in German Syrmisch Mitrowitz.

Metternich: Klemens Wenzel Nepomuk Lothar, Prince of Metternich-Winneburg zu Beilstein. (1773–1859) an Austrian diplomat at the centre of European affairs for four decades as the Austrian Empire's foreign minister from 1809 and Chancellor from 1821 until the liberal Revolutions of 1848 forced his resignation.

Mile stone, milestone: one of a series of numbered markers placed along a road or boundary at intervals of one mile or occasionally, parts of a mile.

Milena: see Dimitrijević, Milena

Milošević: *Slobodan*, Yugoslav and Serbian politician and the President of Serbia charged by the International Criminal Tribunal for the former Yugoslavia (ICTY) with war crimes in connection with the Bosnian War. *See endnote 106.*

Mirković, Zorka, Mrs: essayist, linguist and historian.

Mohach or Mohatsch or *Mohatz or Mohacs*: German: *Mohatsch*; Serbian: *Мохач* or *Mohač*; Turkish: *Mohaç* – a town in Baranya county, Hungary on the right bank of the Danube at the confluence of the Corasse & Danube.

Molk: Now Melk (older spelling: Mölk), an Austrian city next to the Wachau valley along the Danube, best known as the site of a massive baroque Benedictine monastery, Melk Abbey.

Moore, John: Queen's messenger, Appointed 1st November 1824. Retired 1st September 1859. (Wheeler-Holohan, 1935, p. 279)

Moussir. abbreviation of *Moussieren*: sparkling – as in a sparkling wine.

Mussulman: (plural Mussulmans or Mussulmen). (archaic) A Muslim.

Neusatz, Nisatz: now called Novi Sad means 'new orchard' in Serbian. Historically, it was also called Neusatz in German. The fort and settlement of Petrovaradin is on one side of the Danube with Novi Sad on the other.

Nicholson, Elizabeth Frances: (1811-1869) married Mr Gutch in 1832.

Nish or Nissa: Niš is now the third largest city in Serbia. Historically spelt as Nish or Nissa in English. The Niš Eyalet or Pashaluk of Niš was an administrative territorial entity of the Ottoman Empire located in the territory of present-day southern Serbia and western Bulgaria formed in 1846. Its administrative centre was Niš. The Pashaluk of Niš was incorporated into the Danube Vilayet in 1864.

Niška Banja: see *bagnia*. Nine kilometres (six miles) east of Niš and situated at the bottom of Suva Planina Mountain, a spa town known for its hot, radio-active water containing radon.

Niskifor, Nikifor: Nikifor Maksimović. The archbishop of Niš from 1842-1856. Via Zorka Mirkovic.

Nissava: Nišava or Nishava is a river in Bulgaria and Serbia and flows through Niš.

Nördlingen: a town, first mentioned in 898, in the Donau-Ries district, in Swabia, Bavaria, Germany built in a 15 million year old & 25 km diameter impact crater – the Nördlinger Ries – of a meteorite which left 72,000 tons of micro-diamonds. One of only three towns in Germany with a completely intact city wall.

Nuellens Hotel: Hotel at Aachen "*A large elegantly and comfortably furnished house; with a convenient, airy and pleasantly situated salle à manger. The entire establishment is well conducted, with extreme civility and attention on the part of the proprietor and his servants.*" (Coghlan, 1847).

Obrenović, Mihailo: (1823–1868) son of Obrenović, Miloš. The ruling Prince of Serbia from 1839 to 1842 and again from 1860 to 1868. A reformer.

Obrenović, Miloš: (1780 or 1783–1860) leader of the Second Serbian Uprising. Prince of Serbia from 1815 to 1839, and again from 1858 to 1860 and founder of the House of Obrenović.

Oberwesel: above the medieval town of Oberwesel in the Upper Middle Rhine Valley, Rhineland-Palatinate, Germany is a castle called The Schönburg.

Ostler: a person employed to look after the horses of people staying at an inn.

p. jacket: from the Dutch word "pije" meaning coarse wool fabric. A pea coat (or peacoat, pea jacket, pilot jacket, reefer jacket) has broad lapels, double-breasted fronts, large buttons, vertical or slash pockets, originally for naval use or petty officers uniform.

Packet: a boat or vessel travelling at regular intervals between two posts carrying mail, also goods and passengers; a mail boat.

Pallias, palliasse: a straw mattress, usually an under-mattress stuffed with straw.

Palmerston, Lord: (1784–1865) British statesman who was twice Prime Minister of the UK in the mid-19th Century. Palmerston influenced British foreign policy during the period 1830 to 1865 and was foreign secretary from 1846–1851.

Pandour, pandoor or pandwr: a guard, an armed retainer, a member of a local mounted guard. Originally a local force organised by Baron Trenck in 1741 to clear the country near the Turkish frontier of bands of robbers, later a regiment in the Austrian army famed for rapacity and brutality.

Parndorf: (Hungarian: Pándorfalu; Croatian: Pandrof) is a town in the district of Neusiedl am See in the Austrian state of Burgenland.

Pasha, Pacha, Pascha, Paşa, bashaw: a rank in the Ottoman political and military system, typically granted to governors, generals, dignitaries, and others.

Pashaliks, pashalik: a primary administrative division of the Ottoman Empire.

Pashapolanca or Hasan-pašina Palanka or Palanka: now called Smederevska Palanka.

Pavé: cobblestone

Petar: see Žebeljan, Petar

Peterwardein: Petrovaradin – known under the name Pétervárad during the Hungarian administration, Varadin or Petervaradin during Ottoman administration and Peterwardein during Habsburg administration. In Serbian, Петроварадин.

Pfalz: Pfalzgrafenstein Castle, or 'The Pfalz' is a toll castle on the Falkenau island in the River Rhine near Kaub, Germany.

Pisani, Count Alexander Bartholomew Stephen: (1802–1886) a dragoman (interpreter) who worked at the British embassy in Constantinople. *See also endnotes 25 & 26.*

Plenipotentiary minister: a diplomat who has full powers – authorisation to sign a treaty or convention on behalf of his or her sovereign.

Poignon: John Rozel Poignand. Queen's Messenger. Appointed 18th Jan 1845. Retired 2nd Feb. 1867. (Wheeler-Holohan, 1935, p. 281).

Porte: the government of the Ottoman Empire.

Post horse: a horse kept at an inn or post house for use by post riders or for hire to travellers.

Posthouse: a building where post horses were kept. Post riders and travellers would change horses here, exchanging their tired mounts or carriage horses for fresh ones.

Postillion: the driver of a horse-drawn coach or post chaise, mounted on one of the drawing horses, usually on the near, leading horse.

Posting: travelling by means of relays of horses.

Presburgh: Bratislava (Hungarian: Pozsony; German: Pressburg), now the capital of Slovakia.

Prout, Samuel: (1783–1852) British watercolourist, and master of water-colour architectural painting. From 1829 Prout was Painter in Water-Colours in Ordinary to King George IV and afterwards to Queen Victoria.

Quarantine: a period of confinement to stop disease being spread from person to person. Stringent quarantine confinement was practised at the Austrian Empire border, at the border of the Ottoman Empire to guard against the plague and other infectious diseases.

Quarantine, Doctor of: Doctors employed by the state to look after quarantined people, to check them for illness, to treat them if necessary. From

1838, the Ottoman Empire required the Austrian Empire to organise quarantine and the Turkish cordon which extended from the Black Sea to Niš, enlisted the support of Austrian, Italian, German or Polish doctors.

Quarantine Officer: officer who ensured the rules of quarantine were complied with.

Queen's Messenger: Foreign Service Messenger, appointed by the Secretary of State for Foreign Affairs who carries diplomatic despatches, secret and important documents, to and from British embassies, high commissions and consulates around the world.

Quillac's Hotel: Hotel at Calais. *"good and moderate. Charges: bedrooms from 2 fr. to 3 fr.; breakfast, 1 fr. 50c; table d'hote, at 5 o'clock, 3 fr. 50c. Carriages may be hired of Mr Quillac on moderate terms by the journey, month or year."* (Coghlan, 1847).

Radmanović, Ivanka: Serbian poet and translator. Graduated from the Fashion Institute of Technology in New York, where she subsequently worked as a Design Director. In 2013 she returned to Serbia where she writes, translates and teaches yoga. She has three collections of poetry: *Where is My Home* (2016), *Heavenly Cage* (2014) and *Amaranth or About Eternal Love* (2013). *Heavenly Cage* received the prestigious Serbian Milan Rakić Literary Award in 2015.

Raki, rakee, rakis: clear brandy of Turkey and the Balkans made from grapes, plums, raisins or other fruit, flavoured with anise. Usually diluted with water.

Redhouse, Sir James William: (1811–1892) a dragoman (interpreter) to the Porte who wrote a Turkish dictionary which was printed by the Sultan, also produced a published grammar of the Ottoman Language.

Reschid Pasha or Reshid Pasha: Koca Mustafa Reşid Pasha (1800–1858). Ottoman statesman and diplomat, a reformer who was the chief architect behind the Ottoman government reforms known as Tanzimat.

Rheinstein, castle: a castle near the town of Trechtingshausen in Rhineland-Palatinate, Germany.

Rhisto, risto: see Brindish, Rhisto

Rif'at: Turkish Foreign Office Minister, Sadik Rif'at Pasha (1807–1857), Ottoman marshal, statesman and diplomat and twice Grand Vizier of the Ottoman Empire. Sympathetic to the three reforming statesmen of the Tanzimat era (Mustafa Reshid Pasha, Mehmed Emin Âli Pasha and Mehmed Fuad Pasha).

Ridgway, James William: Queen's Messenger. Appointed 13th April 1847. Retired 1st April 1870.

Russie, Hotel de: Hotel at Frankfurt am Main. *"Hotel Russie, first rate establishment; very expensive."* (Coghlan, 1847, p. 156).

St. André, Monsieur Durant: Consul-General of France.

St Stephano: a medieval monastery from the 15th Century built by Despot Stefan Lazarević, St. Stefan in Lipovac, is 25 km from the city. The monastery is built beneath the slopes of Mt. Ozren (1175 m).

Schönbrunn, Palace: the main summer residence of the Habsburg rulers, located in Hietzing, Vienna. The 1,441-room Rococo palace is one of the most important architectural, cultural, and historic monuments in the country.

Schwager: see Postillion. German.

Scimitre, scimitar: a single-edged sword with a convex curved blade.

Semitsch: Aleksa Simić – high-ranking politician. Serbian Prime Minister from October 1843–October 1844 and from March 1853–October 1855 under the rule of King Aleksandar Karadjordjevic (Karađorđević).

Semlin: Zemun, now a municipality of Belgrade, Serbia. It was a separate town until 1934 on the right bank of the Danube, upstream from downtown Belgrade. The development of New Belgrade in the late 20th Century expanded the continuous urban area of Belgrade and merged it with Zemun.

Seraglio: the women's apartments (harem) in an Ottoman palace. From serraculum [Latin] meaning enclosure, place of confinement.

Servia: a historical English term, taken from the Greek language, used in relation to Serbia, Serbs or the Serbian language.

Simplon pass: a high mountain pass between the Pennine Alps and the Lepontine Alps in Switzerland.

Sligovitch, slivovitz: a fruit spirit or fruit brandy made from damson plums, often referred to as plum spirit or plum brandy. In the Balkans, slivovitz is considered to be a type of raki.

Smalt blue: an important pigment in European oil painting, particularly in the 16th and 17th Centuries.

Soave: The Sava, river in Belgrade.

Soko Grad or Sokolac: a medieval city and fortress 2 km east of the spa town of *Sokobanja*. Only a little of the upper town with a gate, walls, and three towers is left.

Sokobanja: a spa town of eastern Serbia situated in the southern part of Sokobanja valley, surrounded by mountains Ozren, Devica, Janior, Rtanj, and Bukovik.

Somlauer: a Hungarian white wine of the second class.

Spencer, Captain, Edmund: prolific British travel writer of the mid-19th Century. Between 1836–1867 published ten books on his visits to the Caucasus, the Ottoman Empire, Prussia, France and the Habsburg Empire.

Staffa: Basaltic columns of the Scottish Island of Staffa.

Stallknecht: groom.

Stambul, stamboul: see Constantinople.

Strengberg: a town in the district of Amstetten in Lower Austria.

Stuttgardt: Stuttgart, the capital and largest city of the German state of Baden-Württemberg, located on the Neckar river in a fertile valley.

Suppositious: fraudulent substitution of another thing or person in place of the genuine one – 1797 (*Shorter OED*, 1933).

Surojee, Soorajee, Serojee: professional groom or porter who accompanied a party to look after the horses. (Wheeler-Holohan, 1935, pp. 157,158)

Surtout: a man's over-frock coat, worn by cavalry officers over their uniforms in the 18th and early 19th Centuries.

Suvla Bay: on the Aegean coast of the Gallipoli peninsula in the Ottoman Empire. The site of a British attempt to break the deadlock of the battle of Gallipoli in the First World War. It began on 6th August 1915 and the British were finally evacuated from Suvla Bay in late December 1915 after heavy losses.

Tambour: small shallow drum.

Tanzimat: or Reorganisation, a period of reform in the Ottoman Empire beginning in 1839 and ending with the First Constitutional Era in 1876.

Tatar: diplomatic couriers of the Principality of Serbia and local couriers for other states. The term comes from Tatar horsemen who were messengers in Anatolia and the Middle East. Tatar came to mean messenger in Ottoman Turkish.

Therapia: a neighbourhood in the Sarıyer district of Istanbul, Turkey (Constantinople) where the British summer embassy was situated.

Tile: Slang – a hat. 1823. OED 1933.

Tower of Skulls: a stone structure embedded with human skulls located in Niš, Serbia constructed by the Ottoman Empire following the Battle of Čegar of May 1809.

Townley, Lieut.-Col. Charles: Queen's Messenger. Appointed 13th April 1840. Retired 1st January 1860.

Trebizond, Trabzon: a city on the Black Sea coast of north-eastern Turkey. Trebizond Eyalet was an eyalet, or administrative area, of the Ottoman Empire. Trabzon Province is now a province of Turkey on the Black Sea coast, the capital of which is Trabzon.

Undine: a popular fairy story of 1811.

Văchitsch: Toma Vučić Perišić, a virulent opponent of Miloš Obrenović was an ally of the Karađorđević Dynasty, against Prince Mihailo Obrenović (son of Prince Miloš Obrenović). He led Vučić's revolt, August 30 to September 7, 1842, proclaiming Aleksandar Karađorđević Prince in Belgrade.

Valet-de-place: a person employed to guide strangers and travellers.

Van John: Blackjack, also called 21 and Pontoon.

Vehigil, Vecihi or Vejihi Pasha: Mehmed Vecihi Pasha, Ottoman military governor of Belgrade Fortress (January 1846–February 1847). Also,

Governor of Bosnia (1835–40), Konya (1841), Diyarbakır (1841–43), Aleppo (1843–45), Mosul (1847–48), Ankara (1848–49 and 1852–55), Bozoka Yozgat (1849–51), Baghdad (1851), Zilka and Kurdistan (1852), Erzurum (1855–57), Selanik (1857–58) and Jeddah (1864).

Verviers: a Walloon city and municipality located in the Belgian province of Liège.

Vidak: see *Maslovarić, Vidak M.*

Vietnam War: Second Indochina War, a conflict in Vietnam, Laos, and Cambodia from 1st November 1955 to the fall of Saigon on 30th April 1975.

Walachia, Wallachia: a historical and geographical region of Romania founded as a principality in the early 14th Century, forced, from 1417 until the 19th Century, to accept partial control by the Ottoman Empire. Wallachia united with Moldavia in 1859, adopted the name Romania in 1866, became the Kingdom of Romania in 1881.

Weinheim: a town in northwest Baden-Württemberg, Germany, known as the 'Zwei-Burgen-Stadt', the 'town of two castles' and is on the Bergstraße.

Wellesley, Henry, 1st Earl Cowley: (1804–1884), also known as The Lord Cowley, a British diplomat. In 1845 he became Minister Plenipotentiary to the Ottoman Empire.

Widin: Vidin, a port town on the southern bank of the Danube in north-western Bulgaria, close to the borders with Romania and Serbia. The name is archaically spelled as Widdin in English. Vidin has a fertile hinterland renowned for its wines.

Wolf's leap: see *Llanwrtyd*

Würtemberg, Württemberg: this kingdom was a German state from 1805 to 1918, located within the area that is now Baden-Württemberg. The kingdom was a continuation of the Duchy of Württemberg, which existed from 1495 to 1805.

Yatagan, yataghan: type of Ottoman knife or short sabre used from the mid-16th to late 19th Centuries.

Žebeljan, Petar: (b.1939) Board Member of the Serbian Writers Association, writer and poet, retired Director of the Radio Belgrade Program and Editor of the Educational Program for RB1. Author of several books about famous Serbian rulers, freedom fighters.

Zinzars: Zinzars or Kutzo-Vlachs are a people of the Pindus range, a mountain range located in Northern Greece and Southern Albania, and Thessaly, a region of northern Greece south of Macedonia, lying between upland Epirus and the Aegean Sea.

Zubović, Branislav: (b.1976) – poet, employed at the 'Danilo Kiš' National Library in Vrbas as editor of the literary and publishing program. Publishes the literary magazine *Trag* (Trans: *Trace*) in Serbia.

Zudcote, Zuydcoote: a commune in the Nord department in northern France and borders Belgium. There was a small French customs and a Belgian customs there.

Zwanziger: an Austrian coin which bore the figure 20 as it represented 20 Kreutzers. In 1846 it was worth about 8d (old British pennies). *"The name Zwanziger properly applies to Austria alone, where this coin which bears upon it the figure 20, goes for 20 Kreutzers. 2½ Zwanzigers make one florin."* (Murray, 1844, p. 2).

Bibliography

(UCTV), U. o. C. T., 2010. *Lunch Poems: Eavan Boland.* [Online] Available at: https://www.youtube.com/watch?v=ERUlybz19H4 [Accessed 8 March 2021].

Anon., 1840. The City of Damascus. *Malta Penny Magazine No. 20,* 25 January, pp. 79-82.

Brewer, E. C., 1894. *Brewer's Dictionary of Phrase and Fable.* London: Cassell & Co.

Burke, J. F. a. C. W. J., 1847. *British husbandry: exhibiting the farming practice in various parts of the United Kingdom /published under the superintendence of the Society for the Diffusion of Useful Knowledge. With a supplement, comprising Modern agricultural improvements /.* London: Robert Baldwin.

Cam., T. C., 1843. Second AENEID of VIRGIL: Aeneas' Tale. A skit.. *Punch,* 16 December, 5(127).

Coghlan, F., 1847. *Handbook for European Tourists through Belgium, Holland, The Rhine, Germany, Switzerland, Italy and France. Including a full description of Paris, the Channel Islands, the fashionable Continental Spas.* 2nd ed. London: H Hughes.

Domeier, E. A., 1830. *A Descriptive Road Book of Germany.* s.l.:Samuel Leigh.

Encyclopaedia Britannica, The Editors of, 1998. *Encyclopaedia Britannica.* [Online] Available at: https://www.britannica.com/place/Wurttemberg. [Accessed 10 March 2021].

Garth, S., n.d. Brave Girls in War. In: *Brave Girls in War.* London: Raphael Tuck & Sons Ltd, pp. 29, 30.

Hall, M. H. B., 1865. *The Queen's Messenger.* London: Jon Maxwell.

Inkel, D., 2005. *Post-chaise Travel.* [Online] Available at: https://www.thetrafalgarway.org/post-chaise-travel [Accessed 14 March 2001].

Knowles, M., 2009. *The Wicked Waltz and other scandalous dances: Outrage at couple dancing in the 19th and early 20th centuries.* London: McFarland & Company.

Lane-Poole, S., 1888. The Life of the Right Honorable Stratford Canning Viscount Stratford de Redcliffe Vol 2. In: s.l.:Longman's Green & Co.

Lewandowski, E. J., 2011. *The Complete Costume Dictionary.* Plymouth: The Scarecrow Press.

Mokyr, J., n.d. *Encyclopaedia Britannica* [Online] Available at: https://www.britannica.com/event/Great-Famine-Irish-history [Accessed 6 March 2021].

Murray, J., 1843. *A Hand-Book for Travellers on the Continent: being a Guide through Holland, Belgium, Prussia, and Northern Germany, and along the Rhine, from Holland to Switzerland. Containing De-*

scriptions of the Principal Cities, their Museums, Picture Galleries, &c.;. London: John Murray.

Murray, J., 1844 . A Hand-Book for Travellers in Southern Gerrmany: Being a Guide to Bavaria, Austria, Tyrol, Salzburg, Syria, &c., the Austrian and Bavarian Alps. London: John Murray.

Murray, J., 1850. A handbook for travellers in southern Germany :being a guide to Würtemberg, Bavaria, Austria, Tyrol, Salzburg, Styria &c., the Austrian and Bavarian Alps, and the Danube from Ulm to the Black Sea.. London: John Murray.

Murray, J., 1873. Handbook for Travellers in Southern Germany: Being a Guide to Wurtemberg, Bavaria, Austria, Tyrol, Salzburg, Styria, &c, the Austrian and Bavarian Alps, And the Danube from Ulm to the Black Sea. 12th ed. London: J Murray.

Ranke, L. v., 1847. History of Servia, and the Servian Revolution: From Original Mss. and Documents. London: John Murray.

Spencer, E., 1851. Travels in European Turkey, in 1850 Through Bosnia, Servia, Bulgaria, Macedonia, Thrace. London: Colburn and Co.

Sumner, I., 2008. Gutch. In: J. Hannavy, ed. Encyclopedia of nineteenth-century photography. s.l.:Taylor & Frances, p. 1587.

Sumner, I. C., 2010. In Search of the Picturesque. The English Photographs of JWG Gutch 1856/59. s.l.: Redcliffe Press.

Taylor, I. a. A., 2000. The Assassin's Cloak. Edinburgh: Canongate Books.

Urquhart, D., 1839. The Spirit of the East: Illustrated in a Journal of Travels. s.l.:Carey & Hart.

Vernon, W. W., 1917. Recollections of seventy-two years. s.l.:John Murray.

Wheeler-Holohan, V., 1935. The History of the King's Messengers. London: Grayson & Grayson Ltd.

Wikipedia, n.d. [Online] Available at: https://en.wikipedia.org/wiki/Serbian_Revolution [Accessed 8 March 2021].

Williams, B., 2001. The Crimean Tatars: The Diaspora Experience and the Forging of a Nation. s.l.:Brill.

Wolff, J., 1846. Narrative of a Mission to Bokhara in the Years 1843–1845: To Ascertain the Fate of Colonel Stoddart and Captain Conolly. 4 ed. s.l.:John W Parker, West Strand.

Yurdusev, E., 2009. The British Ambassadors to Istanbul in the Mid-Nineteenth Century: Sources of Intelligence and Political Reporting. Belleten, 73(267).

Endnotes

1   Eileen Blanche Smyth formerly Gaskell (1895–1981) m. Geoffrey Norman Smyth (1886–1979). They were married Oct 11th, 1924.

2   The international phonetic alphabet is a standardised representation of speech sounds in written form. Speech therapists use IPA in the evaluation, diagnosis, and treatment of communication disorders, and can use IPA to write down distorted speech sounds. Here I have used IPA to present a barrier to the reader. The kind of barrier my mother and uncle lived with daily when trying to make themselves understood to anyone other than close family. For more on IPA see https://en.wikipedia.org/wiki/International_Phonetic_Alphabet.

3   Only we could understand/the assembled/ vowels and consonants / arriving late/ and in disorder.

4   Only the three of them/ could understand his speech/ for us his laugh / became the diagnostic tool.

5   Described at the valuation of property left by Grandpa in March 1979 as 'A George III circular chamber candlestick with beaded edges, the handles with extinguisher fully marked, Maker John Schofield, London 1784, 10 oz.'

6   An extract from my found poem 'Sundry Remarks' first published in *Envoi* magazine. The poem has twelve three-line stanzas, one for each month. Further uses here are noted as 'from my found poem Sundry Remarks'. Details are taken from *British husbandry: exhibiting the farming practice in various parts of the United Kingdom / published under the superintendence of the Society for the Diffusion of Useful Knowledge. With a supplement, comprising Modern agricultural improvements (1847) by Burke, John French and Cuthbert Wm. Johnson.* (Burke, 1847)

7   Described at the valuation of property left by Grandpa in March 1979 as 'A Regency period (1811–1820) black and gold Oriental design lacquer decorated cabinet, the top with neoclassical gallery above five drawers with gilt brass ring handles, enclosed by a door, decorated with chinamen in a pagoda garden, on paw feet.'

8   Mysteriously labelled 'a South Seas small Tekhi of skin'. Grandpa's father, Victor Emmanuel Smyth, whose father owned a grocery shop and wine merchants in St Stephen's Green, Dublin, went on a round-the-world trip in 1875/6 and wrote a journal about it. He travelled with his sister to Australia, New Zealand, Fiji, Hawaii, the United States and Canada. It's possible this artifact was picked up in Fiji on that trip. Of Fiji, he wrote 'We bought some shells off the people on shore and tappa cloth "iperculums" etc. There were lots of curios

for sale at the store in the way of war clubs & spears & but for their inconvenience in travelling I should have purchased heavily.' Victor Emmanuel Smyth, 5th August 1876.

9 HMS Royal George was a Royal Navy ship, launched in 1756, which sank in 1782 with the loss of 800 lives while its hull was being repaired at Spithead off Portsmouth. There is no record of how this fragment was obtained.

10 This penny booklet from Woolworths features my mother, Paddy, and her younger sister Joan (they were born on the same day exactly one year apart), tackling incendiaries in Cardiff during the Second World War. The writer is wrong about their ages and has misspelled their surname which was Smyth: 'Twelve-year-old Joan Smythe and her fourteen-year-old sister Paddy spent hours during a heavy raid tackling incendiary bombs, while high explosives and showers of shrapnel were falling around them. Joan manned the stirrup pump, fetched water and carried urgent messages from warden's post to emergency services through debris-strewn streets' (Garth, n.d., pp. 29, 30). The actual event took place shortly before Saturday March 22, 1941. In a newspaper clipping headed 'It was a darn good show, girls!' below which is a photograph of Paddy and Joan in Girl Guide uniform with bucket and stirrup pump, is an article which says the Girl Guides Association had commended them for 'their fearless efforts in firefighting on a recent night of fire-blitz in one Cardiff suburb. They did a grand job of work, the neighbours say, extinguishing fire-bombs right and left and fighting fires in blazing rooms regardless of the drone of enemy aircraft overhead and the constant shower of shrapnel from our guns. Thirteen-year-old Paddy and 12-year-old Joan, however, say 'It was nothing much...''

11 The handkerchief is attached to a note saying that it belonged to one of the Corkes – Sarah Corke's father, Henry Corke (1776–21st January 1858), who worked for Lord Nelson in 1801. Sarah married George Davies, the writer of our journals, in 1849. Her father had a colourful life. He was sent to France to complete his education and was in Paris during the revolution (1789–99) and she writes that he 'witnessed many of its horrors...'. He barely escaped as, on the way home, he had to disguise himself as a sailor and 'on the voyage they were attacked by a French vessel, captured after a sharp fight, and were being taken back to France when they were retaken by an English man-of-war, after another fight, and brought safely to England. But for this good fortune they would have been consigned to a French prison.' After this, she writes, 'he was sent by his uncle to Gibraltar... Here he obtained an appointment in the Admiralty office and remained some time... He was there when Lord Nelson arrived with the combined fleets and had to sit up all one night

to copy dispatches to send to England, and, not having finished them all as soon as Lord Nelson expected, he was greatly displeased at the delay. This was my father's only meeting with the Admiral.' From an account written for her children by Sarah Davies née Corke.

12 Which may have been brought home by George Davies.

13 The tiny carved ivory elephants are inside a little hollow red seed which comes from the red sandalwood tree, common in India. This seed has a carved stopper on top that fits perfectly.

14 from my found poem 'Sundry Remarks': (Burke, 1847).

15 He had matriculated at the early age of fifteen before studying at Jesus College, Oxford and was enrolled as attorney of Her Majesty's Court of Queen's Bench at Westminster in January 1846, following completion of his Articles of Clerkship, at just twenty-three years old.

16 Mr Gutch, as a qualified Surgeon, would certainly have been considered a gentleman but the regulations for Messengers did not always accord him that treatment, a fact which he considered humiliating and *"obnoxious"*. On April 22nd 1844 in a letter of complaint to Hertslet at the Foreign Office, Mr Gutch makes it very clear that he, and his fellow messengers, should be treated as gentlemen when required to take passage in a war ship, 'When making application for the appointment that I have now the honour of holding; I was given to understand that one of the qualifications required was not only that the candidate should be a Gentleman by birth, but also that he should have received the education of a Gentleman. Possessing both these qualifications, I must own that I could not but feel myself degraded when I was called upon by the regulation of the service to mess daily with the Warrant Officers of the vessel in which I was ordered by Admiral Sir Edward Owen to take my passage. Through the courtesy of Captain Sparkes, the Commander of H M Ship "Polyphemus", this obnoxious regulation was considerately waived, and also in the subsequent instance of Captain Carpenter on board the H M S "Geyser", in both of which vessels I was permitted to mess at the Captain's table; but I must say, much as I felt the kindness and politeness exercised towards me by each of these Gentlemen, still it would have been much more agreeable to my feelings had I been able to claim that as a right which was only conceded to me as a favour: and which, moving in the sphere of life that I have ever been accustomed to, I humbly submit I had a full right to expect'.

17 Byron, who had travelled extensively in Europe and the Ottoman Empire, must have represented for George the romance and adventure of travel. George appears to have had a thorough knowledge of Byron's work, quoting in these journals from *Childe Harold*, *The Curse of Minerva*, *Don Juan*, *The Giaour* and *The Corsair*.

18 George had previously used the first few pages of the notebook to record accounts and clothing details and money which had been borrowed from his mother's sister, Aunt Cordelia, Cordelia J Cox (1807-1864). At the time of the census of 1861, she was visiting Mr Gutch and his wife Elizabeth along with Mr Gutch's brother-in-law James O Nicholson. There may have been a longstanding family friendship which might be how George originally arranged to travel with Mr Gutch.

19 The European Union put paid to the need for internal borders which are completely open between countries that signed the Schengen Agreement of 1985: no passports, visas, and border inspections are required. The euro is the official currency of 19 of the 27 member states of the European Union. Compare this with the borders and currencies our 19th century travellers had to contend with. You'll find just a few of the European currencies in use in the 1840s highlighted in the poem 'In Sight of Mountains'. My favourite of these old currencies is, of course, the Asper which was 'only imaginary'. Borders are apparent everywhere in the text. It should be noted that, Serbia, not in the Union, still presents with borders and currency of its own, and Hungary, in the Union, has its own currency.

20 An English person who thinks England is better than all other countries, and that England should only work together with other countries when there is an advantage for England in doing so.

21 'In 1710 Emperor Joseph I decided to block the chronic spread of diseases from the Balkans by creating a continuous "sanitary cordon" along the Habsburg monarchy's southern frontier with the Ottoman Empire. By the middle of the 18th century, 2,000 fortified watchtowers stood every half mile, punctuated by nineteen border crossings with facilities that registered, housed and isolated everyone entering for at least twenty-one days before granting them passports to enter the [Austrian] empire's territory. Quarters were disinfected daily with sulphur or vinegar and trade goods graded on their susceptibility to transmitting germs. Habsburg agents posted to Ottoman territory provided intelligence that enabled officials to adjust quarantine times—or even temporarily suspend them.' See https://cla.umn.edu/austrian/story/cas-exclusive-emperor-josephs-solution-coronavirus.

22 Stratford Canning, 1st Viscount Stratford de Redcliffe, KG, GCB, PC (1786-1880) was a British diplomat who became best known as the long-standing British Ambassador to the Ottoman Empire. 'At that period there was a struggle for power in Istanbul between the Reform Party, of which Reschid Pasha was the head, and those Turkish statesmen who were opposed to European institutions, which Sultan Mahmoud had previously attempted to introduce into the government of his empire. The most active and powerful of the conservatives was Riza Pasha,

who exercised great influence over the Sultan, Abdul-Mejid. Stratford supported the reform party and established a constant and intimate communication with Reschid Pasha and his principal followers, such as Aali and Fuad Effendis. These communications were carried out in a very secret and confidential manner through Layard (a secret agent).' (Yurdusev, 2009).

23   The Sublime Porte, also called Porte, is the government of the Ottoman Empire. The name is a French translation of Turkish Bâbıâli ("High Gate," or "Gate of the Eminent") which was the official name of the gate giving access to the block of buildings in Constantinople, or Istanbul, that housed the principal state departments. Early in the history of the Ottoman Empire, the grand viziers became powerful, but only in the 17th century did they acquire the official residence, Bâb-ı Âli or Babıali, which became the real centre of government. There, too, were the offices of the foreign ministry and the council of state; hence the application of the term to the government as a whole. (*Encyclopaedia Britannica*).

24   Sir Stratford Canning, British Ambassador at Constantinople, was preparing for a leave of absence, due to start in May, but which was postponed to July of 1846. (Lane-Poole, 1888, p. 143).

25   Count Alexander Bartholomew Stephen Pisani worked at the British Embassy in Constantinople as a dragoman (interpreter). Levantine people were mostly employed as dragomans and many of the Pisani family were employed as such. For more on this fascinating subject see https://deepblue.lib.umich.edu/bitstream/handle/2027.42/133502/castigfr_1.pdf?sequence=1.

26   This letter, from the Hertslet Papers, confirms that despatches were liable to be interfered with by spies and that some *local* couriers were corruptible. Queen's Messengers were employed by the British Government to keep the dispatches they carried safe from any other eyes but those for whom they were intended. There was a thorough investigation following this initial letter of warning and the Foreign Service Messenger, T D Wright, on his return from Alexnitza, was asked to write a report of the incident as it had appeared to him: 'Foreign Office, April 17th, 1845. Sir, the Tatar Tassa delivered to me at Alexnitza the three bags of Despatches and two packets mentioned in Count Pisani's letter; one of these packets, which was directed to the French Chargé d'affaires at Constantinople, was torn open and I examined it in presence of three Tatars who happened to be in the room – I enquired of the Courier Tassa how it had happened & he told me "He did not know". The Turkish Tatar to whom I was about to deliver the Despatches, drew my attention to the binding round the neck of the largest of the bags, which appeared as if it had been drawn off & very badly put on again. Tassa the Tatar told me that it had been broken by the jolting on horseback, which appeared to me not improbable as it was

very large and unsuitable for conveyance on horseback. I examined the two smaller bags & the seals were untouched. I did not observe anything particular in the seals of Mr de Fonblanque's packet. The Tatar Rassab Moustapha's assertion that he refused to take charge of the bags is not true, for I never required him to take them in the state in which they came. I reported the matter to the Embassy at Constantinople, & as I considered the conduct of the Tatar Tassa suspicious (to say the least) I did not employ him to return with me to Belgrade, where I thought it right to mention the circumstance to the Consul General, to put him on his guard against this Tatar. I have the honour to remain, Sir, Your Very Obedient Humble Servant, T D Wright' (Foreign Service Messenger from 1837 to 1862).

27   Tatar – 'hardy Tatar horsemen who were unrivalled for their duration & equine skills served throughout Anatolia and the Middle East as messengers. The Tatar name became so closely linked to this duty that the term Tatar came to mean messenger in Ottoman Turkish' (Williams, 2001, p. 234). In Serbia at that time to be a Tatar was a profession as they were, in addition to their use by other states needing local couriers, diplomatic couriers of the Principality of Serbia. After the outbreak of the First Serbian Uprising, Karadjordj, to retain fast and secure communications, took over from the Turks the well-developed Ottoman network for transmitting messages. Serbian tatars were named for their speed and dexterity, so these were non-Tatar tatars, trusted with important documents. See https://www.011info. com/bilo-jednom-u-beogradu/poslednji-srpski-tatarin. Via Ivanka Radmanović.

28   Miloš Obrenović, leader of the Second Serbian Uprising. Prince of Serbia and founder of the House of Obrenović, or his son Mihailo. See: https://en.wikipedia.org/wiki/Milo%C5%A1_Obrenovi%C4%87_I_ of_Serbia.

29   Mr Gutch married, on 12th December 1832, Elizabeth Frances Nicholson (1811–1869). They had one child in 1838, a son, John, who died at four years and four months. His gravestone was inscribed with the Epitaph *On an Infant*, by Coleridge (1794). Gutch's father had been a friend of Coleridge: 'E're sin could blight or sorrow fade/death came with friendly care/the opening bud to Heaven conveyed/and bade it blossom there'. At the time of this letter, therefore, Elizabeth was thirty-five years old. Their son had died four years earlier. No further children were born. We do not know if she had the operation advised here but she lived on until 1869 when she was fifty-seven and died of heart failure.

30   A list was kept of foreign service messengers who were at home and ready to go out. When the messenger's name came to the top of the list, he would be sent out in strict order to whichever country next

had need of a messenger. It was frowned on to manipulate the list, by illness or other excuses, to do the easy journeys such as Paris and avoid the long arduous journeys such as to Serbia, Constantinople etc. The order was set out thus: 'It is hereby ordered that the First Messenger upon the List for Foreign Service shall henceforward, and unless valid ground of exception be shown to exist, undertake the First Journey or Station that shall be announced to him by the Superintendent, from which moment he shall be considered as fixed for that Duty. Periodical Stations or Journeys shall be considered as announced and fixed, at 6 o'clock of the Third Day immediately preceding that for which a Messenger's departure for such Stations or Journeys is usually appointed.' (signed) H. U. Addington. Foreign Office, April 24th 1844. (Hertslet Papers).

31   Puerperal infection (especially after childbirth) was rife at the time due to doctors passing infection from woman to woman through not washing hands. It wasn't until the 1870s onwards that infection control was more widely acknowledged, and infections were not thought to be vapours in the air, mysteriously carried, and it was well into the 20th Century before the use of antibiotics and strict infection control made childbirth and women's operations in general much safer.

32   A found poem using detail from: (Coghlan, 1847, pp. xvii-xxii).

33   Two months and two days after the letter sent by Mrs Gutch's medical attendant, saying she is seriously ill, Mr Gutch sets off for Serbia with George. Did she have the operation, was she by that time recovered? We simply do not know. The journey to and from Serbia, with time waiting for despatches at Alexnitza, would routinely take messengers about two months so Gutch must have had some anxieties about leaving his wife for so long as she had recently been so seriously ill.

34   'HMS Onyx (1845) was an iron paddle packet launched in 1845 and sold in 1854. From 1820 until 1837 the British Post Office carried mail between Dover and Calais, on steamships which were built specially; and those Government steamers were the most reliable, and so took the ordinary passenger traffic, as well as conveying Queen's Messengers and Royal personages. In 1837 the Post Office transferred the Dover and Calais Mail service from their own vessels to the Admiralty, which continued to carry mail and passengers on the Dover and Calais route for seventeen years. Great improvements were made in the speed and comfort of steam packets on the Passage. Amongst the steamers on the Passage, in 1846, the swiftest were the 'Princess Alice', the 'Onyx', and the 'Violet'. The average time of the 'Onyx' between Dover and Calais from 1846 to 1848 was one hour and twenty-five minutes.' https://www.dover.uk.com/history/1916/annals-of-dover/the-passage/post-office-and-admiralty-packets (retrieved 27/08/21). The Dover to Calais crossing is

currently advertised to take one hour and thirty minutes.

35 Messengers at this time were required to supply their own carriages. Hertslet Papers discussion on messengers' carriages: Memorandum Respecting the Charge for Carriages: 'Messengers might be required to supply themselves with Carriages; – a certain Sum per mile being allowed to them in lieu of all expenses of purchase, hire, repairs, or standing. This is the most simple and probably, the most economic Plan, as the Expense will always be precisely in proportion to the Extent of the Journey performed, wherever the Messenger might land. It is also the most convenient, as each Messenger is already provided with a Carriage purchased by himself; and it will certainly be the best, to insure the employment of good carriages, without which the journeys cannot be performed with the required expedition, as the Messenger will be anxious for their own reputation, as well as advantage, to keep them in the best possible state of repair.' *The National Archives, Kew* FO351/10 (c. 1824).

36 'Aix la Chapelle to Cologne by rail – 2 hrs by fast train or three by the others. Trains three times a day to Cologne.' (Coghlan, 1847, p. 87). The average travel time now is 34 minutes.

37 See (Murray, 1843, p. 245) for more detail on the state of the building of Cologne Cathedral – the crane had been there for hundreds of years 'it was once taken down; but a tremendous thunder storm, which occurred soon after, was attributed to its removal by the superstitious citizens, and it was therefore instantly replaced... Its permanent presence there may have indicated that at no period was the idea of completing this noble structure entirely abandoned'. Murray goes on to say that large annual grants from 1824 to 1842 had been made by the late and present Kings of Prussia to repair the structure rather than build it higher as it had been falling into disrepair. It was finally completed to its original Medieval plan in 1880.

38 'Badische Hof' (Court of Baden). (Coghlan, 1847, p. 165).

39 Lunch of meat or solid food, a French expression from the mid-18th century; lunch with the cup was taken in the morning, lunch with the fork at midday, made up of meat and solid foods requiring the use of fork which then had two tines.

40 But (Coghlan, 1847) has it as Goldene Traube.

41 from my found poem 'Sundry Remarks': (Burke, 1847).

42 *See letter on page 69* dated 20th May 1846 written by Mr Gutch re £100 expenses – this seems likely to have been due to having missed the steamer at Vienna and subsequently having to post with the carriage for 50 to 60 hours, which would have incurred extra expense, rather than going by steamer.

43 Separated by the Danube River, Buda and Pest (old name Pesth), form the two halves of Budapest. The Széchenyi Chain Bridge linked them

in 1849 having been in construction since 1840. Pest is the eastern, mostly flat part of Budapest, comprising about two thirds of the city. It is separated from Buda and Óbuda, the western parts of Budapest, by the Danube. The spelling Pesth was occasionally used in English, even as late as the early 20th century, although it is now considered archaic.

44 from my found poem 'Sundry Remarks' (Burke, 1847).

45 A shortened version of the Hungarian equivalent of 'Giddy up'. George makes a note of this at the end of the 1846 journal. *See p100.*

46 'Selma', by former Yugoslav rock band, Bijelo Dugme (trans: The White Button) in their debut album, *Kad bi bio bijelo dugme* (trans: *If you were a white button*) 1974. Lyrics for 'Selma' written 1949 by poet Vlado Dijak. Translation of the song reproduced in stanza's two and four by Ivanka Radmanović, 2019. The song tells of a young woman called Selma on a train on her way to university.

47 For details see https://en.wikipedia.org/wiki/Novi_Sad_raid. The Raid was a military operation carried out by the armed forces of Hungary, during World War II, after the Hungarian occupation and annex-ation of former Yugoslav territories. 3,000–4,000 civilians died in the southern Bačka region. In Novi Sad at least 1,246 men, women and children were killed of whom 809 were Jews and 375 were Serbs. The commemorative statue by the sculptor Jovan Soldatović was erected in 1971 in Novi Sad, on the spot where the bodies of victims were tossed into the Danube. The inscription at the base of the statue reads: 'Memory is a monument harder than stone. If we are human, we must forgive, but not forget'.

48 'Semlin, from its position upon the frontier of Austria and Servia, (the last Hungarian town upon the right bank of the Danube near the junction of the Danube, Save, and Theiss, and upon the high road from Vienna to Constantinople, is a place of considerable trade and passage. It is the Quarantine Station for travellers coming overland from Turkey, who are compelled to pass 10 days, which are augmented to 20 and 40 (according to the violence or proximity of the plague), in the Lazaretto (Contumatz) here. It is a large piece of ground, fenced in by high walls and stockades, inclosing a number of cottages, each surrounded by a separate palisade, and allotted to a particular lodger, for the period of his detention. The inmates are supplied with meals by a restauranteur in the town. Persons on the outside are forbidden to hold direct communication with those within, but are allowed to approach within a few yards of the paling, and may thus converse with the detenus, and examine them shut within their cages like wild beasts in a menagerie... The distance across the Save to Belgrade is 2 m. but owing to the quarantine extended between the two countries, no one is allowed to cross over from Semlin except he be accompanied by a

health officer or guardian, and he must return to Semlin before sunset. If he breaks these conditions, or touches anything after landing on the Servian bank, or allows anything to touch him, he must go into the Lazaretto for 10 days on his return' (Murray, 1850, p. 502).

49 Kalemegdan, Belgrade Fortress, historically an important site, especially during this period. See https://en.wikipedia.org/wiki/Belgrade_Fortress and also https://www.beogradskatvrdjava.co.rs/o-kompleksu/?lang=en# istorijat

50 See https://en.wikipedia.org/wiki/Princess_Ljubica%27s_Residence

51 Numerous studies have been done to try to identify the cause of the increased cancer rates in Serbia. Some confirm and some deny the theory that they have been caused by depleted uranium. See, for example, https://borgenproject.org/5-facts-about-cancer-in-serbia/

52 Stari dvor (Serbian Cyrillic: Стари двор, lit. 'Old Palace') was the royal residence of the Obrenović dynasty. Today it houses the City Assembly of Belgrade, located on the corner of Kralja Milana and Dragoslava Jovanovića streets in Belgrade, Serbia, opposite Novi dvor (New Palace). See: https://en.wikipedia.org/wiki/Stari_dvor

53 New Belgrade was built after 1948 in a previously uninhabited swampy area on the left bank of theSava River, opposite old Belgrade. Over 200,000 workers and engineers helped build it using rural work brigades for manual labour and high school and university student volunteers. It was backbreaking labour, day and night. Mixing of concrete and spreading sand were done by hand with horses used only for very heavy lifting. https://en.wikipedia.org/wiki/New_Belgrade.

54 The Serbian Writers Association divides up the visiting international poets into groups which are sent out to different areas of Serbia to give readings and meet local writers.

55 Monastery of Rakovica. The event took place at, and was organised by, the Cultural Centre of Rakovica. A literal translation of the name of the event is The Festival of Spiritual Poetry, but a closer translation is The Festival of Religious Poetry, since most of the poetry there is dedicated to God, different saints, monasteries or the religious and/or historical events that at this point have a biblical meaning for Serbs. (via Ivanka Radmanović).

56 Ivanka later told me that the costumes showed episodes in the life of one of the most famous Serbian Poets, Milan Rakić (1876–1938), and that the poetry award, issued every year by the Association of Serbian Writers carries his name.

57 'Eight years ago, there were only a handful of libraries run by volunteers – around 10, estimates *Public Libraries News*. These days, 500 of the UK's 3,800 libraries are operated by ordinary people, working for free in a role once regarded as a profession. The rise of volunteer libraries goes

hand in hand with closures: in 2017 alone, 105 public libraries around the country closed, according to the Chartered Institute of Public Finance and Accountancy, bringing the total number of closures since they began counting in 2010 to almost 600'. 25ᵗʰ June 2018 https://www. theguardian.com/books/2018/jun/25/do-libraries-run-by-volunteers-check-out.

58 Ivanka later told me that her contemporary at school who lived in this house was the only child and heir of the entire extended family because all of them had died young, as he also later did himself.

59 Pandour: usually a soldier noted for brutality, see glossary, but here this retainer seems to be a groom. Perhaps an ex-soldier acting as a groom.

60 He was working on the second treaty of Erzurum which was completed and signed in 1847.

61 Reshid or Reschid – was a reformer and a friend of Canning's. See endnotes 22 & 95.

62 (Lane-Poole, 1888, p. 158). I love the humour in this leave-taking.

63 After 6pm the quarantine rules would have been broken. See endnote 48 for details.

64 The trip to Mehadia is a sightseeing trip.

65 Both spellings [Walachia, Wallachia] are in general use.

66 Possibly this was Mariţica Bibescu, born Maria Văcărescu, also known as Mariţica Ghica (1815–1859), the Princess-consort of Wallachia between September 1845 and June 1848. A boyaress (A boyar or bolyar was a member of the highest rank of the feudal Bulgarian, Russian, Wallachian, Moldavian, and later Romanian, Lithuanian and Baltic German nobility) by birth, she belonged to the Văcărescu family. Her father Nicolae, her grandfather Ienăchiţă and her uncle Alecu were politicians and professional writers; Mariţica herself was an unpublished poet.

67 Xenophon, who wrote *Anabasis*. What the princess might have written after meeting George and while thinking of Xenophon's work, perhaps.

68 Baths of Mehardia or Roman Thermae Herculis, 12 miles from Orşova, in today's Romania. 'Instead of remaining there [Orşova], the best mode of employing the time is to pay a visit to the Baths of Mehadia, about 12 miles distant, where they will find better accommodation than is to be met with at Orsova[...] The road […] passes about half way, a stone aquaduct of 11 arches more than 30 feet high, of Turkish origin, constructed to convey the mineral waters of Mehadia to Orsova. The Baths of Mehadia were known to the Romans under the name "Thermae Herculis" [...] It is a much frequented watering place [...] It consists of about a dozen lodging houses, half-barrack, half inn, and of

an hospital for invalid soldiers, all belonging to the government. The large house built by the Emperor on the left hand is provided with assembly, and billiard rooms, and there is a daily table d'hote during the season[...] The waters are sulphureous [...] and they issue from 22 different sources[...] The situation of Mehadia is very romantic, at the bottom of a very deep and narrow glen of limestone, clothed with wood, except near the summit, which is topped by bare white precipices. The principal Source, that of Hercules, is situated higher up the valley than the rest [...] it is a torrent of hot water [...] nearly 2 feet in diameter, issuing out of a cave or rent in the rock.' (Murray, 1844, p. 459).

69 Belgrade Ethnographic Museum note to the display of walking sticks: 'From the shepherd's hooks to walking sticks and those staked to a man's *grove*, there is a recognised need for the sticks to become one of the symbols of personal, societal, ethnic or confessional identity through their shape function and ornamentation. The shepherds used their sticks as hooks in order to pull sheep closer for milking or administering medicine. The old and the infirm used sticks for walking; sticks were a symbol of status for a kmet, a knez and an obarknez [sic]. They were ornamented with carvings of crosses, eagles or wolves, Serbian coat of arms, and some were coated with snakeskin. In this way the owner of the stick was protected from both real and outworldly forces, while the others were introduced to the social status of the person carrying the stick'.

70 During Ottoman times, a kmet or serf in the Principality of Serbia was not a feudal serf, but a respected individual, often a farmer, chosen by others to be a judge. A knez was a duke and an obor-knez was a Senior Chief of a District.

71 A favourite stick would be staked to a man's *grave*, then engraved on his headstone: 'The walking stick was staked as the masculinity symbol at the head of the new grave of a departed (male), and it would stay there until the headstone was ready to be placed at the grave site. At that point the cane was engraved into the headstone. Many headstones in Serbia have engravings of walking sticks, smoking pipes, umbrellas or a distaff (if it was a female grave). This was done to indicate if the person buried in the grave was male or female, young or old, what was their occupation during their lifetime.' *Bulletin of the Museum of Ethnography of Serbia*, author Milica Matić-Bošković. Trans: Ivanka Radmanović.

72 "Germ" temperature scale is the Réaumur scale, a temperature scale for which the freezing and boiling points of water are defined as 0 and 80 degrees respectively. The actual conversion here would be 112 fahrenheit to 35.55 Réaumur. The Réaumur scale was used widely in Europe, particularly in France, Germany and Russia & was used commonly in some parts of Europe until at least the mid-19th century.

73 'from peak to peak the rattling crags among, leaped the live thunder' Byron, 'Childe Harold'.

74 Details from (Murray, 1844, p. 458) A wooden shed in Orşova where the market was held three times a week. The different nationalities were separated at market due to quarantine regulations, not being allowed to mix or touch each other's goods so as not to carry plague to their respective countries when they returned from trading.

75 From 27th July 1841 the Chief Clerk of the Foreign Office was George W. Lenox-Conyngham.

76 It seems likely that Mr Gutch had to draw extra funds at Vienna because he could not take the steamer at Vienna and had to finance the more expensive 50-60 hours of posting in his carriage instead.

77 Or possibly Rasctchka (the handwriting is very unclear here).

78 The Battle of Navarino was a naval battle fought on 20th October 1827, during the Greek War of Independence (1821–32), in Navarino Bay (modern Pylos). Allied forces from Britain, France, and Russia decisively defeated Ottoman and Egyptian forces trying to suppress the Greeks, thereby making Greek independence much more likely.

79 It is not entirely clear from the text which revolution is being referred to here, but it is most likely to refer to Vučić's revolt, a revolt, led by Toma Vučić Perišić, a virulent opponent of Miloš Obrenović and an ally of the Karađorđević Dynasty, against Prince Mihailo Obrenović (son of Prince Miloš Obrenović). The revolt lasted from August 30 to September 7, 1842, when Prince Mihailo was forced to leave Serbia and his position as prince. Vučić then, as the 'leader of the people', proclaimed Aleksandar Karađorđević Prince in Belgrade. Mihailo Obrenović was again the Prince of Serbia from 1860 to 1868.

80 The simple letter L, in lower or upper case, was used to represent the pound in printed books and newspapers until well into the 19th century.

81 A 24-carat diamond would weigh 4.8 grams, so this is a large and expensive diamond.

82 from my found poem 'Sundry Remarks' (Burke, 1847).

83 Townley, a Queen's Messenger, see glossary, wrote in a letter: 'I had felt some pain in the morning from an old musket wound, but nothing to cause me any uneasiness, and as I had been three days in the saddle without cessation, I attributed it to the great exertion, and thought it would go off after my bath. I found however, on undressing, that my linen was covered with blood' Extract from a letter about his journey from Belgrade to Therapia, a journey of over 500 miles, in November 1849 (Wheeler-Holohan, 1935, p. 195) during which he was taking urgent messages to the Ambassador at Constantinople. See http://www.levantineheritage.com/therap.htm.

84 Found poem using details from Townley's letter (Wheeler-Holohan, 1935, p. 195).

85 These figures are taken from The National Archives, Kew: FO 366/496/ 494 (*Hertslet Papers*).

86　Charles Townley describes Rhisto Brindish in a letter written in 1849 as 'our old and confidential Tatar' 'one of the best men I know' 'I beheld him rush out of the house, and the next moment seizing hold of my hand, cover it with kisses, whilst the tears ran down his weather-beaten face' 'quiet, energetic, attentive'. (Wheeler-Holohan, 1935, pp. 192, 195).

87　*Punch* Volume 5 Issue No 127: 'Since then I have wandered by sea and by land/ Till tossed by a storm on your majesty's strand;/And now, by your leave, we'll have ale and cigars, /And wind up the evening like children of mars!' (Cam., 1843, p. 264).

88　In the 1840s Albania was part of the Ottoman Empire but during the 19th and 20th Centuries political and social movements began to establish it as an independent country. The Reforms of Tanzimat (1839–76), the publication of the first Albanian alphabet (1844), the collapse of the League of Prizren (1881), the publication of Sami Frashëri's nationalist manifesto (1899) all contributed to the establishment of Albania as an independent country within its present borders in 1912.

89　There not being enough proper bedrooms when more than a couple of Messengers were in residence, it seems. Messengers routinely overlapped so that there was a constant messenger presence for movement of despatches in both directions.

90　A re-working of 'An Off-the-shoulder Number', *Bone Monkey*, Shears- man Books, 2014 (p51).

91　Possibly Tchupria (Ćuprija), a station on the second Principal Road described in a list of Stations by Post in the Messenger Regulations, 6 miles or 4 to 4½ hours.

92　Lord Byron, 'Childe Harold's Pilgrimage', Canto III (1816).

93　Henry Peter Brougham, 1st Baron Brougham and Vaux (1778–1868). British statesman who became Lord High Chancellor and played a prominent role in passing the 1832 Reform Act and 1833 Slavery Abol- ition Act. He never regained government office after 1834 but played an active role in the House of Lords. I do not know why George wrote to him.

94　from my found poem 'Sundry Remarks': (Burke, 1847).

95　Reshid (or Reschid) Pasha. Canning wrote 'Among the ministers, whether in office or expectant, Reshid Pasha was the one who in sentiment and policy sympathised most with me'. (Lane-Poole, 1888, pp. 104-110). Reshid was a reformer who had been the Sultan's Ambas- sador in London. Also known as Koca Mustafa Reşid Pasha (literally Mustafa Reşid Pasha the Great; 13 March 1800-7 January 1858). He was an Ottoman statesman and diplomat, known as the chief architect behind the Ottoman government reforms known as Tanzimat. He entered public service at an early age and rose rapidly, becoming ambassador to France (1834), to the UK (1836) and (1838), minister for foreign affairs (1837), and to France (1841) (and 1843). He helped settle the Oriental Crisis of 1840, and aided in peace negotiations of the Crimean War. Between 1845 and 1857, he held the office of Grand Vizier six times. He was well acquainted with European politics and national and international affairs. His efforts to promote reforms within the Ottoman government led to the advancement of the careers of many other reformers, such as Fuad Pasha and Mehmed Emin Âli Pasha. *See also* endnotes 22 & 61.

96 Mrs Redhouse, the wife of Mr Redhouse, a dragoman to the Porte who had written a Turkish dictionary which had been printed by the Sultan and a published grammar of the Ottoman Language. (Wolff, 1846, pp. 450-460). *See also* (Yurdusev, 2009) for more information on Mr Redhouse, and others, on how information was gathered in the Embassies.

97 Turkish Foreign Office Minister, Sadik Rif'at Pasha.

98 (Lane-Poole, 1888, p. 158).

99 Byron, 'Curse of Minerva'.

100 L. slept in another Airbnb for a few days because of my cough.

101 Missing text not inserted into empty brackets. The missing word is probably *raki*, an alcoholic drink made of twice-distilled grapes and anise. It is the national drink of Turkey and is popular in other Balkan countries as an aperitif.

102 Gutch had left Britain for Italy in 1831 to become a private physician in Florence and lived there until 1835 so was likely fluent in Italian.

103 from my found poem 'Sundry Remarks': (Burke, 1847).

104 Skull Tower, Ćele Kula, a stone structure embedded with human skulls located in Niš, Serbia. Constructed by the Ottomans following the Battle of Čegar of May 1809, during the First Serbian Uprising. Serbian rebels commanded by Stevan Sinđelić were surrounded by the Ottomans on Čegar Hill, near Niš. Knowing that he and his fighters would be impaled if captured, Sinđelić detonated a powder magazine within the rebel entrenchment, killing himself, his men and the approaching Ottoman soldiers. The Governor of the Rumelia Eyalet, Hurshid Pasha, ordered that the heads of the rebels be skinned, stuffed and sent to Sultan Mahmud II and a tower be made from the skulls. The tower is 4.5 metres (15ft) high, and originally contained 952 skulls embedded on four sides in 14 rows. Following the Ottoman withdrawal from Niš in 1878, the tower was roofed over. As of 2022, 58 skulls remain embedded in Skull Tower's walls, some were removed

by relatives for burial, others taken. The one that is said to belong to Sinđelić is enclosed in a glass container adjacent to the structure.

105 There is no further reference to this – nor what happened to it.

106 Slobodan Milošević (20 August 1941-11 March 2006) was a Yugoslav and Serbian politician and the President of Serbia (originally the Socialist Republic of Serbia, a constituent republic within the Socialist Federal Republic of Yugoslavia) from 1989 to 1997 and President of the Federal Republic of Yugoslavia from 1997 to 2000. In 1999 he was charged by the International Criminal Tribunal for the former Yugoslavia (ICTY) with war crimes in connection with the Bosnian War, the Croatian War of Independence, and the Kosovo War. He was extradited to the ICTY to stand trial for war crimes in 2001. He conducted his own defence in the five-year trial, which ended without a verdict when he died in his prison cell in The Hague on 11 March 2006. The International Court of Justice found he had had violated the Genocide Convention.

107 Including the theft carried out by George.

108 The current fortification is of Ottoman Turkish origin, built from 1719-1723 but was erected on the site of earlier fortifications – the ancient Roman, Byzantine, and Medieval forts. During World War I it was occupied by Bulgarians who turned it into a prison where Serbian patriots were imprisoned and tortured.

109 'Serbia has a substantial burden of cancer deaths, which might be a consequence of the depleted uranium bombs used by NATO in 1999 during air strikes, according to media reports'. https://www.thelancet. com/pdfs/journals/lanonc/PIIS1470-2045(21)00397-1.pdf

110 Dušan Radović (1922–1984) born Niš, Serbia, was a Serbian journalist and writer who for many years presented a good morning show on Belgrade radio. He was known for his poetry (especially children's poetry), prose, television screenplays, and for his aphorisms. Some of his most influential works are *Beograde, dobro jutro 1* (1977), *Beograde, dobro jutro 2* (1981), *Beograde, dobro jutro 3* (1984), all three collections of aphorisms.

111 Mehmed or Mehemet Emin Âli Pasha, also spelled as Mehmed Emin Aali (1815–1871) – in 1846 Ottoman Minister of Foreign Affairs, was a prominent Ottoman statesman during the Tanzimat period, best known as the architect of the Ottoman Reform Edict of 1856, and for his role in the Treaty of Paris (1856) that ended the Crimean War. Âli Pasha was widely regarded as a deft and able statesman, often credited with preventing an early break-up of the empire, advocating for a western style of reform to modernise the empire, including secularisation of the state and improvements to civil liberties. He held the position of Foreign Minister seven times and Grand Vizier five

times in his lifetime.

112 Missing name left blank in text – possibly Wassif Mehemet Bey, Pasha of Nissa. (Spencer, 1851, p. 154).

113 Might possibly refer to Seignor Georgio Mostrass, a Russian Consul of the 1830s or more likely simply an exclamation about gorging on all the food.

114 Aunt E was Emma Anne Cox (1810–1895) who lived in Bristol. Her sister was Cordelia who is mentioned in the journal as lending money to George. Another sister was Blanche and the three of them are mentioned in George's wife, Sarah's, eight page family history. Their parents were Caroline Fortnum (India, 1778–1850) and Samuel Cox (1753-1809). There were other siblings too.

115 He went back to sleeping in the spare room – entered through hole in wall, described earlier.

116 The messengers overlap – a new messenger arrives at Alexnitza before the messenger already there starts the journey home. There was always a messenger presence at Alexnitza, always someone available to handle urgent dispatches.

117 Probably Soko Grad fortress. See glossary.

118 Very difficult to transcribe due to faded and impossible handwriting, possibly: um zu fragen (in order to ask) lrbrn? für norgt (for worries).

119 Tchupria (Ćuprija).

120 The earliest Serb *gymnasium* was founded here on 3 August 1791. Three years later, an Orthodox seminary was also founded here, the second oldest Orthodox seminary in the world (after the Spiritual Academy in Kiev) and is still in existence.

121 Actually Stuhlweissenburg (German name) or Székesfehérvár known colloquially as Fehérvár ('white castle').

122 As it was the time for women's bathing, 9am until 12 noon, he couldn't have a bath at that time – see note on the Diana Baths below. That is why he went back at 2pm for his bath.

123 Imperial Carriage Museum Vienna (Kaiserliche Wagenburg Wien).

124 The Liechtenstein Museum in Vienna, Austria, contains much of the art collection of the rulers of the principality of Liechtenstein – an important private art collection. The museum had various locations, at the beginning of the 19th century, Prince Johann I of Liechtenstein (1760–1836) decided to transfer most of his extensive art collection into the Garden Palace in the Rossau district. There, from 1810, they were made accessible to the public for the first time.

125 The Diana Baths, 9 Leopoldstadt. 'Dianabad, in the Leopoldstadt, also an excellent Establishment, to which is attached the Winter-Schwimmschule, with 104 dressing rooms, and a swimming-bath 118 Eng. Ft. long, and 68 1/2 ft. wide, and holding 187,000 gallons of filtered

Danube water, constantly renewed. A bath-ticket (including towels, bathing trousers, and attendance) 40 kr. Each person. The bath is set apart for the use of ladies from 9 to 12 a.m.' (Murray, 1873, p. 204).

126 The Volksgarten (English: *People's Garden*) a public park in the Innere Stadt first district of Vienna, Austria. The garden, which is part of the Hofburg Palace, was laid out by Ludwig Remy in 1821. The Volksgarten opened to the public in 1823.

127 The neoclassical sculpture (1805–1819) Antonio Canova (1757–1822) shows the overcoming of animal nature by human reason. The group was ordered by Napoleon for the Corso in Milan. Emperor Franz I of Austria acquired it for the Theseus Temple in the Volksgarten, and since 1891 it has been in the Kunsthistorisches Museum in the Großer Stairwell.

128 'Stuttgardt – the capital of Würtemberg. Railroad in progress, Sept. 1846.' (Coghlan, 1847, p. 221).

129 'The wines of the Neckar are light, but by no means to be despised. The agreeable effervescing wine (Mussirender Neckar-wein) made at Esslingen & Heilbronn should be tasted.' (Murray, 1844).

130 Early trains were sometimes drawn by horses rather than by steam. See, for example, https://en.wikipedia.org/wiki/Saint-%C3%89tienn e%E2%80%93Andr%C3%A9zieux_railway.

131 Ehrenbreitstein, on the eastern bank of the Rhine at Koblenz, over-looks the confluence of the Mosel and the Rhine. The peak of the hill, which shares the name, is 118 metres above the Rhine. After 1815 the Rhineland became a Prussian province and fortification became a Prussian military priority. The Prussians built a ring of fortification around Koblenz, the *Festung Koblenz* ('Fortress Koblenz'), from 1815 until 1834, of which the Festung Ehrenbreitstein was a part. Ehren-breitstein could be defended by up to 1200 soldiers and was ready for service by 1834.

132 Murray, 1843, has this as Löwenberg – a summit of one of the seven volcanic mountains which were crowned with castles. (Murray, 1843, p. 271).

133 See Murray's guidebook of 1843 for much of the detail in this section including the height of the Drachenfels. Trachyte is an igneous vol-canic rock with an aphanitic to porphyritic texture. George used these handbooks assiduously to help with some details in his journal. (Murray, 1843, p. 262).

134 Schloss Johannisberg, a castle and winery in the village of Johannisberg in the Rheingau wine-growing region of Germany which 'discovered' late harvest wine. In 1816 the estate was given by Francis II, Holy Roman Emperor to Austrian statesman Prince von Metternich.

135 Riesling wine is made here.

136 Here he is using information from a travel guide: 'Next follow *Rudes-heim* (Berg) *Markobrunner* and Rothenberg, which possess much body and aroma. Hockreim (which grows on the banks of the Maine, not in the Rheingau) ranks with the best of these 2nd class wines. Of the inferior wines, those of Erbach and Hattenheim are the best. The lighter wines, however, are apt to be hard and rather acid; as table wines.' (Murray, 1843, p. 291).

137 Probably *Slang* for Marijuana. See 'teaed, tea-d (1928) US; applied to someone in a marijuana-induced euphoria; often followed by up; from tea marijuana' *The Oxford Dictionary of Slang* (John Ayto) BCA; First Thus edition (1 Jan. 1998). I've made an assumption here that George smoked cannabis on this occasion since he says he smoked 'a weed' and he usually smokes 'bacco'.

138 Trump.

139 The Minister for Energy and Clean Growth: https://www.gov.uk/government/people/claire-perry.

140 https://pressfrom.info/us/news/world/-303300-huge-swathes-of-the-arctic-are-ablaze-here-s-why.html (26 July 2019).

141 https://www.oregonlive.com/nation/2019/08/amazon-rainforest-is-ablaze-turning-day-into-night-in-sao-paulo.html (Published: Aug. 21, 2019, 1:51 p.m).

142 Bolsonaro to the U.N. General Assembly 24th September 2019.

143 Halberstadt / Halbestadt is a town in the German state of Saxony-Anhalt, the capital of Harz district. Located north of the Harz mountain range and is way out of range for their journey – so this looks like an error. It seems more likely to be Eupen, where there was a border post. *See also* endnote 277.

144 See *endnote 34* for detail on packet boats.

145 Atmospheric railway – in 1844, the London and Croydon Railway was given parliamentary authority to lay an additional line next to the existing track and test an atmospheric railway system. Pumping stations were built at Portland Road, Croydon and Dartmouth Arms, which created a vacuum in a pipe laid between the running rails. A free-running piston in the pipe was attached to the train through a slit sealed by a leather valve. The piston, and hence the train, was propelled towards the pumping station by atmospheric pressure. The pumping stations were built in a Gothic style, with a very tall ornate tower, which served both as a chimney and as an exhaust vent for air pumped from the propulsion pipe. The railway experienced many problems with the pumping engines during 1846. In 1847, the atmospheric experiment was abandoned. The engine house at Dartmouth Arms was largely demolished in 1851. According to one historian the use of the atmospheric system cost

the railway £500,000 and was 'a sad fiasco'. For lots more detail see: https://en.wikipedia.org/wiki/Atmospheric_railway#London_and_Croydon_Railway.

146 Bricklayers Arms was a railway station in Southwark opened by the London and Croydon Railway and the South Eastern Railway in 1844 as an alternative to the London and Greenwich Railway's terminus at London Bridge. The station was at the end of a short branch line from the main line to London Bridge and served as a passenger terminus for a few years before being converted to a goods station and engineering facility.

147 from my found poem 'Sundry Remarks': (Burke, 1847).

148 This looks wrong as Gheorghe Bibescu(1804–1873) was a *hospodar* or *Gospodar* (Ruler or Prince) of Wallachia, not Serbia, between 1843 and 1848. His rule coincided with the revolutionary tide that culminated in the 1848 Wallachian revolution.

149 Possibly Miloš Obrenović.

150 Karadjordje, George Petrović, Serbo-Croatian Karađorđe, or Đorđe Petrović, (born 1762, Viševac, Serbia–died 1817, Radovanje), leader of the Serbian, not Wallachian people in their struggle for independence from the Turks and founder of the Karadjordjević (Karađorđević) dynasty.

151 Alexandru II or Alexandru D. Ghica (1796-1862), a member of the Ghica family, was Prince of Wallachia from April 1834 to 7 October 1842 and later caimacam (regent) from July 1856 to October 1858.

152 A naval officer, a Frenchman in the Turkish Service.

153 Possibly Mehmed Vecihi Pasha, Ottoman military governor of Belgrade Fortress (1846-47) whom they had met with Fonblanque on the 23rd of May in Belgrade.

154 Possibly Mushir (field Marshal) of Belgrade – In a military context, mushir became associated with the idea of the ruler's personal counsellor or advisor on military matters, and as such became the highest rank in Arab countries and the Ottoman Empire. It is used as the highest rank in most armed forces of the Middle East and North Africa, for armies, navies, and air forces. It is therefore equivalent to the ranks of Field Marshal and Admiral of the Fleet.

155 The German 'Handschrift' is hard to decipher. A note to refer to while making house calls, perhaps.

156 An area in Istanbul. '[…] famous for its beautiful promenade, wooden houses, cafes and fish restaurants. As most of the settlements on the upper Bosporus, Büyükdere had long been a cosmopolitan enclave. After a French ambassador had obtained the Sultan's permission for the settlement of foreigners in this area, the bay of Büyükdere […] was discovered by the embassies and their entourage in the second half of the 18th century'.

157 My transcription of letters held at FO519 96, The National Archive, Kew. They were copied by scribes from the originals into logbooks as a permanent record of correspondence. This series dates from The Lord Cowley taking over the post from his predecessor Sir Stratford Canning, hence the numbering starts at 1 and we can see him gradually taking up the reigns of his new job.

158 HMS Hecla (1839) was a 4-gun Hydra-class wooden paddle sloop launched in 1839, run aground off Gibraltar on 23 January 1855, and sold in 1863.

159 From the Hertslet Papers, National Archives at Kew.

160 from my found poem 'Sundry Remarks': (Burke, 1847).

161 The town of Dunkirk erected a statue and named a public square after him. The statue survived intense bombing in the Second World War. Jean Bart (1650–1702) was a French naval commander and privateer. The statue is indeed disproportionate.

162 Pfalzgrafenstein Castle, a toll castle on the Falkenau island in the River Rhine. The pentagonal tower keep was erected 1327 with later additions. As a toll-collecting station it worked with Gutenfels Castle and the fortified town of Kaub on the right side of the river. A dangerous cataract and a chain across the river forced ships to submit. Uncooperative traders could be kept in the dungeon, a wooden float in the well, until a ransom was paid. 'The Pfalz' was never conquered or destroyed. Its Spartan quarters held about twenty men.

163 'In one of the towers of the castle a room is shewn where it is said the wives of the Counts of the Palatinate came to be confined. It has likewise several dungeons, used as state prisons; and a remarkably deep well, which is cut out of the rock, and does not receive its water from the Rhine'. (Coghlan, 1847).

164 Edward, his younger brother – Edward John Cox Davies born 1826.

165 Riesling wine, dry.

166 John Ruskin, who often emulated Prout, wrote in 1844, 'Sometimes I tire of Turner, but never of Prout'.

167 Durlach is a borough of the German city of Karlsruhe.

168 Possibly referring to Pope's 'Odyssey of Homer' 'Each drinks a full oblivion of his cares, And to the gifts of balmy sleep repairs.' *The British Poets*, C. Whittingham (1822).

169 Geislingen an der Steige is a town in the district of Göppingen in Baden-Württemberg in southern Germany. The name relates to its location "on the climb" (an der Steige) of a trade route over the Swabian Jura mountain range.

170 St Mary Redcliffe, an Anglican parish church, renowned for the beauty of its Gothic architecture, in the Redcliffe district of Bristol. Constructed from the 12th to the 15th Centuries. Described by Queen Elizabeth I as 'the fairest, goodliest, and most famous parish church in

England'.

171   Neu-Ulm is the capital of the Neu-Ulm district and a town in Swabia, Bavaria. In 1810 the sovereignty over Ulm city changed from the Kingdom of Bavaria to that of Württemberg. The Danube became the boundary between Bavaria and Württemberg. Neu-Ulm remained under Bavarian sovereignty with only a few houses, taverns, and the village of Offenhausen and was known as 'Ulm am rechten Donauufer' (Ulm on the right-hand side of the Danube). Growth began in 1841, with the building of the Federal Fort of Ulm, the Bundesfestung. King Ludwig I, decreed that Neu-Ulm be included within the fort. After Neu-Ulm was connected to the Augsburg railway line in 1853, soldiers arrived and a garrison was created there.

172   Oktoberfest, annual festival in Munich, Germany, held over a two-week period and ending on the first Sunday in October (Oct 3rd 1847 was a Sunday). The festival originated on October 12th 1810, in celebration of the marriage of the Crown Prince of Bavaria, who later became King Louis I, to Princess Therese von Sachsen-Hildburghausen.

173   The old station mentioned was built in Marsfeld and was a simple wooden station building including two toll booths. There were two waiting rooms and several work spaces. The line to Augsburg was opened in October 1840 and was used by about 400 passengers daily. It was too far out from the centre of Munich and when the station suffered a major fire, on 4th April 1847, the new one was built nearer the city. The new station opened on 15th November 1847. See https://en.wikipedia.org/wiki/M%C3%BCnchen_Hauptbahnhof for further details.

174   Byron, 'Don Juan'.

175   'A town and fortress of the Innviertel, situated on the river Inns' (Domeier, 1830).

176   Dürnstein Castle in Dürnstein, in the Lower Austrian Wachau region on the Danube River, is the ruin of a medieval rock castle and one of the places where King Richard I of England, returning from the Third Crusade, was imprisoned after being captured near Vienna by Duke Leopold V of Austria, from December 1192 until his extradition to Emperor Henry VI in March 1193.

177   Vienna: 'Soon after leaving the station the traveller is stopped at the Linien or Lines – i.e. gates in the outer lines of fortifications, which are kept up more for revenue purposes than for defence. Here a carriage-toll of 4 kreuzer per horse is levied, and the duty upon any provisions, which are all liable to octroi or city dues.' (Murray, 1873, p. 201). 'By 1840 urban Vienna had expanded towards the west by up to a mile and a half [...] the boundaries had reached the Linienwall, the custom barrier'. (*The City as a Work of Art: London, Paris, Vienna* by Donald

J Olsen, 1986 Yale University Press). The Linienwall was an outer line of fortifications for Vienna, between the city's suburbs and outlying villages. Construction was ordered by Emperor Leopold I in 1704 to protect against attacks by the Turks and the Kuruc (a group of anti-Habsburg rebels). It formed part of a defensive line that followed the Austro-Hungarian border. All Vienna residents between eighteen and sixty had to work on the fortifications (a zigzagging, palisade-reinforced, earthen rampart, 4 metres high by 4 metres wide, and a 3-metre-deep ditch). Construction took just four months. The most important arterial roads entered the city via drawbridges and gates; each of these locations also included a custom house where a toll, the Liniengeld was charged. The Linienwall was razed in 1894 to make way for the Vienna Beltway.

178 Wilder Mann (the oldest inn in Vienna) (Murray, 1873, p. 201).

179 The Messengers would stop to drop off and pick up despatches at British Embassies along their route.

180 There is no information about who this is, and I have not been able to identify him.

181 'The Sperl, which opened in 1807, was another well-known dancing palace. The ballroom there was so large that one end of the room was barely visible from the other". "At Sperl's there were soft rugs, palm trees, flowers, mirrors, a dining room with many hundreds of candles, a winter-garden, and a large park". In 1833 Heinrich Laube wrote, 'An evening and half the night at Sperl's is the key to Vienna's sensuous life, which means Vienna's life'. 'A venue for many of the city's most important balls, Joseph Lanner and Johann Strauss I often played there. The Sperl eventually became the artistic home of Strauss and the site where he premiered many of his waltzes.' (Knowles, 2009, p. 29).

182 Probably Strauss the elder, Johann Strauss I, (1804-1849), one of the principal composers of Viennese waltzes, who 'established his reputation as a composer of Viennese waltzes in 1830 by conducting at the "Sperl," a popular dance hall in the Leopoldstadt'. *Encyclopaedia Britannica*. However, Johann Strauss II (Johann Strauss the Younger, Johann Sebastian Strauss) (1825–1899) also played at Sperl Gardens, so it is difficult to be sure which Strauss was leading the orchestra on this occasion.

183 Unfortunately, this was not handed down through the family.

184 Odessa is the third most populous city of Ukraine on the NW shore of the Black Sea. From 1819 until 1859 the city was a free port. It had an extremely diverse population of Albanians, Armenians, Azeris, Bulgarians, Crimean Tatars, Frenchmen, Germans (including Mennonites), Greeks, Italians, Jews, Poles, Romanians, Russians, Turks, Ukrainians, and traders representing many other nationalities.

Pushkin, who lived in internal exile in Odessa between 1823 and 1824 wrote that Odessa was a city where 'the air is filled with all Europe'.

185 Circassia is a region in the North Caucasus and along the northeast shore of the Black Sea. It is the ancestral homeland of the Circassian people. Circassia was located in Eastern Europe, near the north-eastern Black Sea coast. Before the Russian conquest of the Caucasus (1763-1864), it covered the entire fertile plateau and the steppe of the north-western region of the Caucasus, with an estimated population of between 3 and 4 million. As part of its conquest of the Caucasus, the Russian empire became involved in a series of wars and battles in Circassia, starting in the late 18th Century and building in intensity to 1864, when the war was declared over. From the 1860s the Russian policy was one of ethnic cleansing and mass expulsion of the population to the neighbouring Ottoman Empire, events that have become known as the Circassian Genocide. Among the main Circassian tribes that were affected were the Shapsugs, Kabardins, Abzakhs and Natukhajs. It is estimated that the population of Kabardins in Circassia was reduced from 500,000 to 35,000; the Abzakhs from 260,000 to 14,600; and the Natukhajs from 240,000 to 175 persons. The Shapsugh tribe which numbered some 300,000 were reduced to 3,000 people. Calculations, including those of the Russian Government's own archival figures, have estimated a loss of over 90% of the original Circassian population. *See also endnote 231.*

186 The word is very badly written but appears to be Taheran which makes geographical sense as Teheran – an alternative spelling for Tehran. Most commonly it was called Teheran eg by Sir Stratford Canning in his memoirs, however I have found it spelt as Taheran and Teheraun, and indeed, George may have misspelled it.

187 This is probably one of the reasons George is travelling with Mr Gutch – as German translator – it seems Mr G did not speak much German and German was spoken by over 70 per cent of the population in Presburg at that time.

188 St Martin's Cathedral, a church in Bratislava, Slovakia, the cathedral of the Roman Catholic Archdiocese of Bratislava, situated below Bratislava Castle. It is the largest and one of the oldest churches in Bratislava, known for being the coronation church of the Kingdom of Hungary between 1563 and 1830. https://commons.wikimedia.org/wiki/File:Jakob_Alt_-_Die_Domkirche_in_Pressburg_-_1842.jpeg.

189 The Primate's Palace is considered one of the most beautiful neo-classical buildings in Slovakia.

190 Possibly the Holy Trinity Column, a religious column dedicated to the Christian Holy Trinity, a popular theme for a monument in Czech Republic and Slovakia for celebrating the end of the Plague. Every city

in this region has one, including Bratislava. A central column is topped with the Holy Trinity at the base of which are sculptures of saints. A low wall encloses the column. The column can be found on the western edge of Bratislava Old Town.

191 Possibly half-bastion behind the convent or Polveža za kláštorom, Halbturn hinter dem Kloster at the end of Františkánska Street. The original name of Františkánska Street was Street behind the convent (Ulica za kláštorom, Gassl hinter dem Closter). The system of fortifications of medieval Bratislava contained several bastions and guard towers.

192 The Slovak National Theatre now stands on the site of the former city theatre which was built in 1776. The current building opened in 1886.

193 Dissolving views were a popular 19th Century magic lantern show where pictures gradually changed from one projected image to another, for example, landscapes that dissolved from day to night or from summer to winter. Two matching images were aligned, then the first was slowly diminished while the second was introduced. Diorama theatre paintings had originated in Paris in 1822 and were similar in effect. The terms 'dissolving views', 'dioramic views', or 'diorama' were often used interchangeably in 19th century magic lantern playbills. The oldest known use of the term 'dissolving views' occurs on playbills for the Adelphi Theatre in London in 1837. Double or biunial lanterns in the 1840s and later triple lanterns enabled the addition of more effects, for instance the effect of snow falling while a green landscape dissolved into a snowy winter version. All early dissolving view slides seem to have been hand-painted.

194 In 1962/3, the year I was five, there was a very hard winter. My mother caught pneumonia and was very ill and we, my sister, Alison, and I, were sent off to stay with Aunty Joan for six weeks or so while she recovered in hospital and in a convalescent home in Bournemouth. Joan had four children of her own. After her recovery, my mother noticed the first signs that she had inherited the familial cerebellar degeneration which affected her mother and her brother. The disease affects balance and speech and leads to severe physical disability in old age.

195 you have come to this unexpected place/ a tract of snow where snow keeps falling/ only a thread of sound/ your breath/ your breath. *International Phonetic Alphabet.*

196 To protect the despatches, they were carrying.

197 Visegrád is a small castle town in Pest County, Hungary. It is north of Budapest on the right bank of the Danube in the Danube Bend. Visegrád is famous for the remains of the Early Renaissance summer

palace of King Matthias Corvinus of Hungary and the medieval citadel. The castle of Visegrád is called Fellegvár (Citadel) in Hungarian.

198 https://historycampus.org/2015/erect-a-memorial-erase-the-past-the-memorial-to-the-victims-of-the-german-occupation-in-budapest-and-the-controversy-around-it/.

199 The official wording said the sculpture commemorates 'Hungary's German Occupation on March 19, 1944'. As a result of the scandal the wording was changed to read 'the victims of the occupation'. Hungary was a faithful ally of Hitler's Germany during the Second World War and was the first in 1940 to join the Axis Powers. On March 19th, 1944, the arriving German troops were met with flowers not bullets. The state administration, unchanged by the Germans, effectively organised and executed the mass deportations. Antisemitism in Hungary had started in 1920 with laws increasingly stripping rights from Hungary's Jews. The protestors say that by erecting the monument the government concedes to Hungary's far right and deliberately rinses clean the memory of Admiral Miklós Horthy who governed the country between the wars.

200 Raoul Gustaf Wallenberg (1912–disappeared 17 January 1945) was a Swedish architect, businessman, diplomat, and humanitarian. He is remembered for saving tens of thousands of Jews in Nazi-occupied Hungary during the Holocaust from German Nazis and Hungarian Fascists during the later stages of the Second World War. While serving as Sweden's special envoy in Budapest between July and December 1944, Wallenberg issued protective passports and sheltered Jews in buildings designated as Swedish territory. On 17th January 1945, during the Siege of Budapest by the Red Army, Wallenberg was detained by SMERSH (an umbrella organization for three independent counter-intelligence agencies in the Red Army operating 1942–1946) on suspicion of espionage and subsequently disappeared. He was later reported to have died on 17th July 1947 while imprisoned by the KGB secret police in the Lubyanka, the KGB headquarters and affiliated prison in Moscow. The motives behind Wallenberg's arrest and imprisonment by the Soviet Government, along with questions surrounding the circumstances of his death and his ties to US intelligence, remain mysterious and are the subject of continued speculation. See https://en.wikipedia.org/wiki/Raoul_Wallenberg.

201 By July 1944 when Wallenberg arrived there were only 230,000 Jews remaining in Hungary. With fellow Swedish diplomat Per Anger, and Miklos "Moshe" Krausz they issued "protective passports" (German: Schutz-Pass), which identified the bearers as Swedish subjects awaiting repatriation and thus prevented their deportation. Although not legal, these documents looked official and were generally accepted by German and Hungarian authorities, who sometimes were also bribed. The

Swedish legation in Budapest also succeeded in negotiating with the German authorities so that the bearers of the protective passes would be treated as Swedish citizens and be exempt from having to wear the yellow badge required for Jews. When the German government said the travel passes were invalid, Wallenberg appealed for help from Baroness Elisabeth Kemény, wife of Baron Gábor Kemény, Hungarian Minister for Foreign Affairs in Budapest. She convinced her husband to have 9,000 passes honoured.

202 Sándor Petőfi (1823–1849) was a Hungarian poet and liberal revolutionary and one of the key figures of the Hungarian Revolution of 1848. Author of the *Nemzeti dal* (National Anthem), said to have inspired the revolution in the Kingdom of Hungary that grew into a war for independence from the Austrian Empire. It is likely he died in the Battle of Segesvár, one of the last battles of the war. *John the Valiant* (1844) is a folk-epic recounting the adventures of a shepherd boy.

203 Read about the politics of the statue here: https://en.wikipedia.org/wiki/Liberty_Statue_(Budapest).

204 "A Tiszttartó Kikocsizik" by Lotz Károly. (The title would be something like "The bailiff ventures out by carriage". Tiszttartó is an old word, so bailiff is only my best bet. A farm bailiff, perhaps.) via email from Imre. Lotz Károly (1833-1904) was a German-Hungarian painter.

205 'Join Me in Death' a single by the Finnish band HIM, taken from their second studio album *Razorblade Romance* (BMG, 2000). See https://www.youtube.com/watch?v=1V4AscLidWg HIM

206 For more on the debacle around the Beograd Centar station see https://en.wikipedia.org/wiki/Belgrade_Centre_railway_station.

207 As at 2020: 'The number of Jews currently residing in the "Jewish Quarter" in the old city of Damascus is twelve, distributed in half between men and women. All of these people are elders, unmarried and over 70 years old, according to Bikhor Shamentop, a Jew living in Damascus and a resident of the Jewish Quarter.' https://english.enabbaladi.net/archives/2020/11/damascuss-jewish-quarter-devoid-of-its-residents/. The article was written on 4/11/2020. Jews left Damascus in successive migrations in the 1990's.

208 Damascus, Syria 'There are several very opulent Jewish merchants in Damascus who carry on considerable business. I was unable to ascertain the number of Jews residing here; they have six synagogues,…According to a very late census, the number of persons who paid the Ferdi, or poll tax, amounted to 25,000, and this being exclusive of women, children, strangers, and those who by protection are exempted from payment, the entire [Jewish] population of Damascus may be estimated at 125,000'. (Anon., 1840)

209 See (Lane-Poole, 1888, pp. 89-99) for the history behind reforms

in dealing with such cases. In 1843 a young Armenian man had been executed by the Porte for leaving Christianity, becoming Moslem and then turning back to Christianity (women would have been imprisoned rather than executed). 'The details may be read' says Lane-Poole, 'in the Correspondence relating to Executions in Turkey for Apostasy from Islamism, laid before the House of Commons in 1844'. Canning, through dogged persistence, managed to achieve reform and the executions for apostasy stopped.

210 The Congress of Vienna in 1814 and 1815 had granted the UK full sovereignty over all of the Ionian islands, Corfu, Paxoi, Lefkada, Cephalonia, Ithaca, Zante, and Kythira, using the term 'exclusive amical protection'. 'The United States of the Ionian Islands' was created, and along with allowing British rule, the islands had to grant the Austrian Empire commercial status equal to the UK, allowing Vienna to trade freely in this part of the Mediterranean. The blockade of the coast of Albania by the Ottoman Empire because of an Albanian revolt which prevented Ionian trade was therefore a matter for the UK Ambassador to address. The tone of the letter clearly addresses also the "*desolation and bloodshed*" experienced by the Albanian population at the hands of their Ottoman rulers. On May 28, 1864, the Ionian Islands were officially united with Greece.

211 From this point the roads are unsuitable for carriages, so they use posthorses instead. They would change horses at posthouses along the way – the distance being too far for one horse to travel.

212 For an account of the job of a postboy (Inkel, 2005). The History of the King's Messengers states: 'The Soorajee was a professional groom or porter who accompanied a party to look after the beasts'. There are several spellings of this word.

213 Jim Crow hat: Man's felt hat with wide, flapping brim (Lewandowski, 2011). The term Jim Crow has racist origins: 'The character of Jim Crow is thought to have been first presented about 1830 by Thomas Dartmouth ("Daddy") Rice, an itinerant white actor. Rice was not the first performer to don rags and use burnt cork to blacken his face to present a mocking exaggerated imitation of an African-American, but he was the most famous, and his success helped establish minstrelsy as a popular theatrical form that thrived from about 1850 to 1870'. https://www.britannica.com/story/what-is-the-origin-of-the-term-jim-crow.

214 Palanka (now Smederevska Palanka). According to the official list of stations, noted in the archives at Kew, *see p75*, they are travelling on the second principal road.

215 English miles were substantially different from other country's measures of length. The Bohemian mile, for instance would have been 5 English

miles, 6 furlongs and 17 yards. There were 1,760 yards in one English mile. The wildly varying measures in use for length, mass and time were often impractical for trade between countries which paved the way for the introduction of the metric system.

216 from my found poem 'Sundry Remarks': (Burke, 1847).

217 See: http://edition.cnn.com/WORLD/europe/9904/06/serb.town.hit and also see: https://www.wsws.org/en/articles/1999/04/bomb-a07. html (both accessed 28/10/2021).

218 Ivanka Radmanović notes that it would be very unlikely that George could see the mountains stretching all the way southwest to Albania. He may possibly see nearby mountains such as Kopaonik (west of Aleksinac). There are several mountain ranges including the Dinaris range that extend down to the Adriatic coast and to Albania, but it seems highly unlikely that he can see them from where he is.

219 Palanka is between Kolari and Batochina.

220 Mentioned in posting routes of the 18th and 19th century – Jagodina to Raschna 10 hours posting, Raschna to Nissa 19 hours posting.

221 Probably Mount Ozren, a mountain in central Serbia, near the town of Sokobanja. Its highest peak, Leskovik, has an elevation of 1,178 m (3,865 ft).

222 Plovdiv is the second-largest city of Bulgaria and is one of the oldest cities in the world. Plovdiv used to be known in the West by the name Philippopolis, "Philip's Town" after Philip II of Macedon, who conquered the city in the 4th Century BC. Originally Thracian, it was invaded by Persians, Greeks, Celts, Romans, Goths, Huns, Bulgars, Slavs, Rus people, Crusaders, and Turks. In 1878, at the end of the Russo-Turkish War (1877–1878), Plovdiv was taken from Ottoman rule by the Russians. In July 1878 it left Bulgaria and became the capital of the autonomous Ottoman region of Eastern Rumelia. In 1885, Plovdiv and Eastern Rumelia joined Bulgaria.

223 Captain Spencer describes how he ended up in Quarantine: 'Having set out from Alexinitz to extend my excursions through the Knejine of Gorgouschavatz and Mount Rtagn, we inadvertently, in a frontier so ill-defined as that of Servia, crossed the Turkish frontier, and entered the province of Bosnia. On our return into the principality, we were reminded of the indiscretion by a troop of Servian pandours, who, without much ceremony, conducted us to the establishment at Alexinitz. But as the offence was committed through ignorance, our imprisonment in the quarantine was, as a great favour, reduced from five to three days, which term may be extended to forty, when an epidemic prevails in any of the adjoining provinces' (Spencer, 1851, p. 71).

224 Here used to mean a backhander or bribe.

225 George notes the following books by Spencer on the first page of the

journal: Spencer's *Travels in the Circassia Crim Tartary and Eastern Turkey* – Coburn. Spencer's – *Germany and the Germans*. Spencer's *Prophet of the Caucusus. European Turkey, Greece and Ionian Isles*. These are as follows and still available as facsimiles: *Travels in Circassia, Krim-Tartary &c, Including a Steam Voyage Down the Danube from Vienna to Constantinople, and Round the Black Sea, in 1836* – Edmund Spencer (free to download online). *Sketches of Germany and the Germans: With a Glance at Poland, Hungary, & Switzerland in 1834, 1835, and 1836, Volume 2*. Edmund Spencer, Whittaker, 1836. *The Prophet of the Caucasus: an Historical Romance of Krim-Tatary: Volume 1*. Edmund SPENCER (Captain.) January 1, 1840 Whittaker& Company. *Travels in European Turkey, in 1850: with a visit to Greece and the Ionian isles* ... 2 vol, Spencer.

226 'Monastir, or Bitolia, is the long-established seat of the chief Governor of Turkey in Europe, the centre of all the communications of Roumeli' (Urquhart, 1839). Now known as Bitola, a city in the south-western part of North Macedonia. Known since the Ottoman period as "The City of The Consuls", since many European countries had consulates there. During the Ottoman Empire it was known as Manastir/Monastir, founded as Heraclea Lyncestis in the middle of the 4th Century BC by Philip II of Macedon. It was the last capital of Ottoman Rumelia, from 1836 to 1867.

227 Bukhara is the fifth largest city in Uzbekistan, rich in historical sites and inhabited for at least five millennia. Located on the Silk Road, the city has been a centre of trade, scholarship, culture, and religion. Bukhara was known as Bokhara in 19th- and early 20th-Century English publications. Since the Middle Ages, the city has been known as Buḥārā in Arabic and Persian sources. The modern Uzbek spelling is Buxoro.

228 "Christopher North" was a pseudonym of John Wilson of Elleray FRSE (1785–1854) who wrote for the Tory monthly, *Blackwood's Edinburgh Magazine*.

229 Messengers were exhorted to bring books and magazines with them and leave them at Alexnitza for the next messengers to read so that there was literature to fill the long days of waiting. George notes a couple of books at the beginning of his journal which he may have encountered at Alexnitza. These were: *Hints to all parties by a man of no party* – Pub Whittaker and Pollock's *Course of life. Hints to all parties by a man of no party*, London Bach and Co, 1834 (available on Google Books). Robert Pollok (1798-1827) was a Scottish poet best known for *The Course of Time*, published in the year of his death (from tuberculosis), a ten-book poem in blank verse which sold more than 78,000 copies.

230 Upper Moesia was a Roman province first established in AD 86, its

boundaries changed frequently over the centuries, but what is usually taken as its perimeter is the one that emerged in the first half of the 2nd Century which is most of today's central Serbia (except a smaller Western part which belonged to the province of Dalmatia), the north-west portion of today's Bulgaria to the Tsibritsa (Ciabrus) river, and the region of Tetovo in the north of today's FYR Macedonia.

231 As part of its conquest of the Caucasus, the Russian Empire became involved in a series of wars and battles in Circassia, starting in the late 18th Century and building in intensity to 1864, when the war was declared over. From the 1860s the Russian policy became one of ethnic cleansing and mass expulsion of the population from their country to the neighbouring Ottoman Empire, events that have become known as the Circassian Genocide. Calculations, including those taking into account the Russian Government's own archival figures, have estimated a loss of 90%, 94% or 95-97% of the original Circassian population. *See also* endnote 185.

232 Pasha of Three Tails – there are three grades of pashas distinguished by the number of horse-tails on their standard. In war the horse-tail standard is carried before the pasha and planted in front of his tent. The highest rank of pashas are those of three tails; the grand vizier is always such a pasha. Pashas of two tails are governors of provinces; it is one of these officers that we mean when we speak of a pasha in a general way. A pasha of one tail is a *sanjak* or lowest of provincial governors. (Brewer, 1894, p. 947).

233 It seems likely that this is Draževac (Serbian: Дражевац) a village in the municipality of Aleksinac, Serbia since it lies between Aleksinac and Niš where the border with the Ottoman Empire lay at that time. Via Ivanka Radmanović.

234 Possibly *Jelen* (deer, stag) Serbian.

235 Srna (doe or red deer) Serbian.

236 Lepa Gora, a mountain between Mt. Kopaonik and Mt. Jastrebac to the west of Aleksinac. See https://www.srbijapodlupom.com/lepa-gora/.

237 sluga pokorni (obedient servant).

238 dobro zdravlje (good health).

239 'At Tchoupria [Ćuprija] we traversed a fine wooden bridge thrown over the Morava, the toll was twenty-five pari for our two horses. I amused myself while Georgy was roasting a string of fat ortolans, I had shot during our route, by strolling through this little town, which contains a few hundred houses. The principal occupation of the inhabitants, both men and women, seemed to be weaving. When at work the aspect they presented was almost ludicrous, since the loom being placed in a hole in the ground, nothing but the head and shoulders of the operator remained visible' (Spencer, 1851, p. 61).

240 (Spencer, 1851, p. 35)

241 Her ingredients: take five mixed river fish (some of carp, catfish, barbel, perch, pike, sturgeon), 5½ tbs sunflower oil, 3 bay leaves, 7 peppercorns, 2 yellow onions (chopped), 2 carrots (diced), 1 parsnip (chopped), 2 potatoes (quartered), 5½ tbs celery root (or white part of stem), 2 cloves of garlic (optional), ½ tbs sweet red paprika powder, ½ tbs hot paprika powder, ½ cayenne pepper (whole), 1 tomato (chopped) water (2 pints), handful of parsley, handful of lovage, few basil leaves, a few leaves of dill, 1 tsp thyme, pinch of anise seed, salt, pepper, 11 tbs tomato juice, 1tbs red wine vinegar. Fry onions in sunflower oil till transparent, add chopped vegetables, herbs and spices and continue to fry until softened. Add liquid ingredients together with cubed fish, check seasoning and simmer until done. Recipe adapted by JS.

242 Hannah Glasse (1708–1770) was an English cookery writer. The instruction 'First catch your hare' is sometimes wrongly attributed to her but her recipe for roast hare begins 'Take your hare when it be cas'd', meaning simply to take a skinned hare.

243 The German is hard to translate here because the text is crabbed and hard to read. Trans: Tony Frazer and Gertraude Klemm.

244 The Four Lions Fountain, built in 1799. Another legend says 'that everyone who drinks water from it will return to Karlovci and get married.' See https://en.m.wikipedia.org/wiki/Four_Lions_Fountain.

245 Unfortunately for me he did not complete this task!

246 'Curse of Minerva', Byron.

247 Possibly a place called Tchupelirck which is mentioned in the messenger regulations lists of posting stations on one of the minor routes but which I cannot identify on current maps. The National Archives, Kew: FO 366/496/494 (*Hertslet Papers*).

248 A Greek Monk from Byron's 'The Giaour', a fragment of a Turkish tale. 'The Bride of Abydos' was written between 1813 and 1815 in various editions. The story 'contained the adventures of a female slave, who was thrown, in the Mussulman manner, into the sea for infidelity, and avenged by a young Venetian, her lover'. "How name ye yon lone caloyer?" A caloyer is a monk of the Eastern Church.

249 George Cox 1806–1855.

250 See https://en.wikipedia.org/wiki/Dummy_whist. Dummy whist is one of many variants of the classic trick-taking card game, Whist. The general rules of Dummy Whist are similar to that of Bid Whist, with two notable exceptions. Bid Whist is played by four players, whereas Dummy Whist is played by only three – as Mr G would not play with them. Secondly, instead of dealing a kitty, a dummy hand is dealt to be on the team of the player who wins the auction.

251 A Rubber is three games.

252 A found poem using references from George's journal and: *A*

Handbook for Travellers in the Ionian Islands, Greece, Turkey, Asia Minor, and Constantinople, John Murray (London 1840). *A handbook for travellers in southern Germany*, John Murray (London 1837). *A handbook for travellers in southern Germany*, John Murray (London 1873). *Hand-book for central Europe*, Francis Coghlan (London 1845). *Travels in European Turkey, in 1850*, Edmund Spencer (London 1851).

253 Time to travel in sight of mountains – we shall find the last gold here / a gift for strangers.

254 from my found poem 'Sundry Remarks': (Burke, 1847).

255 *Henrietta Temple* (published 1837), ninth novel by Benjamin Disraeli, later Prime Minister. First volume written in 1833 as he began an affair with Henrietta Sykes, on whom the novel's heroine is based. Second volume completed three years later, soon after the affair ended. The volumes reflect the affair. Disraeli's heavy debts were eased by its success. The novel's hero escapes debt by marrying into a wealthy family and entering Parliament, both of which Disraeli did in the three years following the novel's publication.

256 from my found poem 'Sundry Remarks' (Burke, 1847).

257 See pages 65, 66 & 67.

258 Urinating. "And at stations where horses are changed a delay of half an hour is authorised (signed Stoyan Ltd, Stephen Stephanovitch and others) Belgrade 20 July 1843. Foreign Office notes on Stations. It appears that after a long post, horses would customarily urinate and especially if they were in harness to a carriage this would take more time. They would not urinate while moving.

259 See sick note and doctor's letter on his return – this was in fact a rather serious injury and Mr G must have been feeling very ill on the long and difficult journey home. See p.182, 183 & 184.

260 They made good time – Foreign Office workings suggest "Journey usually done in 32 hours" and this journey was done in November in poor weather.

261 Bajloni Market, founded in 1927 by Ignjat Bajloni, of Czech origin. Probably one of the most popular markets in Belgrade. See https:// belgrade-beat.com/attractions/bajloni-market.

262 This may be Rtanjski čaj (Rtanj Mountain tea) – helpful with bronchial problems, originates from Mt. Rtanj, near Sokobanja, made with a variety of wild hand-picked herbs. Via Ivanka Radmanović.

263 He had been a surgeon, before being a Queen's Messenger, so this was well within his skill set.

264 Likely to be a phonetic spelling of Szekszárd, a small city in S. Hungary.

265 See endnote 177.

266 The Noric Alps (German: Norische Alpen), a collective term for various mountain ranges of the Eastern Alps. The name derives from

the ancient Noricum province of the Roman Empire on the territory of present-day Austria and the adjacent Bavarian and Slovenian area. In the 19th century, the German term Norische Alpen covered the whole group of ranges of the Central Eastern and Northern Limestone Alps east of the Dreiherrnspitze peak.

267 Possibly Traunstein.

268 By 1936 there were 192 Jews living in Harburg – *The Encyclopedia of Jewish Life Before and During the Holocaust*, Vol. 1 (New York University Press, 2001, p. 498).

269 The new bridge was the stone-arch bridge, the Neckar Bridge near Ladenburg (11km from Heidelberg) which was started in 1844 and finished in 1848. The temporary bridge they used was a wooden structure.

270 See https://www.rothschildarchive.org/business/business_premises/frankfurt.

271 During the 19th Century, Johann Heinrich von Dannecker's marble sculpture 'Ariadne on the Panther' (1803–14; today in the Liebieghaus Skulpturensammlung, Frankfurt) was the most famous sculpture in Germany. Its installation in the private museum of the banker Simon Moritz von Bethmann in 1816 coincided with a travel boom after the end of the Napoleonic Wars. Numerous travel accounts and guides described the statue and its display, focusing primarily on the red lighting and its rotating pedestal, both of which had been suggested by the sculptor. https://online.liverpooluniversitypress.co.uk/doi/abs/10.3828/sj.2017.26.2.2?journalCode=sj.

272 Probably George has this incorrectly as it was not *Pittman* but Simon Moritz von *Bethmann* who acquired the sculpture in 1810 and in 1816 put it on display in the so-called Odeon, the first museum in Frankfurt to be open to the public. The sculpture was recommended by every guidebook as one of the most important sights of Frankfurt.

273 Written on left lower side of this page at right angle to words above at the beginning of the notebook are these notes on the paintings: Foolish Virgins, Schadow [Parable of the Wise and Foolish Virgins Schadow, Friedrich Wilhelm von, 1789–1862 now displayed Städtische Galerie im Städelschen Kunstinstitut Frankfurt am Main.]; Huss bef. [Constance Council], Lessing [Huss before the Council of Constance, 1842, now displayed Städel Museum, Frankfurt am Main.]; Römerberg Markttag, Schütz [Markttag am Frankfurter Römerberg von Christian Georg Schütz, now displayed Städel Museum, Frankfurt am Main; Daniel in Lions Den, Rethel [*Daniel in the Lion's Den* by Alfred Rethel, (1816–1859), now displayed Städel Museum, Frankfurt am Main.]; Ezzelin III in Kerker Lessing [Carl Friedrich Lessing: Ezzelino da Romano im Kerker, Gemälde 1838,now displayed Städel Museum,

Frankfurt.]

274 Frankfurt Cathedral, Imperial Cathedral of Saint Bartholomew, is a RC Gothic church in the centre of Frankfurt am Main, the largest religious building, but not a true cathedral. Named the Kaiserdom (Imperial Great Church) or the Dom. From 1356 emperors of the Holy Roman Empire were elected here as kings in Germany, and from 1562 to 1792, emperors-elect were crowned here. Destroyed by fire in n 1867, and rebuilt. During World War II more than a thousand half-timbered houses of the old town were destroyed, St. Bartholomew's was also destroyed and reconstructed in the 1950s.

275 Had the weather not been foggy they would have gone by steamboat up the Rhine to Cologne as they had done before on the previous journeys.

276 'The first electrical telegraph line in continental Europe was installed in Germany along a steep railway track between Aachen and Ronheide in 1843. The locomotives available were too weak to climb this section which had a slope of 1 in 38 m. therefore a stationary steam engine was located at Ronheide to pull the train up by rope from Aachen Herbestal over a distance of 2.74 km. To communicate between the stations, two telegraphs were ordered by which messages could be sent by electrical telegraphy. By 1855 locomotives were powerful enough to pull the train up the incline and the stationary steam engine and telegraph were taken out of service.' *The Worldwide History of Telecommunications*, Anton A. Hurdeman (John Wiley & Sons, 2003) p74.

277 Halbestadt in Germany is not on this route so this must be an error of George's part. The border crossing between Aix la Chapelle and Liège was at Eupen in Belgium at that time. *See also* endnote 143.

278 Mechlin lace or Point de Malines is an old Flemish bobbin lace, originally produced in Mechelen. It is fine, transparent, often worn over another colour. Popular until 1910, used for coiffures de nuit (evening hair-styling), garnitures de corset (corset trims), ruffles and cravats.

279 The first railway to reach the coastal port of Calais was only completed in 1848 hence they had to post for that part of the journey.

280 Not listed as a Messenger in the History of the King's Messengers by V Wheeler-Holohan (1935) however he is listed as a messenger in documents in *The Hertslet Papers* at the National Archive, Kew, as serving in 1847.

281 Lord Byron, from 'The Corsair': "The exulting sense—the pulse's maddening play,/ That thrills the wanderer of that trackless way?/ That for itself can woo the approaching fight, / And turn what some deem danger to delight;"

282 Suggesting that the despatches they carried were urgent.

283 The first station at London Bridge was opened at Tooley Street on 14 December 1836 by the London & Greenwich Railway (LGR), along with its line as far as Deptford. It had a complicated early history as routes were developed. More detail can be found at https://www.networkrail.co.uk/who-we-are/our-history/iconic-infrastructure/the-history-of-london-bridge-station/.

284 Possibly Adamberger, although I have not been able to find out what the box for Mrs Hertslet would have contained.

285 Grocka to Kolari now takes 32 mins by road (30.4km). Belgrade to Grocka 44 mins by road (35.3km).

286 Kolari to Smederevska Palanka now takes 40 mins by road (29.5km).

287 Hasan-pašina Palanka – Smederevska Palanka to Rača now takes 23 mins (18.8km).

288 Rača to Batočina now takes 18 mins by road (13.2km).

289 Batočina to Bagrdan by road now takes 15mins (13.8km).

290 Bagrdan to Jagodina by road now takes 15 mins (12.8km).

291 Jagodina to Paraćin by road now takes 29 mins (20.2km).

292 possibly two different towns: Paraćin and Palanka – Paraćin to Ćuprija by road now takes 11 mins (8.3km).

293 Ćuprija to Aleksinac by road takes 39 mins (60.2km) or Paraćin to Aleksinac 36 mins (50.5km).

294 Aleksinac (Grocka to Aleksinac now takes 1 hour 47 mins by road (171km).

295 The notebook ends with these Serbian words and phrases – an informal dictionary of useful words, phrases and commands, written phonetically by George as he was taught them, with his translation written beside each word. Translations and/or correct Serbian in [brackets] by Ivanka Radmanović.

296 Mr Gutch was a very early photographer, as we have seen, but did not take his camera on these trips as far as we know.

297 *Punch* was taken to Alexnitza for the messengers staying there to read. George quotes from *Punch* when he says they came home drunk 'like children of Mars'.

298 (Mokyr, n.d.)

299 Victor Emmanuel Smyth, my maternal Grandpa's father, jokes in his journal on his arrival in Boston 'In the public gardens there is a monument to commemorate the discovery that the inhaling of ether causes insensibility to pain, first proved at the Mass. Gen. Hospital in Boston, Oct 1846. On the other side of pedestal is inscribed "Neither shall there be any more pain" just as if St John referred to the inhaling of ether.' Saturday 7th October 1876.

300 https://en.wikipedia.org/wiki/Yugoslav_Wars#:~:text=The%20Yugo-slav%20Wars%20were%20a,Yugoslavia%20from%201991%20to%20

2001. The Yugoslav wars lasted from 31 March 1991–12 November 2001 and included the Slovenian War of Independence, Croatian War of Independence, Bosnian War, Insurgency in Kosovo, Kosovo War, Insurgency in the Preševo Valley, and the Insurgency in Macedonia.

301 See https://en.wikipedia.org/wiki/Timeline_of_abolition_of_slavery_and_serfdom.

302 https://www.worldometers.info/coronavirus/ (accessed 5/12/2022). A conservative estimate.

303 A period in the early 1840s when Britain experienced an economic depression, causing much misery among the poor. In 1839 there was a serious slump in trade, leading to a steep increase in unemployment, accompanied by a bad harvest. The bad harvests were repeated in the two following years and the sufferings of the people, in a rapidly increasing population, were made worse by the fact that the Corn Laws seemed to keep the price of bread artificially high. In 1845 potato blight appeared in England and Scotland, spreading to Ireland later in the year and ruining a large part of the crop. The potato blight returned in 1846, bringing the Irish Famine. *A Dictionary of World History* (2 ed.) Edited by Edmund Wright.

304 See a fuller account here: https://www.thehistorypress.co.uk/articles/the-slavery-abolition-act-of-1833/.

305 See Sarah Corke's note, endnote 316, that she had a governess while her brothers went to school. George and Sarah's children also had a governess who lived with them at their house in Crickhowell.

306 Vaccination gradually replaced the riskier variolation for smallpox and by 1853, thirty years after Jenner's death, smallpox vaccination became a standard practice.

307 (Wikipedia, n.d.).

308 In my copy – a facsimile of a copy held in Stanford Library – the name of the translator has been firmly crossed out, presumably because she is a woman.

309 The United States of the Ionian Islands was a Greek state and amical protectorate of Great Britain between 1815 and 1864. It covered the territory of the Ionian Islands, in modern Greece, and was ceded to Greece as a gift of Britain to the newly-enthroned King George 1 of Greece in 1864.

310 He matriculated on 14th Dec 1837 aged 15: 'Davies, George Sydney ('serviens'), is. George, of Crickhowell, co. Brecon, gent. JESUS Coll., matric. 14 Dec, 1837, aged 15; B.A. 1841.' https://archive.org/details/alumnioxonienses01univuoft.

311 In 1843 he began Articles of Clerkship for Geo Augustus Spruce Davies. Trainee solicitors and training contracts were formerly known as articled clerks and articles of clerkship, respectively. The articled clerk

signs a contract, known as 'articles of clerkship', committing to a fixed period of employment.

312 'Sworn in court this 27th January 1846: Let George Sydney Davies of Crickhowell in the County of Brecon Gentleman be sworn admitted and enrolled at attorney of Her Majesty's Court of Queen's Bench at Westminster. Dated this 26th day of January 1846. Articles dated 7th January 1843. Denman. To the Masters of the said Court.'

313 'The Ottoman Grand Tour could be a natural extension of the European Grand Tour. Particularly in the eighteenth century, when defeat in the plains of Hungary had diminished the Ottoman Empire's appetite for wars, it was common for English, Scottish and Irish travellers on the Grand Tour to sail on from Naples or Venice – as Byron would sail on from Malta – to visit Greece, Constantinople and beyond.' *Philip Mansel Lecture given to the Byron Society*, House of Lords, London, March 2003.

314 In 1837 objections were put forward to messengers carrying passengers by Lord Palmerston, however Hertslet countered the objection saying that a second person in the carriage might speed the journey especially at night 'when after several successive Days' and Nights' travelling, the Messenger is overcome by fatigue, and his companion can relieve him, and thereby keep up the constant vigilance which is required to prevent delays, at the Post Stations, at the Frontiers, and on the Road' *Hertslet* (Wheeler-Holohan, 1935, p. 62).

315 See p30 to read a letter preserved in *the Hertslet Papers* in the National Archives at Kew, about spies interfering with despatches in 1845 which confirms that some local couriers were indeed corruptible. Queen's Messengers were employed to keep the dispatches they carried safe from any other eyes but those for whom they were intended.

316 She wrote a short family history of both sides of the family for her children. This is the account of their meeting 'My father, when he found himself bereft of the property he had always considered his own, had to find some way of adding to his means to support himself and his family, and for this reason he went into partnership with a cloth manufacturer at Woodchester, near Stroud, Gloucestershire. Leaving Clifton where he had previously lived, he bought a small estate called Stanley Hall in the village of King's Stanley, beautifully situated on the side of the Cotswold Hills, not far from Woodchester, where he lived for many years; but the partnership which was to have lasted 7 years proved very disastrous. My father discovered that he was being defrauded and, only just in time to save himself from bankruptcy, he dissolved the partnership, and when the affairs were wound up, he found that he had lost all the money he had put into it. After this he made no further attempt at work of any kind, but with what he had

left and my mother's money, he was able to remain at Stanley. I can remember the event of my father's giving up Woodchester, but it did not trouble us children. My two brothers and myself had a very happy life; they went to school and I had a governess at home, and when my brothers were old enough, the eldest, Henry, was placed in a merchant's office in Bristol, and Charles, the youngest was articled to Mr Sidney Wasbrough, a solicitor in Bristol, and a cousin of my mother's and he lived with his aunt Mrs Longmore, my mother's eldest sister. My father and my mother and I lived a very quiet life at Stanley. We had no near neighbours and my father disliked visitors. My life was brightened by visits to my Aunt at Bristol who was a widow and had no children (Mrs Longmore of Clifton Wood). I was her godchild, and very dear to her always. On one of these visits your father and I became acquainted, and the result was our marriage in 1849. Our wedding took place from the house of this dear Aunt, whose age and failing health made it impossible for her to go to Stanley. We were married at the old parish church of Clifton and my cousin, the Rev Joseph Theophilus Toye, then Rector of St Stephens, Exeter, and afterwards Rector of St David's in that city, came on purpose to marry us.' From a typescript copied by Barbara Collins from one lent to her by Pamela Seys which itself was a copy of the original which is now lost.

317 (Sumner, 2008, pp. 627-629).
318 Note the passages where George Davies helps with beetle collecting – shaking them into an umbrella.
319 (Wheeler-Holohan, 1935, p. 276).
320 Boyles London Court and Fashionable Guide Directory for April 1847 confirms Mr Gutch was living at 77 Great Portland Street.
321 Queen's Messengers were required to live no more than two miles from Downing Street where the Foreign Office was located at that time so that they were available at short notice to set off on journeys. There was a systematic list ordering who would travel next, but this could easily be put out of order by sickness, travel difficulties or other problems.
322 Mr Gutch did not have a military background but as a qualified Surgeon would certainly have been considered a Gentleman. See endnote 16.

Ingram Content Group UK Ltd.
Milton Keynes UK
UKHW010622160423
420233UK00001B/2